ROUTLEDGE LIBRARY EDITIONS:
MANAGEMENT

Volume 18

PLANNING AND THE
GROWTH OF THE FIRM

PLANNING AND THE GROWTH OF THE FIRM

JOHN BRIDGE AND J.C. DODDS

Routledge
Taylor & Francis Group

LONDON AND NEW YORK

First published in 1978 by Croom Helm Ltd

This edition first published in 2018
by Routledge
4 Park Square, Milton Park, Abingdon, Oxon OX14 4RN

and by Routledge
605 Third Avenue, New York, NY 10017

Routledge is an imprint of the Taylor & Francis Group, an informa business

British Library Cataloguing in Publication Data
A catalogue record for this book is available from the British Library

ISBN: 978-1-138-55938-7 (Set)
ISBN: 978-1-351-05538-3 (Set) (ebk)
ISBN: 978-0-8153-9194-4 (Volume 18) (hbk)
ISBN: 978-0-8153-9195-1 (Volume 18) (pbk)
ISBN: 978-1-351-20031-8 (Volume 18) (ebk)

Publisher's Note
The publisher has gone to great lengths to ensure the quality of this reprint but points out that some imperfections in the original copies may be apparent.

Disclaimer
The publisher has made every effort to trace copyright holders and would welcome correspondence from those they have been unable to trace.

Preface

Although this book was completed some 40 years ago, growth and planning are still key elements for policy makers in the corporate and public sectors. What has changed for the corporate sector in particular is the increased integration of economies and financial systems. With GDP growth rates of emerging economies exceeding the mature, developed economies, for example China is now the second largest economy in the world, firm's seeking a growth strategy cannot ignore opportunities for offshoring production through FDI and seeking funding sources in global financial markets. Off shoring has also occurred with the Japanese auto makers producing in the US and Canada.

Today with significant changes in telecommunications and transportation it is possible for firms to manage subsidiaries abroad and develop global supply chains. This is not just the domain of US, European or Japanese firms as we now have the emergence, through M&A's in particular, of firms from Brazil, India and in the case of China, both the private sector and state enterprises. We can add to this that with the growth of financial institutions such as pension funds, foundations, insurance companies, private equity funds and sovereign wealth funds, they are all searching for yield and diversification of their assets from their home market. Many are making investments not just in financial markets, but directly through minority or complete ownership of firms. Some will play an activist role in seeking to bring about a change in the management and direction of the firm by selling off non-core assets. Many policy issues arise from this cross border activity, including country risk, operating and translation currency exposure. Corporate governance issues will also arise not just from the span of control of a parent and its subsidiaries, but in the different laws and cultures found in the host country.

In the public sector we have witnessed the privatisation of many crown corporations, particularly in the UK, and many aspects of health service and social care provision now involve the private sector. Most developed countries are facing demographic changes and ageing populations, such that the management and financing of health care services have become critical issues. Public finances have come under increasing pressure since the financial collapse of 2008, and subsequent attempts to cut the deficit.

Many western economies experienced a prolonged slowdown after the financial crisis, creating a less favourable outlook for business. Few economists had foreseen the events of 2008, and there has been further recent criticism of their inability in the UK to promote a consistent view of the impact of Brexit. While these failings have caused a great deal of concern, the discipline has always needed to review its predictive limitations and adapt its theoretical models (both macro and micro), in the light of experience.

Following our earlier text "Managerial Decision Making" (1975), the present book was written in an era which had seen extensive debate around the methodological issues concerning the so-called theory of the firm. Doubts were frequently voiced about the extent to which microeconomic theory had a place in management education where analysis of "real" firms was necessary. Fritz Machlup in 1967, commenting on the misunderstanding by the theory's critics, stated that it was not "designed to serve to explain and predict the behaviour of real firms", and "the firm is only a theoretical link, a mental construct helping how one gets from the cause to the effect".

The various behavioural and managerial theorists whose contributions are summarised and evaluated in the present text believed that revisions were necessary, whilst accepting Machlup's contention that some abstraction was justified in explaining resource allocation in a market economy, these revisionists sought increased realism in various aspects of the firm so that it would no longer be just a black box or "mental construct" within the wider theory.

The most extensive departure from conventional theory came in the guise of Cyert and March's behavioural theory of the firm, in which the decision-making process and internal resource allocation of the firm were major considerations. Profit was no longer the sole objective, and maximising was replaced by *satisficing* – achieving what is satisfactory, or good enough, rather than the optimum. Moreover, information was not given, but revealed during a search process, and the assumption of perfect knowledge thereby eliminated.

The managerial theories of Baumol, Marris and Williamson, likewise dismissed profit as the sole objective. Baumol, even relegated it to being a constraint, rather than the purpose of the enterprise. However, these theories maintained the assumption that the firm had knowledge about the main variables impacting on the firm, such that optima could be determined within a fairly conventional graphical analysis of their models of the firm.

Another feature of the present text was its attempt to link economic theory to the literature of corporate strategy. To this end, Ansoff's writings on this subject were of interest, since his classification of product-market and diversification strategies extended and enriched the concepts as used in the Marris growth model. It was the association of these works from different, but related, disciplines which encouraged us to use the latter as the main vehicle for our analysis of planning and the growth of the firm.

Ansoff has continued to receive mention, in the literature of strategic management and marketing, particularly in the context of his product market matrix, but in the evolution of the analysis of the firm in modern microeconomics, it is Williamson rather than his contemporaries of the sixties and seventies, who has stood the test of time. In addition to his managerial theory of the firm, attention was given in the present text to his analysis of organisational form on enterprise behaviour. Williamson has remained prominent in developments of the analysis of organisations and he became a Nobel prize winner in 2009 for his work on transaction cost economics.

PLANNING AND THE GROWTH OF THE FIRM

JOHN BRIDGE and J.C. DODDS

CROOM HELM   LONDON

© 1978 J. Bridge and J.C. Dodds
Croom Helm Ltd, 2-10 St John's Road, London SW11

British Library Cataloguing in Publication Data

Bridge, John
    Planning and the growth of the firm
    1. Industries, Size of   2. Corporate planning
    I. Title   II. Dodds, James Colin
    658.4'06   HD69.S5

ISBN 0-85664-362-9

Printed in Great Britain by
Biddles Ltd, Guildford, Surrey

CONTENTS

ACKNOWLEDGEMENTS

In the writing of this book we have benefited from discussions with many of our colleagues and in particular we can cite C.W. Neale who read all the chapters of a previous draft, A.J. McGuinness who read chapter 3 and K.W. Wilson who read chapters 2 and 4. We must, however, add the usual rider that we accept responsibility for the material in (and omissions from) this book.

J. Bridge would like to thank the Welsh Office and the Department of Health and Social Security for the material which they have provided, primarily for a research project which is in progress, but which has also proved useful in the preparation of chapter 6 in this book. J.C. Dodds would like to thank the Esmee Fairbairn Charitable Trust for the endowment of the fellowship at Sheffield University which he currently holds.

The manuscript was expertly typed by Mrs S. Watts and Miss M. Pugh and the proof reading undertaken by Mrs M. Burton. We have been granted permission to reproduce certain copyright material specifically Figure 2.1 which is from Richard M. Cyert and James G. March, *A Behavioural Theory of the Firm* (1963), p. 126, which is reprinted by permission of Prentice-Hall Inc. Figure 3.1 is from R.L. Marris and A. Wood (eds.) *The Corporate Economy* (1971), Macmillan, p. 14, and is reprinted by permission of the Presidents and Fellows of the Harvard College; Figures 3.8 and 3.9 and Table 3.1 are from H.K. Radice, 'Control Type. Profitability and Growth in Large Firms', *Economic Journal*, September 1971, pp. 548-9, 555 and Table 5.3 is from G. Meeks and G. Whittington, 'Giant Companies in the United Kingdom, 1946-69', *Economic Journal*, December 1975, pp. 132-3 and are all reprinted by permission of Cambridge University Press and the authors. Table 5.1 and Figures 5.8 and 5.9 are from A.D. Bain, C.L. Day and A.L. Wearing, *Company Financing in the United Kingdom* (1975), Martin Robertson, pp. 6, 27, 29 and reprinted with the authors' permission; Figures 5.1, 5.3 and 5.4 are from *Economic Trends*, February 1977 and Table 5.2 from G. Meeks and G. Whittington, *The Financing of Quoted Companies in the UK*, background paper to Report No. 2 of the Royal Commission on the Distribution of Income and Wealth 1976 and are all reprinted by permission of the Controller of Her Majesty's Stationery Office.

To Nicholas and James

PREFACE

This book has emerged from our interest in the neo-classical theory
of the firm and its many revisions and additions. It takes up some of
the issues which were raised in our earlier book *Managerial Decision
Making*, but which could not be developed fully within the framework
we adopted.

The task which we set ourselves in writing the present volume was
to bring together some of the more important contributions to the
economic theory of business behaviour, broadly defined to include
both behavioural and managerial theories, and to determine the
implications of these works for micro-economic theory and managerial
economics. In surveying this literature, one finds that different levels
of decision are explored – for example, R.M. Cyert's and J.G. March's
behavioural theory is mainly concerned with decision processes at the
operating level while the contribution of R.L. Marris is directed more
towards decisions of a strategic nature. In being selective, we have
tended to concentrate on the strategic level given that few previous
works have examined the theoretical developments of micro-economics
in relation to corporate planning practice. For this reason rather more
weight is given to Marris than to the other authors, and our exploration
of the topics of diversification and the financing function follows this
emphasis, as does the prominence of the growth objective throughout
this book.

The firm of prime interest to us in this study is the large manager-
controlled business organisation in contrast to the firm of traditional
theory which is small relative to the size of the market, controlled by
an entrepreneur and without an explicit organisational structure. The
increasing size of firms has brought a high degree of concentration in
many industries and opportunities to exploit market power either by
making profits in excess of the 'normal' rate, or by pursuing
alternative objectives. An additional feature of the growth process
has been the spreading of activity by firms over a number of products
and markets – diversification. Both concentration and diversification
have been brought about by mergers as well as by internal or
organic expansion and a number of conglomerate enterprises have
evolved largely through merger or take-over.

Although the analysis we present is geared to the large, privately owned concern which figures in the 200 or so biggest quoted companies in the UK, it is not restricted to this kind of entity. In particular, firms of all shapes and sizes are finding it increasingly necessary to plan, particularly in environments characterised by a rapid wave of innovation and technological change. Moreover the government and its agencies have adopted planning systems which have to resolve complex strategy issues for an uncertain feature in the same way that comparable business systems have to function. Explicit recognition of this fact has been made in our inclusion of a chapter devoted to the public sector in which defence and health planning systems are outlined.

This book is intended for postgraduate students reading Management, Business Studies, or Managerial Economics and it presupposes a knowledge of micro-economics to second-year undergraduate level and some background in managerial economics. Final year honours students reading specialist options in these subject areas will also find the coverage appropriate.

1 CORPORATE OBJECTIVES, DECISIONS AND PLANS

1.1 Introduction

Economics revolves around human decision making, despite attempts by some practitioners in this discipline to deny the fundamental importance of the decision process itself. The fact remains that resource allocation reflects choices made by individuals, and groups of individuals, whether we are concerned with market economies and the price mechanism or with socialist economies and central planning. In neo-classical micro-economics, firms and households are regarded as the key actors in the functioning of the market economy, but it is the market which is the main object of study. Since individuals are credited with complete knowledge and rational behaviour, the response to any stimulus is unique and the choice process is entirely mechanistic. Rationality in the context of the firm is seen as the pursuit of maximum profits by the entrepreneur and in the idealised world of perfect competition, rational behaviour of this sort would be ensured by the market, since survival could only be guaranteed through the maximisation of profits in the long run. Some firms might survive by chance,[1] in which case their unintended 'rationality' would in retrospect be seen to involve behaviour patterns similar to other surviving firms responding to similar circumstances.

In the real world where competition is less than perfect and where markets are often dominated by just a few large companies the behaviour of firms is only partially circumscribed by the market. Moreover, the notion of rational behaviour becomes ambiguous in practice, since what is rational for the owners of the firm may not be so for the decision makers when there is divorce between ownership and control. The manner in which large firms allocate resources can thus only be understood through a closer investigation of decision processes and objectives than that undertaken in neo-classical micro-economics. In order to analyse the workings of a modern economy it seems more fruitful to take the firm as the basic unit rather than the market and this is the approach that we shall be adopting throughout this book. The firm will be treated as an active entity which influences and reacts to the environment in which it finds itself, rather than as a mere cog in the system, which in effect is the treatment given in

9

neo-classical analysis. Indeed, it can be argued that firms have been the vehicle for expansion and change in the economy. In consequence the large firm emerges (as we shall see in chapter 3) as a dynamic organisation continually searching for new outlets for its expanding product base. This is well illustrated by a quotation from R.L. Marris (93), commenting on E.T. Penrose (127).

[Mrs Penrose] sees the firm as an administrative and social organisation, capable, in principle, of entering almost any field of material activity. The firm is not necessarily limited to particular markets, industries or countries; indeed, there is no theoretical reason why firms should not venture anywhere in the universe. In practice, of course, they find advantages in specialisation, but this represents a deliberate choice whose direction and degree may be varied at will. Every firm, at any one moment, inherits a degree and direction of specialisation from its own past, and this is represented in the knowledge and talents of the existing members and the sphere of technical and commercial activity with which they are familiar (as well as, of course, in the nature of the physical assets). But new members and new assets can always be recruited; the firm is a changeable bundle of human and professional resources, linked through the corporate constitution to a corresponding bundle of material and financial assets. [p. 113]

In understanding the 'administrative and social organisation' described by Penrose, the nature of management and its functions assumes an importance not previously encountered in micro-economics. It is beyond the scope of this book to examine each and every management function in detail, and since decision making lies at the heart of managerial activity, it is to this aspect of management which we shall devote most attention.

In an earlier book[2] we argued that economic analysis does have a vital part to play in the decision process, particularly in the evaluation of alternatives, but there is a large gap between what we may call *traditional economic theory* and the needs of practising economists and managers in industry, particularly as one moves to the higher level, strategic decisions (see Section 1.3 below). However, we are able to draw on revisions to traditional theory and supporting empirical studies, which take the firm rather than the market as the basic unit and which, in some cases, encompass strategic as well as operating decisions. Other revisions, despite their orientation to the large firm and its decisions have little to say about strategic decisions, but these theories are still valuable for the insight they give into objectives and decisions in general and, accordingly, will be examined in this volume. A study of revisionist micro-economics not only promotes an understanding of the impact of modern business on resource allocation,[3] it also offers an insight into the firm of the real world and the influence of economic variables on business decision making itself. Before proceeding to the newer theories of the firm which are covered in Chapters 2 and 3, it is necessary to establish a framework within which their distinct but complementary contributions can be analysed. The approach we have adopted here is to consider the case for incorporating objectives other than profit into the alternative formulations of the theory of the firm and, in doing so, to pay particular attention to growth as a long-term objective for large firms. A consideration of objectives leads naturally to the managerial processes of decision making and planning which guide the firm towards those objectives, and here we highlight the special requirements of strategic decision making. We shall proceed now with the first of our tasks — a consideration of the firm's objectives.

1.2 The Large Firm and its Objectives

Traditional economic theory incorporates the assumption that firms will pursue an objective of profit maximisation, but the theories to be discussed in this book all adopt objective functions which differ from this. Indeed this is really the only feature which the various managerial and behavioural theories have in common in their analysis of the large firm, but the rejection of profit maximisation is a highly significant departure from traditional orthodoxy and it warrants further consideration at this stage.

Strictly speaking, *maximisation* of any objective function is a meaningless concept when knowledge is less than perfect, so let us just regard this part of the profit maximisation objective as a convenient simplification which facilitates theoretical analysis. Rather than debate the conceptual difficulties surrounding maximisation we shall question here the emphasis given to *profit* in traditional theory. This emphasis follows from a consideration of what would be rational for an 'entrepreneur' who owned and managed the firm and, clearly, as the recipient of all proceeds, the entrepreneur would at least give high priority to the making of profits. Even if the entrepreneur exhibited a preference for some other kind of reward, a competitive market would constrain his ability to deviate too far from profit-making activities.

Nowadays, large firms occupy a place of some importance in the industrial structure of Western economies (exhibited in overall concentration figures), these firms have market power (indicated in concentration ratios[4] for industries and markets) and they are often *companies* (or corporations) owned by large numbers of shareholders but controlled by managers − giving rise to the separation of ownership and control.[5] Consequently the validity of the entrepreneur concept and the relevance of motivational assumptions developed in the context of a 'perfect competition' model has been increasingly questioned in recent years. The possession of market power and the separation of ownership and control gives the large corporation a measure of discretion and opens up the possibility that this discretion will be exercised in the pursuit of objectives which serve managerial rather than shareholder needs. Before considering the alternative objectives which companies may pursue, let us take a brief look at the kind of data which are often used to justify an investigation into managerial discretion.

Measures of overall concentration for British industry show that 45 per cent of manufacturing net output was accounted for by the largest 100 firms in 1970. This compares with 42 per cent in 1968, 37 per cent in 1963 and 31 per cent in 1958.[6] Thus a relatively small number of large companies accounts for a very large proportion of net output, a proportion which appears to be increasing, and the same tendency is exhibited in the control of net assets.[7] Concentration ratios for individual products, measured as the proportion of net output produced by the five largest firms in the industry, have also increased substantially.[8] If the rate of growth in concentration experienced during the 1958 to 1968 period is maintained, approximately two-thirds of products will have concentration ratios greater than 80 per cent by 1993. In Hansard 1970 (63), are listed 156 products including both consumer and producer goods where just one firm supplied over half of the UK market.[9]

Turning to the separation of ownership and control, we find satisfactory measures rather harder to come by, and a limited number of studies looking into the phenomenon. The classic work in this field is that of P.S. Florence (48) who used the median percentage of shares held by the directors of very large companies[10] as a measure of the overlap between ownership and control. The fact that this percentage had fallen from 2.8 per cent in 1936 to 1.5 per cent in 1951 was seen as evidence of a wide and growing separation. In another analysis, T. Nichols (118) reconsidered the data for several large British companies with boards whose shareholdings amounted to 5 per cent or less and included in these were British American Tobacco, Courtaulds, Dunlop Rubber, ICI, and Imperial Tobacco. Despite the smallness of these holdings in relation to the total, some were significant in absolute terms with average director's holdings in excess of £40,000 for Imperial Tobacco in 1951 (nominal values).

In recent years, managers of some large companies in the US and UK have been encouraged to take shareholdings through stock option plans and thus their pecuniary interests have become more closely identified with those of the shareholders. The observation that managerial stock-holdings may be a significant source of income has been supported by the study of W.G. Lewellen (85) who noted a sharp increase in the value of such holdings as revealed by data over the period 1940-63 in the US. He concluded that management

> . . . may not be so inclined to disregard the interests of its share-holders in making managerial decisions . . . A separation of ownership and management *functions* clearly exists; it seems that a significant separation of their pecuniary interest does not. [p. 320]

The contention that the separation between ownership and control has weakened the influence of shareholders rests, in part, on the belief that the holdings of shares are too diffuse[11] for concerted action to be mounted by the owners of the firm. However, the growth of institutional shareholdings may force a re-examination of this belief, since the holdings of these institutions – life assurance companies, superannuation funds, unit trusts, etc. – now account for a large proportion of the market value of marketable ordinary shares in the UK (44 per cent in 1974).[12] The shareholding body may also have become better informed in recent years thanks to an active and frequently highly critical financial press, but obviously such attributes are unmeasurable.

It is thus difficult to draw conclusions concerning how far managers or directors will pursue interests which conflict with those of the shareholders, and we shall find that all the theories in which managerial or organisational objectives are proposed make some recognition of shareholder interests. Thus although profit ceases to be the sole objective of the firm, it remains either as part of a multiple objective function or as a constraint on the firm in its pursuit of other objectives.[13] The constraint may take the form of security, as in R.L. Marris's (92, 93) theory, rather than profit *per se*, but this too is related to the shareholders' valuation of the firm and, in particular, the threat of take-over which could ensue from managerial failure to deploy the firm's resources efficiently.

A complication which arises in assessing the relevance of a profit objective is the time period to which the objective pertains. A number of attacks on profit maximisation have been directed towards its use as a short-run objective within the theory of the firm, since a firm which pursued short-run profit to the detriment of investment, research or promotional expenditures might jeopardise its prospects for the longer term. It may thus not only be possible, but also desirable, for the firm to pursue objectives other than profit in the short run, so long as it maintains a rate of return on investment which will ensure survival in the long run.[14]

It is our view that despite the checks which may exist to bring managerial actions into line with the interests of shareholders, the possibility of conflicting objectives must be recognised. Although there are still many economists who defend the traditional (profit maximisation) view of motivation there are an increasing number who have proposed managerial or organisational alternatives. These may take various forms. W.J. Baumol (18, 19) argues that sales revenue is likely to be a key managerial goal in the short run and growth of sales in the long run, provided there is a minimum acceptable level of profits to ensure survival by providing the means for expansion and an adequate return for the shareholders. Those views are also held by J.K. Galbraith (49) and R.L. Marris (92, 93) although their emphasis is on long-term growth. The growth objective is a recurrent theme in this book and we shall have more to say about it presently. O.E. Williamson (170, 171) proposes that managerial 'utility' depends partially on profit, but he also includes expenditure on managerial perquisites and staffing in specifying an objective function. The inclusion of sales, by Baumol, and staff, by Williamson, in their respective objective functions, reflects in part the impact which these dimensions are alleged to have on managerial salaries. This argument is related to the R.J. Monsen and A. Downs (113) hypothesis that managers wish to maximise their own lifetime incomes.

The 'behavioural', as distinct from the 'managerial', approach to the theory of the firm (the latter referring to the recognition of managerial objectives) is to view the firm as an organisation in which objectives are determined through a bargaining process. Participants in this bargaining process include not only managers, but employees and other interest groups. The objectives, or goals as R.M. Cyert and J.G. March (38) prefer to call them, are thus 'organisational' rather than 'managerial'. In their behavioural theory of the firm, multiple goals of profits, sales, market share, production and inventory are proposed and the targets set are supposed to change over time as aspirations change. Sales and marketing personnel would normally work towards a sales or market share goal while employees in production departments would generally strive towards production targets. The goal of profit retains some importance as it is the only goal which all parties are involved in, regardless of which department they work in or their seniority in the hierarchy.

The various interest groups form, what Cyert and March call, a 'coalition', and it is interesting to note how broadly this coalition is sometimes defined in the context of the modern business organisation. Originally the interests of the shareholders were regarded as supreme so that, notwithstanding the divorce between ownership and control, managers were supposed to accept their role as trustees for the shareholders.[15] Nowadays managers are often seen as trustees for the whole community,[16] so that the relevant coalition in the determination of a company's objectives includes managers, employees, shareholders, customers and even the public at large. It may be that an accommodation of the public interest would lead to an objective of social responsibility,[17] but this is often seen as stemming from enlightened managerial self-interest rather than from altruistic motives.

The social responsibility doctrine does have a bearing on the acceptability of growth as a business objective. Marris regards growth primarily as a means of satisfying managerial needs. Galbraith argues that most employees of the organisation will also be well served by the same end, and governments are seldom averse to business expansion if it facilitates the achievement of their own employment, balance of payments, and macro-growth objectives. If we accept that shareholder needs are, at least in part, also accommodated within the objective functions of firms, then growth would seem to be an objective with widespread appeal. However, the interests of society at large, in particular those of future generations, may not be so well served and, although we do not see it as our task to comment on moral or ethical issues in this book, we shall discuss shortly some of the objections which have been raised against growth both at macro- and micro-levels.

For the moment let us examine the reasons why growth is seen as a key objective and thereby justify the emphasis given to growth in this book. In his 1963 article, Marris (92) begins by discussing the sources of managerial utility and the nature of managerial preferences, and in so doing makes the following observation,

> . . . the various sources of positive managerial utility would appear
> to be strongly correlated with a single observable attribute of the
> firm, that is, its size. Thus managers have been supposed to value
> salary, power, and status.[18] 'The firm' has been supposed to
> value aggregate profits, aggregate turnover, aggregate capital, share
> of the market and public image.[19] All of these things, except
> perhaps public image, are correlated with almost any measure of
> size and some are themselves measures of size. [pp. 186-7]

The next step in Marris's argument is to propose that since managerial
mobility is supposedly low,[20] managements will see the growth of their
own organisation, rather than moves to other larger organisations, as
the route to higher levels of personal utility.

Galbraith (49) arrives at the same conclusion in his chapter on
'The Goals of the Industrial System' in his book *The New Industrial
State*. He refers to the complex organisation of modern business as the
'technostructure', and proposes that the goal of growth commends
itself to the whole organisation (technostructure).

> Expansion of output means expansion of the technostructure
> itself. Such expansion, in turn, means more jobs with more
> responsibility and hence more promotion and more compensation.
> [p. 177]

In stressing the advantages of growth to the technostructure, Galbraith
points to the pitfalls of contraction in modern industry, with its
high overhead costs which can quickly create losses when production
falls. He also explains that since group working is common in the
technostructure, it becomes difficult to discharge individual
employees should falling output dictate the need to do so. Consequently
as a safeguard against contraction, firms will pursue expansionary
strategies.

Galbraith's discussion of goals leads on to the adoption of growth
as a national policy objective. The respectability of growth as a social
goal makes business growth a consistent and acceptable end to pursue.
Galbraith describes how the success of a society seems to be judged in
terms of its rate of increase in Gross National Product, with Britain
consequently being regarded as a failure. The relationship between
growth at a national level and growth at the level of the firm is not

uni-directional according to Galbraith. Admittedly expansionary fiscal
and monetary measures will facilitate business expansion but, according
to Galbraith, growth as a national goal may reflect the interests of
industry rather than vice versa.

> The acceptance of economic growth as a social goal coincides closely
> with the rise to power of the mature corporation and the techno-
> structure. [p. 180] [21]

Politicians, nevertheless, seem to favour growth as a means of
promoting general well-being and not just that of the business sector.
It is not difficult to see why this objective finds favour in political
circles since votes depend to a large extent on living standards, and
a sustained improvement in the latter can only be achieved through
an expansion in GNP. Re-distribution of wealth and income could
increase welfare, but not for all individuals and not over a prolonged
period. Certainly economic growth opens up the possibilities of
increased welfare if the additional resources which are generated can
be used to eliminate poverty, bad housing and poor health. In Britain,
high priority has been given in the past to public expenditures directed
towards these problems, but industrial expansion has not kept pace,
and our ability to maintain a high level of public spending has
been threatened. A view seems to be emerging that industrial expansion
is a prerequisite for economic prosperity on a wider scale, but Galbraith
would argue against its being a sufficient condition. He doubts whether
expansion biased towards advertising-intensive consumer goods,
especially consumer goods like automobiles, and towards defence
expenditures, really increases national welfare if sectors such as health,
education and housing are left to stagnate. It is on these grounds that
he is highly critical of growth in the 'affluent society'[22] of the US.

The arguments of E.F. Schumacher (140) are often heard in the
growth debate, particularly in the context of 'high technology'
industries. Schumacher would like to reverse the trends which have
brought large-scale production techniques to industry and the
concomitant needs for 'bigness'. His thesis that 'small is beautiful'
implies that the diseconomies, both internal and external, exceed the
economies of large-scale production, but this remains unproven.
One or two observations are, however, worth making on this subject.
We shall see that the growing firm relies to a large extent on
diversification of products and markets, which means that expansion
may not be accompanied by the kind of economies which are

associated with single-product expansion. At the same time the diversity of activities may bring increasing organisational complexity in its wake and the sort of administrative problems which give rise to diseconomies. (We shall have more to say on this subject in Chapter 4.) Turning now to *external* diseconomies, it is apparent that industrial progress has often come about at the expense of our environment. The ecological system has been disturbed by the pollution of atmosphere and rivers, the landscape has been spoiled in the extraction of minerals and the dumping of waste, and natural resources have been depleted at an alarming rate. The development of alternative sources of energy is becoming urgent as oil reserves shrink throughout the world and it is highly likely that nuclear power will play an increasing role in the future, despite the horrific possibilities of plutonium poisoning and the size of the waste disposal problem in general. Indeed it is not just private manufacturing industry which must exercise social responsibility in its pursuit of growth. Public agencies, particularly in the energy sector need to consider the wider interests of the community, both for present and future generations, in the development and execution of their plans.

Industrial growth has undoubtedly left a trail of dereliction, pollution and scarred landscapes, but the more prosperous nations are now able to direct resources to restoration programmes and it would be unfortunate if the UK continued to suffer from the ravages of industrialisation without the benefits that a high rate of economic growth can bring. Although high consumption rates will certainly pose resource depletion problems, the growth of firms is frequently accompanied by technological advance and a concomitant switch to new types of resource inputs. The research departments of a number of large firms are also examining the possibilities of recycling waste and recovering material which would normally have been disposed of, spurred on by the desire to use resources more efficiently at the level of the firm but, at the same time, enabling national output to increase without a corresponding increase in the rate of input usage.

The growth of the large corporation has not taken place behind national frontiers, but has been of an international nature, especially in the case of some large American firms, for example, Ford and General Motors which have subsidiaries throughout the world. To some observers the multinational corporation is an undesirable phenomenon, given the absolute power which it wields, especially when it plans expansion or contraction for one of its subsidiaries. The decision may be of minor significance in the context of the worldwide operations of the parent company, but of immense importance to the industry of the country concerned. The employment consequences of Chrysler UK's threat to run down operations in this country were of such a magnitude that the British government felt obliged to provide public money in order that Chrysler might remain in business here. Yet Chrysler is not one of the really big multinational companies and the actions of its big brothers could have had a massive impact on the investment and employment prospects of a national economy.

At the present time Britain is said to need more industrial investment and, although expansion within this country by British firms is the preferred route to the recovery in investment, there is no active discrimination against incoming foreign capital; on the contrary, a number of Japanese firms have been encouraged to invest here in recent years. In addition to providing investment and employment, it is hoped that those Japanese firms can be of help to the UK balance of payments instead of a threat to it.

In conclusion, despite the drawbacks associated with the growth of firms, in the UK at least, the advantages seem likely to be stressed for many years to come. The so-called 'industrial strategy' seeks to develop a strong, growing, 'wealth producing', industrial base.[23] Consequently, although we shall examine the wider implications of corporate strategy from an efficiency point of view (for example, in Chapter 4 when we shall be discussing diversification), in much of what follows we shall not question the objectives of the corporations, but rather seek to understand their impact on the options open to the firm and their effect on resource allocation both internally and externally.

1.3 Types of Business Decision

Whether it pursues growth, or some other objective, the modern large business firm has to respond not only to changes in the environment and to pressures generated internally, it also anticipates change, and influences its own environment and accordingly needs a decision-taking capability which can meet these wide-ranging demands.

Business organisations are usually hierarchical, and the type of decision that is made by a manager, its importance and its complexity generally reflect his seniority in the hierarchy. *Strategic* decision-making which in H.I. Ansoff's (10) classification is concerned with the relationship between the firm and its environment, takes place in the upper echelons; it is the prerogative of senior management and the board, although it is frequently argued that grass-roots participation in the decision process facilitates the implementation of such decisions.

Operating decisions, again using Ansoff's terminology, are the every-day routine repetitive decisions which pervade the organisation, and timing is normally critical so that decisions of this type tend to receive priority. Senior management is often preoccupied with operations to the detriment of the firm's strategic decision-making capability. In part this may reflect deficiencies in organisational design, hindering the effective delegation of authority, but managerial perception may also be significant in that a remedy to declining performance is typically sought locally, as R.M. Cyert and J.G. March (38) have observed. More widespread search, including strategy reappraisal may only come about if localised search fails to yield a solution which works.

Administrative decisions are inward looking and are concerned with the structuring of authority and responsibility relationships within the organisation and the resultant information flows, acquisition and development of resources, the location of facilities and other internal problems concerned with the structure of the firm's resources.

Since search is initially localised in many organisations, an administrative solution to a problem might be put forward when the problem is essentially strategic. Perhaps the administrative solution would follow the failure of management in finding an operating solution, with the problem only being recognised as strategic when all else has failed. Important administrative decisions, for example, where a fundamental re-organisation is involved, will naturally be taken at senior management level with less complex decisions being made at appropriate lower levels.

A fundamental difficulty in decision-making is thus providing senior management with the time to consider strategic problems when operating and administrative matters may stake a prior claim, but perhaps more important is the question of problem recognition and perception so that strategic problems are treated as such and not as administrative or operating problems.

1.4 The Process of Decision Making and Planning

In discussing the types of decision in the preceding section we have inevitably introduced some concepts with which the reader may not be familiar. The concepts of 'problem recognition', 'search' and even 'decision' all need further explanation.

Management may be viewed as a system in which a management process receives inputs of the organisation's problems and delivers outputs of solutions to these problems. This approach emphasises the

problem solving nature of management, problems being solved by
making appropriate conscious choices (or decisions) from alternative
courses of action, with decision being followed by implementation.
The complete decision process may be represented thus:

(1) problem recognition;
(2) search for alternative courses of action;
(3) evaluation of alternatives;
(4) choice from among alternatives (this is the act of decision);
(5) implementation of the decision;
(6) monitoring the consequences of the decision, which in turn
indicates the need for further decision if the problem persists either
wholly or partially.

Problem recognition may stem from consideration of feedback data
such that if, for example, order books are lengthening and stocks of
finished goods are falling, it is fairly obvious to management that there
is an imbalance between the demand for the firm's products and the
rate of production. Suitable alternatives are generated in what is called
a search process to restore the balance, for example, raising the price
of the product, reducing advertising expenditure (to curtail demand)
or installing extra productive capacity to increase supply. The latter
option will not provide an immediate solution if it takes time to
order and fit new equipment and this may be regarded more properly
as a *planning* problem, where planning is *anticipatory* decision making.
Consequently the range of alternatives is far greater if one can foresee
a problem rather than wait for events to take their course, which
results in crisis management with a limited range of feasible alternatives.
   Planning is vital where strategic decisions are concerned but this
does not mean that the two are synonymous, since managers can
anticipate problems and search for alternatives without contemplating
strategic change. The options open to the firm when it is contemplating changes in its relationship with the environment include the
entering of new markets and the creation of new products. The firm
is thus not tied to a particular product-market posture, it may diversify
internally or through acquisition and either way it will require a long
gestation period before change is effected.[24]

1.5 Problem Recognition

Let us now examine each of the separate parts of the decision process
starting with problem recognition, considering in particular how a

strategic problem can be recognised as such. Clearly response to feedback like sales data and stock movements can only serve as a very imperfect guide, perhaps indicating the continuance of a long-term trend, since feedback indicates current or recent performance and not the future, so how can one be sure that the problem, perhaps identified as a fall in sales or profitability, requires strategic change? Perhaps a comparatively simple change in the marketing mix or a minor administrative change will restore performance to the desired level. To reply that 'managerial judgement' is called into play provides no meaningful answer to this question even if one argues that managers should be selected on their abilities to 'weigh up a situation' so that there is sufficient 'flair' in the management team to recognise the extent and nature of a problem. Even if it can be assumed that personnel of the required calibre have been selected for decision making at this level, it is still essential that a mechanism exists to indicate the need for strategic change. This mechanism may involve special organisational arrangements, for example, the creation of a corporate planning team divorced from operating decisions and charged with the identification and solution of strategic problems.[25] The mechanism adopted must enable comparison to be made between desired performance and that anticipated. Desired performance depends upon the objectives of the firm which we have already discussed in Section 1.2. It was apparent from our discussion that growth is a key long-term objective so that performance measures will include not only profits and sales in absolute terms, but also the rates of change in these attributes. If it is seen that such long-term objectives cannot be attained with the present product-market posture, then new products, markets, or both must be sought. It may be that a gap between desired and anticipated performance is revealed, but correction can take place through an operating or administrative decision such as price change, or the creation of a new managerial post in marketing. Strategic change is then dictated when a company is unable to fill the gap even when the optimal administrative and operating decisions have been determined.

It is an established fact, however, that many organisations only begin to seek an optimal pattern of internal resource allocation under duress.[26] On the other hand if a firm is willing to plan, rather than manage by crisis, it can relate its current pattern of resource deployment to its long-term objectives and thereby identify inconsistencies which can be remedied before the need to take corrective action becomes desperate. Problem recognition should perhaps therefore begin with taking stock to see how far the firm's deployment of resources deviates from the ideal.

Let us now consider how future performance is to be anticipated. The most important factor here is undoubtedly the sales forecast, since the sales of a particular product, or product range are unlikely to show continuous expansion and it is therefore this attribute which is likely to constrain long-run performance.[27] Even though firms can undoubtedly manipulate demand and do not regard it as given, determined exclusively by consumers' tastes, there will generally be a saturation point beyond which sales cannot be expanded at all or only by a very high cost in terms of advertising. Various types of forecast are possible but as these have been described elsewhere[28] they will only be briefly summarised here:

Mechanical Methods – e.g. simple extrapolations and moving averages, with or without exponential weighting.

Statistical Methods – using techniques of econometric analysis, in particular, multiple regression.

Questionnaire and *Interview Approaches* – where opinions of managers, employees and customers are surveyed.

Experiments – both in the market itself and in a controlled (laboratory) environment.

Leading indicators are useful guides in the short run but are unsuitable for forecasting long-term movements in sales.

Forecasting is facilitated if the economy as a whole is subject to a planning system. Indeed this is one of the prime aims of *indicative* planning which involves the setting of targets for the national economy and its constituent industrial sectors and public services. We shall assess further the potential of this kind of approach in Chapter 6, but it should be fairly obvious that, since the growth of national income is one of the most significant variables in demand forecasting and one of the big problem areas, national economic planning may facilitate planning at company level. Certainly the 'management by crisis' of the British economy in the post-war era, the so-called stop-go policy of successive governments, has not been conducive to planning at the micro-level. This has been manifest in a low rate of investment, particularly notable when viewed against the performance of our Western European neighbours and of Japan. One may retort that a low and fluctuating growth rate in the UK should have encouraged firms to mount an export drive to countries enjoying higher, more predictable growth rates. This is a valid argument and points to the lack of planning by British companies, but the fact remains that improved knowledge concerning the national economy's future performance would facilitate planning and might also stimulate investment through the creation of confidence.

1.6 Search, Evaluation and Choice

The forecasting and comparison involved in strategic problem recognition may be regarded as preliminary 'intelligence' activity, following which alternatives are enumerated and evaluated and a decision is made. Another kind of intelligence activity is involved in the determination of feasible alternatives and this is usually referred to as 'search' activity. Even when dealing with operating problems, it is found that decision alternatives are not given but rather are generated or sought in response to a particular problem. We thus read of 'problem-oriented search' or 'problemistic search' in behavioural approaches to the study of decision making.[29] This contrasts with the traditional (economist's) theory of the firm in which the entrepreneur is completely informed about the alternatives open to him. According to Cyert and March[30] search will continue so long as the problem remains unsolved, but when a workable solution has been found, search will cease. Ansoff suggests that the same is sometimes true of strategic decision making, that is problem-oriented search replaces regular, planned search. Strategic change is then a one-off phenomenon where perhaps a traumatic experience stimulates search, with the company reverting to operating and administrative problems once a workable solution to the strategic problem has been found. As we argued earlier, strategic change needs planning if it is to be successful and not only must problems be recognised in advance but also the solutions to these problems. Sporadic problem-oriented search cannot hope to bring success to firms in industries characterised by rapid technological advance, for example, chemicals, petro-chemicals, electronics and aerospace. To ensure survival, firms in such industries must continually scan the environment for new opportunities. Some firms may find that a periodic review of strategy is all that is necessary, but this should be seen as a minimal requirement since no firm can be regarded as immune from saturation of demand or product obsolescence.

It is difficult to distinguish between changes which are strategic and those which are not and indeed many long-range company plans do not involve drastic changes, presumably because their objectives can be met without them. Quite often a company will plan a new product variety but this may amount to a relatively minor modification of an existing product. In time, however, successive modifications incorporating improvements brought about by advances in R & D may result in the evolution of a product which serves a rather different purpose from the original and which sells to a different kind of customer. The firm's basic activities may be extended in a number of ways; market penetration, market segmentation, market development, product development and diversification. All of these may be incorporated into a company plan but apart from diversification, which inevitably involves strategic change being a simultaneous departure from both product and market, the boundary between strategic and other changes is very difficult to draw. This is a matter to which we shall return in Chapter 4.

Assuming now that the firm has been able to identify a number of feasible alternatives possibly, though not necessarily, including diversification, the next stage is to evaluate these alternatives in terms of how well each satisfies the firm's objectives, in particular how far the gap between anticipated and desired performance will be bridged. As we shall explain shortly, our concern must be with the performance of the firm as a corporate whole, hence 'corporate planning' or 'corporate strategy'. If the proposed alternative involves the addition of a new activity, in the extreme case a merger with another business organisation, then the new entity thereby created must be appraised in total, since the whole may be more than the sum of its constituent parts. Sometimes this is called a 'synergy' effect.

The relationships at work should then be specified in a formal model, relating the pertinent causal factors, embodied in the proposed alternatives, to their effects measured in terms of the degree of attainment of the company's objectives. A model in this sense then is a means of relating the inputs and outputs of a system. The simplest kind of model which might be adopted for evaluation purposes is a statement that in an assumed set of circumstances (i.e. states of nature and competitive strategies in the terminology of decision theory and game theory), strategy 1 will have an impact of magnitude X_1 on the company's performance, however measured, strategy 2 will have an impact of magnitude X_2 on performance and so on. A more refined type of model would specify the effects of differing assumptions concerning states of nature, reactions of competitors, or both, so that for each strategy a range of possible outcomes could be listed. A system of mathematical equations from which responses to changes in variables can be calculated is one type of model which could be used for evaluation purposes, for example a set of possible strategies might involve a range of diversification rates and profit margins. The growth of demand may be seen to depend on these variables as may the growth in productive capacity (as Marris in fact argues in his growth theory). Provided that estimates of the parameters can be made for the growth of demand and growth of supply equations, it will then be possible to determine the growth potential of each strategy. In practice, it would generally be inadequate to build a model for evaluation purposes around the rate of diversification and the profit margin as the dependent variables. Nevertheless, we shall return to Marris's theory in Chapter 3 since it gives an insight into the workings of 'managerial capitalism' even though it involves a degree of abstraction so far as the decision *process* within firms is concerned.

'Simulation' involves an approach rather different from mathematical modelling and in some instances can prove a very powerful technique for evaluation purposes. Precise mathematical solutions of some business problems simply is not possible, since the complex, often dynamic relationships at work cannot always be expressed in terms of mathematical relationships. What one can do in analysing a problem, however, is to examine how a system responds to a sample of possible situations rather than attempt a complete mathematical specification. The simulation method tries to predict what would happen in practice if the actual project went ahead, but arrives at the answer without making changes in the real world situation which would generally be impracticable or too costly. That is not to say that simulation is without cost since the use of computer time may involve considerable expense and the structure of the data and the sampling method must be chosen with great care to ensure that a fair representation of the real world, and of the full analysis, is being presented. Applications in strategic decision making do not as yet appear to be widespread and the potential for this approach and indeed most other modelling techniques is limited by the wide range of strategies and random variables involved at this level of decision.

The difficulties which surround the construction of models appropriate for the task in hand may discourage elaborate analysis at the evaluation stage of strategic decision making. Sensitivity and contingency analysis, which are essential when planning for an uncertain future, become all the more difficult when adequate models are not forthcoming. Sensitivity analysis is often described as an exploration of 'What if?' questions: is a particular decision alternative attractive if national income only grows by 1 per cent per annum instead of the assumed 3 per cent? What happens if the actual rate is 2 per cent? Cleaily for testing the sensitivity of an alternative to such changes, some kind of model, however crude, is essential. Where sensitivity analysis ends and contingency analysis begins is not important. It is a matter of degree with contingency analysis examining the implications of rather more drastic changes in assumptions – an economic crisis or trade war. 'Contingency planning' generally refers to making provision for some kind of emergency; for example a contingency plan consisting of arrangements with overseas suppliers might be prepared to cope with a local strike interrupting the supply of vital components. This undoubtedly represents forward planning to cope with an uncertain future, but is rather different conceptually from strategic decision making incorporating a contingency analysis. The latter is concerned with choosing the appropriate product-market strategy to achieve the company's objectives after allowing for the major uncertainties which surround the decision.

The actual decision which is a conscious choice from among the alternatives is a trivial matter in conventional economic theory. All the known alternatives can be assessed in terms of cost and revenue, and as profit maximisation is assumed, the optimal decision is readily apparent. 'Uncertainty' in the real world means that no single performance figure can be attributed to a strategy. It is the purpose of sensitivity and contingency analysis to determine the limits within which a particular result applies, but implicit in this approach is the possibility of another alternative being preferred outside these limits. The best decision then depends upon the assumptions that are made, but even if the future and the consequences of the decision, are anticipated perfectly, the decision might only be optimal in terms of one objective.

Decision criteria will be multiple for strategic plans designed to satisfy more than one objective. The extension of profit maximisation to cover capital budgeting decisions involves the net present value (NPV) or the internal rate of return (IRR) criterion. Either of these provides a technically sound method of comparing the financial returns anticipated from a project (output) with the capital invested (input). For ranking purposes,[31] the NPV criterion is generally regarded as superior, and in capital rationing situations this is modified to NPV per pound invested to take account of the scarcity of finance for investment, which may be a limiting factor in many instances. Strategic plans will in part be directed towards a profitability objective so that the NPV criterion in pure form, or in terms of each pound invested, will be one of the yardsticks by which competing alternatives should be assessed.

Growth in sales or assets as we have suggested may, however, be a more important consideration to the firm than profitability, although the latter is bound to act at least as a constraint on strategic decision making. Each alternative will then be assessed in terms of how effective it will be in meeting the required growth performance, and efficiency in resource allocation dictates that the criterion adopted here should also relate effectiveness to input cost. Provided that limits on demand growth can be removed (using diversification if necessary), the most likely constraint for the majority of firms will be availability of finance, so that any criterion used to rank alternatives in terms of their growth potential will also need to relate performance to financial requirements (for example growth in sales or assets per £1 invested).

Security[32] is another possible objective, although regarded as a constraint in the Marris model. A number of indices may serve as measures of security, for example the level of gearing (ratio of debt finance to equity finance) which indicates the financial risk and the likelihood of the company's liquidation. This has to be related to the stability of the company's earnings and here the variance or standard deviation of cash inflows or profits can serve as a useful guide. The proportion of liquid assets will also be an important consideration since too low a level can lead to insolvency and too high a level can reduce investment, the share price, and lead to a threat of take-over (and therefore the possibility of redundancy for management).

Cost-effectiveness in meeting social responsibilities, objectives concerning market standing, reputation for innovation, public image and so on lengthen the list of criteria by which plans might be appraised. The ranking problem is compounded by the presence of risk and uncertainty. A number of criteria, including *maximin, maximax, expected value* and *minimax regret* which are examined in decision theory and game theory, may, and usually do, rank strategies differently. No single criterion has universal applicability since individuals and organisations have different attitudes to risk and uncertainty. Pessimistic decision makers will tend to prefer strategies which avoid catastrophe and implicitly adopt the maximin criterion whilst the more adventurous might assess proposals in terms of their maximum potential and use maximax as a criterion. Furthermore, since no two decision makers have the same personal values, the exercising of managerial (value) judgement will compound the difficulties involved in making an optimal choice. Perhaps, in consequence, optimising is not feasible. Certainly we can see that conflicting choices viewed against different criteria are inevitable. For example, a growth maximising plan might require such a substantial raising of debt finance that the gearing level would become critical and violate the security constraint. Where optimisation is not possible, 'satisficing' takes its place — this term being coined by H.A. Simon (143) to describe behaviour directed towards some level of satisfaction or aspiration. Thus, instead of firms being profit maximisers, they aim for target rates of return and pursue other objectives, like sales and production also set in terms of satisfactory performance levels. In the long run firms will be more likely to pursue a growth target which is regarded as good enough rather than the highest rate possible. Profit and security levels will then be aimed for which are consistent with the desired rate of growth and vice versa. This means that a compromise is reached whereby satisfactory performances are sought for each objective rather than maximum performances which could be inconsistent with one another and make conflicting demands on resources.

If strategic planning is satisficing in nature, objectives are set in terms of target performance measures, as far as possible achieving a consensus between the various interest groups which constitute the organisation. Although Cyert and March (38) have been more concerned with operating decisions than with strategic planning, their description of a bargaining process during which satisfactory-level goals are established will have its parallel in goal setting for strategic plans. The alternatives ultimately selected will frequently be based therefore on satisficing criteria. At its extreme, satisficing may discourage extensive research and evaluation particularly when information costs are high so that search may cease when a solution which seems to work is discovered. Strategic planning would then be very limited in its scope and it is unlikely that any notable change in direction would be brought about. Satisficing can be condoned to the extent that goals with conflicting demands on resources dictate a compromise position and uncertainty renders optimisation, in its strictest sense, unworkable. However, satisficing in the sense of limited search and evaluation is not recommended as a planning philosophy. To quote R.L. Ackoff (3):

> The most serious deficiency of this type of planning is that it seldom increases understanding of either the system being planned for or the planning process itself. The satisficer tends to use

only available knowledge and understanding of the system; he seldom engages in research designed to expand such knowledge, and understanding. His planning is not research oriented. [p. 9]

1.7 Implementation and Monitoring

The implementation and monitoring stages of the management process are not, strictly speaking, part of decision making or planning. Nevertheless, no decision or plan can be made without consideration of the subsequent implementation, not can its success be determined without monitoring: measuring actual performance and comparing it with what is desired. The strategic plan must first of all be feasible and this means that objectives must be set at target levels which are attainable and that the decision alternatives put forward are capable of being implemented. There is no point in proposing diversification into a field where there is no readily accessible expertise either within the company or outside it, though some companies do in fact diversify in this way. Likewise there is no sense in deciding to merge with another company if the government is likely to reject the proposal. Some strategic plans may not be feasible within the existing organisational structure so that administrative changes inextricably bound up with the plan, and diversification, either within the company or through acquisition, will frequently call for such changes; for example regrouping or production and selling activities, re-location of facilities, acquisition and training of operatives and so on.

Implementation of the corporate plan will also call for subplans for each division and department of the company. Every member of the organisation must be aware of his contribution to the overall aims of the company and indeed successful implementation can probably best be assured by encouraging widespread participation in the decision process at an early stage. Once the plan has been effected and results become detectable, monitoring becomes possible. However, information which is suitable for control of operations is not necessarily helpful in monitoring plans. For example, cost accounting is invaluable in controlling operations; it highlights variances from standard cost and facilitates investigation of inefficiency and waste, so that corrective action can be applied where necessary. Strategic planning on the other hand incorporates decisions which are frequently non-repetitive and non-reversible so that if an expensive project has exceeded the budgeted outlay, there may be no scope for corrective action after the event. (Although cost control during construction can often save large sums of money!) There is frequently a paradox in the provision of information; managers complain that there is insufficient *relevant* data on which to base their decisions, yet at the same time suffer from an excess of *irrelevant* information. If the monitoring process is to provide relevant information, it must show the degree of attainment of each objective and the contribution of each activity towards it. Moreover it must be forward looking so that current experience is projected forward and problems anticipated as we stressed earlier. To this end, new information systems may have to be designed. Accounting systems in the past have concentrated too much on the *historical* cost of system *inputs* and too little on the *anticipated* cost of achieving system *outputs*. This has hindered the measurement of cost-effectiveness, particularly in non-profit making organisations. 'Programming Planning Budgeting' or PPB for short, represents an attempt to correct the balance, by specifying programmes, each contributing to some well defined objective with the aim of comparing their costs and effectiveness and we shall examine some of the applications of PPB in the final chapter.

1.8 The Systems Approach

Complex organisations tend to be subdivided into specialised units, and the breaking down of tasks into simpler, more closely defined ones, i.e. division of labour, has been partially responsible for the expansion of our gross national product. Specialisation occurs in every walk of life — we have only to look at the subdivisions of economics, accountancy and management education to appreciate this much. Despite the advantages of specialisation, it often reduces one's awareness of the composite whole, and the systems approach sets out to correct such myopic vision by regarding an organisation, a complex machine or any other entity engaging in purposeful activity as a *total* system which consists of a process, an input and an output. A firm, for example, can be regarded as a system for the achievement of profit and sales (and usually growth in these attributes) achieved by producing outputs of goods and services from inputs of financial, human, and physical resources through a process. The appropriate arrangements for the production process or for the administration of the firm cannot be established without regard to the total organisation and, in particular, its objectives. Ansoff's book *Corporate Strategy* (10) and Ackoff's book *A Concept of Corporate Planning* (3) emphasise the systems approach by their reference to the firm as a *corporate* entity. Ansoff, moreover, describes a business firm as '. . . a *purposive* organisation whose behaviour is directed towards identifiable end purposes or objectives' (p. 36). Ackoff comments, in discussing improvements in organisation:

> A concept of the organisation as an integrated system is essential if an improvement in one of its parts is to be kept from producing a compensating deficiency in another of its parts.
>
> Even small corrective measures cannot be evaluated effectively unless one has a conception of what the organisation *should* be like as a *whole* and *ideally*. [p. 59]

When an author says that he is using the 'systems approach' for problem solving or decision making he usually means that he is concentrating on the wood rather than the trees, the whole rather than the parts, throughout his analysis — from defining the system and its objectives, through search, evaluation and choice to implementation and monitoring. The systems approach seldom finds one point of view or a single discipline adequate. It is multi-disciplinary and may call upon any expertise, that of the mathematician, engineer, economist, sociologist, psychologist or whatever is necessary for a complete study of the problem.

In strategic planning, the boundaries of the system may change according to the proposals selected. Diversification will change the relationship between the firm and its environment by incorporating new types of product, perhaps embodying a new technology and catering for different kinds of consumer need. In the acquisition of another enterprise we can see an even more immediate re-drawing of the system's boundaries. It is inadequate therefore to evaluate simply the proposed extensions of the firm's activities on their own. The planners must visualise the alternative systems in total and evaluate the strategies in terms of their contribution as part of the system and not in isolation. In this context Ansoff emphasises the analysis of 'synergy' which he describes as:

> ... the 2 + 2 = 5 effect to denote the fact that the firm seeks a product-market posture with a combined performance that is greater than the sum of its parts. [p. 72]

Following this, Ansoff lists four types of synergy: sales synergy, operating synergy, investment synergy[33] and management synergy, but part of his discussion seems to be concerned with little more than economies and diseconomies of scale; for example, investment synergy which, according to Ansoff, results from:

> ... joint use of plant, common raw materials inventories, transfer
> of research and development from one product to another, common
> tooling, common machinery. [pp. 75-6]

However, there is no doubt that the concept of synergy is a useful one
in strategic planning if only to remind the planner that the enterprise
in total can seldom, if ever, be understood from an analysis of its
separate parts. We shall see shortly, in our discussion of the 'Behavioural
Theory' of Cyert and March that a subunit view is often taken in
practice with problems tackled locally and without consideration of
their impact on the organisation in total. It is to this, and other theories
which examine business behaviour from a positive standpoint,[34] that
we now turn.

Notes

1. See A.A. Alchian (5).
2. J. Bridge and J.C. Dodds (26).
3. An issue which has policy implications for the government in its relationships with industry.
4. For a detailed coverage of 'overall' and industrial concentration see
   S. Aaronvitch and M.C. Sawyer (1), S.J. Prais (129, 130), L. Hannah
   and J.A. Kay (62), M.C. Sawyer (139) and L. Hannah (61).
5. A phenomenon first explored by A.A. Berle and G.C. Means (21) in 1932.
6. See S.J. Prais (129).
7. In 1969 the top two hundred companies in the UK accounted for 65 per
   cent of the total net assets (book value) based on a sample of quoted
   companies' accounts published by the Department of Trade and Industry,
   compared with 50 per cent in 1957 and 46 per cent in 1948.
8. See for example, D. Elliott's (47) analysis of data from the 1968 Census
   of Production, in which increases in average concentration in the order
   of 4 to 5 per cent were shown as compared with 1963.
9. See K.D. George (54).
10. For a discussion of the effect of firm size on the benefits to shareholders
    see G.D. Newbould, S.J. Stray and K.W. Wilson (117).
11. For a recent coverage see K. Midgley (107).
12. See Stock Exchange Fact Book (153).
13. Many economists take the line that the alternative objectives which
    have been proposed can be reconciled with profit, at least in the long
    run; see for example W.L. Baldwin (15).
14. Return on investment is normally termed 'profitability', and it is this
    concept rather than 'profit' in an absolute sense which appears in the
    literature on strategic decision making and corporate planning. See H.I.
    Ansoff (10) (Chapter 3).

15.   See, for example, A.A. Berle and G.C. Means (21).
16.   See, for example, J.L. Weiner (166).
17.   See, for example, M. Heald (66), H.R. Bowen (25), G. Goyder (58) and E. Morgan (115).
18.   Referring to R.A. Gordon (55).
19.   Referring to R. Dorfman (40).
20.   To substantiate this supposition one can point to pension schemes which are non-transferable, the difficulties of middle-aged managers in finding new employment and the preferences a firm may have for its own employees and thus internal promotion.
21.   For a discussion of the relationships between the growth of firms and the growth of the economy see R.L. Marris (97).
22.   See Galbraith's book *The Affluent Society* (50).
23.   In time, the removal of the balance of payments constraint, the growth of tax yields and the higher GNP per head will, it is hoped, permit a resumption of expansion in public expenditure to ensure that economic development is balanced and not biased towards industrial output.
24.   With possible government intervention if merger is involved.
25.   Some organisations have adopted an annual planning cycle to provide a logical planning sequence and to promote strategic thinking – see Chapter 6.
26.   See Chapter 2 where we introduce the concept of organisational slack.
27.   If a firm is aiming for sustainable growth, it also has to ensure that the supply of finance grows at such a rate as to permit capacity growth to match the growth in demand. See Chapter 3.
28.   See for example our earlier work on managerial decision making (26) (Chapter 5, Section 5.12 to 5.16).
29.   See R.M. Cyert and J.G. March (38) (pp. 120-2) and our discussion of this in Chapter 2.
30.   Idem.
31.   For a fuller discussion of ranking and capital rationing see A.J. Merrett and A. Sykes (106) and also Chapter 8 of our earlier work (26).
32.   Security can also be achieved in the context of the wider environment by a policy of take-over so as to give greater control over the environment. This was found to be an important motive for the period 1967/8 in the UK by G.D. Newbould (116). Apart from this defensive motive there are of course strategic motives for a merger policy – to increase the value of the firm and growth. In this respect, therefore, a merger policy can be set in the context of corporate planning.
33.   Investment includes the purchase of whole firms, and thus mergers, in this context.
34.   Much of our discussion about decision making and planning has been concerned with the decision taking capability a large firm *ought* to have and has thus been normative rather than positive.

2 BEHAVIOURAL AND MANAGERIAL THEORIES

2.1 Introduction

The newer theories of the firm all incorporate changes to the classical objective function of profit maximisation, in recognition of two facets of the modern corporation: (1) market power; (2) separation of ownership and control.

Increasing market power is implied in rising concentration ratios, and firms with this power may exercise some discretion by pursuing objectives other than profit maximisation, since the latter ceases to be a long-run prerequisite for survival when competition is less than perfect. On the other hand, without the separation of ownership and control, there would be little justification for supposing that any other objective would be pursued by a rational being.

Two alternative methodologies have been employed in the theories of the firm discussed in this chapter. The behavioural approach which we examine first, rests on the view that once external market constraints are relaxed, the behaviour of the firm becomes governed in part by organisational factors. The behavioural theory examines, amongst other things, goal formation, the decision making process and internal resource allocation in business organisations. The managerial approaches of O.E. Williamson (170, 171) and W.J. Baumol (18, 19), which we discuss later in the present chapter, are less concerned with organisational features but the scope for managerial discretion is recognised by changing the objective function to reflect managerial rather than shareholder needs. The growth theory of R.L. Marris (92, 93), although usually regarded as being of the managerial type, warrants consideration in its own right since it is richer than the others in its implications for corporate planning. Consequently the whole of the next chapter is to be devoted to growth and the theory of Marris.

2.2 Organisational Aspects of Business Behaviour

We have seen that ownership and control may be separated in the modern corporation, particularly in large complex business organisations where shareholdings are diffuse, and professional managers are employed. The need for professional line managers and advisory staff becomes apparent even in a medium-sized firm. Organisation can be regarded as the harnessing and arrangement of specialist skills to

35

facilitate the solving of complex business problems which cannot be tackled by a single decision maker. The corporation has become a large organisation with a hierarchical administrative and decision making structure. The economist's concept of an entrepreneur as a single minded owner-manager making all the decisions for himself may be re-interpreted in terms of a peak co-ordinator[1] who uses group effort for decision making.

S. Cleland (32) argues that the firm should be studied within the framework of general organisation theory and that the entrepreneur should be seen as a manager-executive who adopts different roles as he performs different functions of organising, planning and controlling. He develops specific policies and establishes standard procedures for control to enable subordinates in the organisation to make numerous operating decisions. These policies and procedures become constraints, replacing the market constraints which regulate the behaviour of the firm in traditional theory. The establishment of a control system should be an intermittent activity, as should all organising activity which Cleland describes as establishing the structure of the firm, its inputs, outputs and workflows and designing of decision processes. Having performed his basic organising and control activity and delegated routine work in those areas to subordinates, he will have more time for planning. In particular it is recognised that growth-oriented firms must plan if expansion is to be successful. Although Cleland's attempt to extend the entrepreneur concept forms a useful bridge between traditional models and the behavioural and managerial theories which we are exploring in this book, his analysis remains very much a framework within which planning, organising and operations are distinguished, and the impact of organisational structure on the behaviour of the firm is left largely unexplored. However, in a world where behaviour is not rigidly constrained by the market, where oligopoly rather than perfect competition is the market structure under scrutiny, the nature of the organisation cannot be neglected in analysing the behaviour of the firm. In hierarchical organisations, authority is delegated, ultimately from the shareholders, the board, and thence to the managing director or chief executive. He in turn delegates authority to sales, production and finance executives who head their respective departments. Of course, in some organisations the degree of departmentalisation at this level of hierarchy may be greater, including for example personnel, purchasing, inventory, and research and development activities, or there may be delegation by product type or by territory. Even if there is only a tripartite split, we see the emergence of specialised competences and restriction of attention to a limited part of the firm's total experience.

P. Selznick (141) argues that departmentalisation brings a bifurcation of interests among the subunits in the organisation and that the commitment to subunit goals assumes an importance over and above their contribution to the total organisation programme. The needs of the individual then become dependent on the continued success and, perhaps, expansion of the subunit and this in turn may lead to increased conflict between subunits. The firm, therefore, is an entity which is not only subject to external pressures but also internal pressures brought about by the bifurcation of interests within the organisation. This is stressed by R.M. Cyert and J.G. March (38) who believe that a bargaining process occurs among the coalition of participants with disparate demands, and that the goal structure which emerges reflects the subunits or departments contained in the organisation. In the contemporary firm, they argue that the most relevant goals are production, sales, market share, inventory and profit. Thus, while profit will be of general significance for the organisation, the sales executive and his subordinates will strive towards sales or market share goals, and the production subunit will be primarily concerned with the production goal.

Much of post-war organisation theory has been concerned with decision making in organisations, particularly the work of H.A. Simon. According to his theory of Administrative Behaviour (143), decision makers in organisations can only 'satisfice' in contrast to the entrepreneur of economic theory who is able to optimise. Cyert and March have used Simon's notions of satisficing, problem-oriented search and the aspiration level model in their *Behavioural Theory of the Firm* which, unlike the earlier models of organisation theory, is specifically directed to the business firm and the environment in which it operates and the decision variables which characterise the firm's operation.

2.3 The Behavioural Theory of the Firm

R.M. Cyert and J.G. March (38) in developing their behavioural theory regarded the following as their terms of reference:

(1) the firm should be the basic unit;
(2) the purpose of the theory should be to predict the behaviour of the firm with respect to such decisions as price, output and resource allocation;
(3) the research should be directed explicitly towards the actual

process of organisational decision making. (p. 19)

The theory incorporated a substantial amount of earlier organisation theory, notably the work of Simon, but we see in the behavioural theory a specific interest in the firm and its decisions. Research was conducted to establish the sequence of behaviour leading to the decision itself, this sequence being specified in a flow diagram and programmed for computer simulation. The resulting model was subject to empirical test against the actual behaviour of selected firms and the predictions were sufficiently promising to suggest that other firms' behaviour could be likewise simulated. However, each firm would need a separate computer programme to include its own particular procedures, and as such no general predictions are available from the programmes constructed by Cyert and March. Nevertheless, these authors have claimed that their approach can be extended to other business organisations and to that extent their theory has general applicability.

The composite theory comprises four sub-theories of:

(1)   organisational goals;
(2)   organisational expectations;
(3)   organisational choice;
(4)   organisational control.

We shall examine the first two of these individually but shall take the sub-theories of choice and control together since they are closely intertwined, being dominated by the standard operating procedures of the firm.

The Theory of Organisational Goals

It was suggested in the preceding Section (2.2) that the goals of subunits may be in conflict and assume an overriding importance for the individuals working within those subunits, so much so that the goals of the organisation as a whole may be pushed from the forefront of attention. This theme of conflict is developed by Cyert and March who regard the firm as a coalition of different interest groups including: shareholders, managers, employees and customers. Provided that the membership of the coalition is fairly stable over time and that the organisational structure remains unchanged, it is possible to identify the parts of the coalition which are most concerned with particular types of decision and the goals towards which they are working.

As a result of bargaining between members of the coalition a measure of agreement will be reached as to (a) departmental allocations of resources and (b) the policy commitments of the organisation. Conflict is resolved through the making of side-payments which represents the central process of goal specification in this model. However, the objectives which emerge are imperfectly rationalised and may not have been fully tested for consistency with current policy. Indeed, the illusion of consensus may be better preserved by a less than thorough test for consistency. Some of the objectives may be stated fairly specifically in the form of targets or levels of aspiration, while others may be stated in non-operational form (such as an aim to have a good public image), which increases the probability of agreement being maintained. The stability of the objectives is enhanced through the use of mutual control systems which include budgetary control to enforce the agreed allocation of resources, and role specification to ensure that the allocation of functions is preserved. Thus much of the organisational structure is taken as given and, to the extent that precedents are regarded as binding, coalition agreements become semi-permanent arrangements. The memory of the organisation consists in part of precedents formalised in terms of standard operating procedures and in part of precedents less formally stored. The fact that such a memory exists removes the need for re-consideration of agreements, decisions and commitments. Thus, today's departmental budgets will serve as the basis for future budgets and likewise today's targets for production and sales will largely shape those for subsequent periods.

To explain how the demands made on the coalition change through experience, Cyert and March (38) use 'the aspiration level model' which they summarise as a set of three propositions:

(1)   in the steady state, aspiration level exceeds achievement by a small amount;
(2)   where achievement increases at an increasing rate, aspiration level will exhibit short-run lags behind achievement;
(3)   where achievement decreases, aspiration level will be above achievement. (p. 34)

Aspiration level movements are, however, not the only type of demand changes; others occur through shifts in attention focus. In particular since individuals concentrate on different demands at different points in time, the organisation may be able to survive by focusing on a subset of the organisational goals at any one time. Conflicting goals may, therefore, not be seen simultaneously, but tackled sequentially

and, in consequence, there may be no strong pressures to resolve
apparent inconsistencies. Attention focus may change in response to a
particular event — for example the firm might become safety conscious
after the experience of a fatal accident.

It is in connection with the discussion of the coalition's viability
that one of the most valuable concepts of the theory is developed,
namely that of 'organisational slack'.[2] There is normally a disparity
between the resources available to the organisation and the resources
needed to maintain a viable coalition. Payments, in their various forms
to coalition members, are usually above the minimum necessary to keep
them within the organisation, largely as a result of uncertainty concerning the minimum acceptable factor payments and a consequent leaning
towards over-provision. Although there may be a long-run tendency for
payments and demands to be equal, short-run frictions will generally
result in the disparity known as organisational slack. The notion of
organisational slack includes not only excessive payments to individuals
or allocations to subunits, but also an over-zealous pursuit of certain
organisational goals. Either way, the firm's behaviour can be deflected
away from the pursuit of maximum profits but, on the other hand, in a
crisis when resource scarcity brings on renewed bargaining, organisational slack can be pared until the firm is able to make adequate profits
to ensure survival. This option is not open to the profit-maximising
firm which would already have seized any opportunities for eliminating
slack and, of course, in traditional theory the firm has perfect knowledge of factor prices and would not need a safety margin of over
provision.

It must be emphasised that organisational slack is not a phenomenon
deliberately created to cushion the firm, although it does act as a
stabiliser by absorbing excess resources during a period of prosperity
and providing a pool of resources in an emergency. It is more properly
regarded as a by-product of the bargaining process and its nature and
magnitude will vary from firm to firm according to the composition of
the coalition and the relative strengths of individuals and subunits in
the bargaining process. The existence of slack can be seen in numerous
instances of firms on the verge of liquidation which have been able to
discover economies virtually overnight. Unprofitable plants are closed
to rationalise production, staffs are slimmed, product ranges are
reviewed and streamlined where necessary. A profit maximiser would
have taken such opportunities to increase profits at an earlier date and
a firm which engaged in planning activity would have anticipated the
crisis and taken remedial action earlier. But there is little doubt that

many firms exist with organisational slack which is only scrutinised
when crisis threatens. This can be illustrated by the energy crisis of
the winter of 1973/4 which affected most of British industry. For a
period, industry was compelled to work to a three-day week as a fuel
saving measure. Despite the drastic reduction in inputs available to
firms, down to 60 per cent of the normal availability in many cases,
the output of British industry held up remarkably well with many
firms able to produce over 80 per cent of normal output, some over
90 per cent, and others nearly 100 per cent. It was argued at the time
that this apparent increase in efficiency was but a short-term phenomenon, that the intensity of production during the truncated week
could not be tolerated by man or machine over a prolonged period,
but, to the authors, the experience of the three-day week provides
compelling evidence for the existence of organisational slack.

Returning now to the main theme of the sub-theory of organisational goals, Cyert and March argue that once the relevant goals have
been identified, they can be assumed to be fairly stable over time.
Though stable, these goals will not be static, and changes in aspiration
level and attention focus will occur over time. The empirical work
of the behavioural theory suggests that five goals are of significance
in decisions about price and output. These are, as indicated above:
production, sales, market share, inventory and profit. *Inventory* is a
consideration which is absent from traditional static models but, in
reality, there are time lags between purchasing, production and selling.
Moreover, the level of sales is uncertain at the time of production,
so the size of inventories is an important issue. How small should
inventories be allowed to become, given this uncertainty? How large
can they be allowed to grow given the cost of keeping capital tied up
in this way? The changes in inventories of finished goods also provide
feedback data on the state of demand such that stocks of final products
are decreasing, then demand exceeds the rate of production, and vice
versa if stocks are increasing. The *sales* and *market share* goals (which
are often alternatives for one another), although particularly pertinent
to the demands of the sales subunit, also seem to hold high priority
among other coalition members. The reasons for this emphasis towards
sales are enumerated by Baumol (18, 19) who takes this objective as
the maximand for his managerial theory. The *production* goal represents, to a large extent, the demands of coalition members directly
involved in production. It is concerned not just with the level of
production, but also the variance from one period to another, given the
pressures towards stable employment and ease of scheduling. The reader

will observe that the production goal cannot remain independent of
the sales or market share goal for any length of time, but organisations
do seem to give varying emphasis to their production and sales goals
according to the most pressing problems they face. On the one hand
an organisation may have adequate productive capacity and no
production scheduling problems but, on the other, experience
difficulties in filling its order books. A different firm may enjoy long
order books but fail to meet delivery dates because of inadequate
capacity, poor scheduling or stoppages in production. The former
organisation would have a production goal dictated by sales potential
while the latter's attention focus would be towards the production
goal with its sales goal predetermined by its success in meeting that.

In common with all theories of the firm, a *profit* goal or constraint
is necessary. Whereas this enters as a constraint in Baumol's model
(18), rather than a goal, profits in the behavioural theory are seen as
one of the key goals pursued by the firm.[3] According to Cyert and
March (38), the profit goal summarises two things:

(1)   demands for accumulating resources in order to distribute them
in the form of capital investments, dividends to stockholders, payments to creditors, or increased budgets to subunits;
(2)   demands on the part of top management for favourable
performance measures. (p. 42)

The Theory of Organisational Expectations

This part of the behavioural theory deals with the broad issue of
information generation, gathering and handling, and in so doing covers
the search and evaluation aspects of decision making. The concept of a
perfectly informed entrepreneur, who scans all alternatives continuously and evaluates these in terms of marginal returns against marginal
costs, is replaced by that of an organisation which is not completely
informed about its environment and which, moreover, suffers from
internal communication difficulties, which searches for alternatives
intermittently — when problems arise — and which evaluates alternatives using simple rules of thumb. According to this model then,
information is not given but revealed by search activity which is
stimulated when a problem is recognised. The empirical studies of Cyert
and March have revealed that, initially, rough data are generally used
to screen the alternatives, whereupon a short list of feasible options is
drawn up for more detailed evaluation. In most instances, search did
not proceed very far and alternatives were evaluated in order of

generation, i.e. sequentially rather than simultaneously. Frequently, the first alternative expected to yield a satisfactory solution to the problem was selected even when other alternatives were known to exist but which had not been evaluated. Thus optimising behaviour was replaced by satisficing behaviour[4] — finding a workable solution rather than the best. Conspicuous alternatives or pet projects were frequently chosen and a fairly firm commitment to action was taken before search had become either deep or widespread. Such favoured projects appeared to be supported by biased cost and revenue estimates so that 'expectations' were dependent upon the hopes and wishes of those party to the decision process. Bias can also occur in communication, a topic discussed by Cyert and March (37) in an earlier work in which it was regarded as a critical variable in decision making. If this were so, one would doubt the reliability of a predictive model, but the phenomenon is somewhat played down in the behavioural theory on the grounds that biases are recognised by the recipients of communications and are then corrected, and also that organisations tend to focus on easily verified data, especially feedback, in preference to more remote anticipations about the uncertain world in which organisations exist.

Localised search, besides leaving less favoured alternatives uncovered, implies a partial, fragmented approach to problem solving. Instead of examining the implications of a problem for the firm as a whole, the problem is classified according to departmental function, for example sales or production, it being the responsibility of the sales manager or production manager to find a workable solution. In the studies undertaken by Cyert and March, it was only when localised search failed to yield a satisfactory solution that search became more intense and widespread, and there was thus no real evidence of the systems approach which we argued earlier was central to corporate planning. It must be remembered, though, that the behavioural theory is concerned more with operating decisions than with strategic decisions, but even so some of the case studies reproduced by Cyert and March (38) in their fourth chapter do cast light on fairly major decisions, for example, that concerning accelerated renovation of old equipment which involved expenditures totalling $ 600,000. From this case, three major features of the decision process were regarded as being of particular significance in the context of expectations in decision making:

(1) it is clear that search behaviour by the firm was apparently

initiated by an exogenous event, was severely constrained and was distinguished by 'local' rather than 'general' scanning procedures;
(2)   the noncomparability of cost expectations and expected returns led to estimates that were vague or easily changed and made the decision exceptionally susceptible to the factors of attention focus and available organisational slack;
(3)   the firm considered resources as fixed and imposed feasibility, rather than optimality, tests on the proposed expenditure. (p. 52)

Concerning the third feature, it seemed that cost-effectiveness only became a significant consideration when funds became scarce. In the other case studies there was some limited evidence of financial appraisal but using crude methods like the 'payback' approach rather than the more technically correct 'discounted cash flow' techniques. It would be wrong to predict marked deviations from optimal investment patterns, since rules of thumb would provide some constraints on resource allocation. On the other hand, the weakness of *market* constraints on oligopolists does permit organisational slack, and any alternative which satisfies the *internal* constraints of the firm and which meets with the approval of powerful factions within the organisation has a high probability of being adopted. Perhaps the most significant finding, from our point of view, to emerge from this sub-theory is the conclusion that:

> ... decision making is likely to reflect a response to local problems of apparent pressing need as much as it will reflect continuing *planning* on the part of the organisation. [p. 79] [5]

Standard Operating Procedures in Choice and Control

Before examining the standard procedures used by business organisations, Cyert and March developed 'a partial model of organisational choice' (Section 5.1), but they felt that a theory of the firm directed specifically at decision making would have to include standard procedures. For this reason, and because such procedures also dominate the control function of management, we shall discuss standard operating procedures first and then examine their roles in choice and control.

In the coverage of these standard operating procedures, they propounded three principles. The first of these is concerned with uncertainty avoidance and it is claimed that firms typically use short-run feedback as a trigger to action, rather than predictions of uncertain future events, and that they then adopt standardised decision rules. The second is that once a feasible set of rules has been determined, change is seldom envisaged, except under duress. The third states that simple rules are adopted, but that it is quite common for a list of conditions to be added, describing the circumstances under which procedures may be modified.

Numerous studies on both sides of the Atlantic have revealed that cost-based pricing is common in many industries and the full-cost pricing rule typifies the general choice procedure described by Cyert and March as revealed here. Short-run feedback frequently provides the decision maker with demand information in the shape of inventory movements, and length of order books. This kind of information seems to be preferred to forecasts of sales, which are prone to error, and hence provides a means of 'avoiding uncertainty'. The pricing procedure itself which involves the addition of a percentage markup to full unit cost at the estimated sales volume is, in many instances, rigidly adhered to, even to the extent of maintaining a rigid markup on cost. During periods of depressed economic activity the rule may be abandoned, with firms content to set prices which cover only the avoidable costs of production. Quite often nowadays the simple rule is given a fair amount of flexibility so that the markup can be varied in response to demand circumstances but typically the demand estimates are based on feedback rather than forecasts. Pricing is a recurrent operating decision and it is generally for decision making at this level that procedures are developed. Strategic problems do not recur in the same form and consequently there are no set responses which the firm can learn or develop for decision making at this level. On the other hand it is possible to formulate a routine for the creation of plans to ensure that certain steps are followed before any decision is taken. Thus while a strategic decision may itself be unique, it may have resulted from an established sequence of goal formation, forecasting, problem recognition and definition and so on, perhaps set out in an annual planning sequence or cycle.

The kind of planning described by Cyert and March in their section on standard operating procedures is not long-term planning which they thought 'plays a relatively minor role in decision making within the firm' (p. 110). It is the kind of short- to medium-term planning manifest in budgets (which also serve as control devices) that is discussed in this context. In the first place the budget is used to state the anticipated results on a company or departmental basis for all or part of its activities. Subsequently achievement is checked against the expectations detailed in the budget and corrective action triggered where necessary (i.e. the control function).

Four observations on plans are made in the behavioural theory:

(1)   plans contain targets for sales, costs, profits, etc., and therefore embody organisational goals;

(2)   plans often consist of schedules with details of intermediate steps to the anticipated end product; in so doing they specify acceptable achievement levels for subunits and the organisation as a whole and for segments of the planning period as well as for the period as a whole;

(3)   a plan can be regarded as a theory to the extent that relationships between sales, costs, and profit are stated; thus although it is difficult to assess profit month by month and department by department, sales and cost data can serve as guideposts to the achievement of a target level of profit;

(4)   a plan is a precedent since it provides a statement of the decisions arrived at for one period and, so long as satisfactory results arise, there is a strong case for using it as the basis for future decisions.

Referring back to the theory of organisational goals, it was recognised that mutual control systems enforce coalition agreements and so budgets have an important part to play in that part of the behavioural theory as well. Coalition agreements, if specified in budgets, will tend to remain stable, only changing slowly over time. Cyert and March believe that such changes as do come about tend: 'to reflect the expansionist inclinations of subunits rather than systematic reviews by top management' (p. 112). It is concluded, following this section on standard operating procedures, that procedures are followed in avoiding uncertainty and, to this end, reacting to feedback is preferred to forecasting the environment; also that the organisation uses standard procedures (and rules of thumb) to make and implement choices. Decisions are dominated by these procedures in the short run and control too is focused on them. Thus, if the standard decision rules of an organisation can be determined, the possibility of simulating its behaviour is heightened. We shall now draw the strands of the theory together to see how a predictive model, based on simulation, can be constructed.

The Structure of the Organisational Decision Making Process
The standard operating procedures of the organisation are acquired

through a 'learning' process. Cyert and March believe that organisations exhibit adaptive behaviour and this is a central feature of the decision making process together with the concepts of: quasi-resolution of conflict (from the theory of organisational goals); uncertainty avoidance (mentioned in the theory of organisational expectations and the section on standard procedures); and problemistic search (the theory of organisational expectations). Organisations can be regarded as adaptive institutions in so far as they change their goals, their focus of attention and revise their procedures in the light of their experience. It is assumed in the behavioural theory that organisational goals, in a particular time period, are a function of:

(1)   organisational goals of the previous time period;
(2)   organisational experience with respect to that goal in the previous period;
(3)   experience of comparable organisations with respect to the goal dimension in the previous time period. (p. 123)

Initially a simple linear function is hypothesised:

$$G_t = a_1 G_{t-1} + a_2 E_{t-1} + a_3 C_{t-1}$$

where G is the organisational goal, E the experience of the organisation, C a summary of the experience of comparable organisations, and where $a_1 + a_2 + a_3 = 1$.

Organisations are also alleged to learn to attend to some parts of their environment and not to others. In particular they learn which performance evaluation criteria are useful and which are not, and which aspects of their environment they should make reference to for purposes of comparison. Adaptation in search rules occurs when an organisation, having tackled a particular problem successfully in a specific manner, tends to follow the same kind of search activity when similar problems recur in the future. Thus the sequence of consideration of alternatives will change in response to the success and failures of the organisation. If the order of search is known, the likelihood of predicting an organisation's decisions is enhanced. The general structure of the decision making process will now be represented in the flow chart which we reproduce from the principal reference as Figure 2.1. The main elements of this chart are:

(1)   *Quasi-resolution of Conflict.* This leaves the organisation with a

48   *Behavioural and Managerial Theories*

Figure 2.1: Organisational Decision Process in Abstract Form

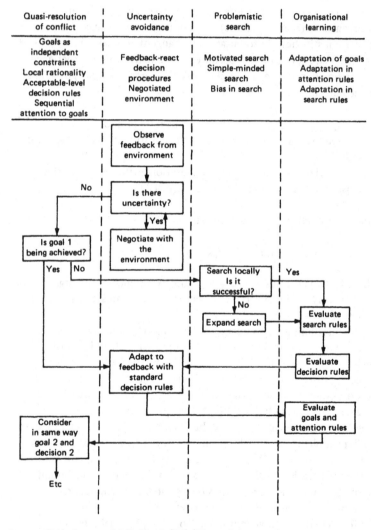

Source: R.M. Cyert and J.G. March (38) (Figure 6.1, p. 126).

set of goals which, though incompletely tested for consistency, represents the demands of coalition members. Though these demands may be conflicting, attention focus and the pursuit of goals sequentially, enables the organisation to survive. There are two aspects of the goals which must be considered. There is the subset which is operational, attention focus perhaps reducing the suggested set of five to a smaller subset, and then there is the aspiration level for each goal which is normally greater than, or equal to, the currently attained level, except for inventory which is a special case having an upper and lower limit.

(2)   *Uncertainty Avoidance.* The organisation avoids uncertainty by responding to feedback as a trigger to action and by 'negotiating' with the environment. The latter expression means that organisations try to make their environment controllable by entering into contracts with suppliers and major customers, by using business conventions which are understood and followed by rivals and by internal budgeting as a mutual control system. Conventions, which arise from the industry-wide adoption of standard rules, have been seen as devices which permit tacit collusion. Baumol, for example, regards conventions as sufficiently potent in oligopoly to remove interdependence as a consideration from more routine decisions.

In their flow chart, Cyert and March have inserted the sequence: is there uncertainty? If the answer is yes, negotiate with the environment, and then determine whether there is still uncertainty. The present authors doubt the relevance of this particular sequence since the activities which Cyert and March describe under the heading 'negotiated environment', such as entering into contracts, use of conventions, internal budgeting, would surely be matters dealt with throughout the financial year rather than in response to a test for uncertainty. In fairness to Cyert and March, they do state explicitly that the decision process is continuous and that the starting point in the flow chart is arbitrary. We still feel, however, that this part of the sequence is of dubious validity.

(3)   *Problemistic Search.* The terms used in this part of the flow chart need little commentary apart, perhaps, from 'Bias in search'. This does not include *communication* bias which is ignored on the grounds that counter-bias tends to negate its influence. The bias which is incorporated into the model is that which occurs in adjusting expectations to hopes and this has the consequence of decreasing the amount of

time devoted to search, and of stimulating the growth of organisational slack — slack which tends to be eliminated in periods of adverse fortune for the firm.

(4)   *Organisational Learning.* In this part of the chart, the boxes: 'evaluate search rules' and 'evaluate decision rules' follow from the organisation's experience in selecting a feasible alternative. If the customary localised search does not reveal a solution early in the process, the order in which alternatives are considered may be revised for future reference, with unsuitable alternatives being relegated to the bottom of the list and the more suitable ones promoted to higher places in the order. Moreover, since decisions are heavily dependent on standard procedures, the latter too will be subject to change if found unsuccessful. It must be remembered, however, that standard rules used for decision making have often stood the test of time and are rigidly adhered to, and one should only expect change following *repeated* failure. On the other hand the search rules, concerned with the order in which alternatives are considered may be less stable. Cyert and March believed that the organisational decision making process, as represented in Chapter 6 of their behavioural theory, would serve as a useful basis for the study of decision making in business organisations. We propose here to examine two features of behavioural theory in our appraisal: (a) its positive implications as revealed by its predictive power; and (b) its implications for normative analysis, i.e. how firms *should* plan and make decisions.

(a)   *Positive Implications.* In Chapter 7 of *The Behavioural Theory of the Firm* — 'A Specific Price and Output Model' — the general decision process described hitherto is applied to a retail department store. The decision process of the latter is simulated, predictions are obtained and compared with actual observed behaviour. The principal goals are sales and markup, and the decision variables are price and order levels (output not being an appropriate decision variable for a department store). The results were encouraging: 95 per cent of 'predicted' prices were correct and, although paucity of data precluded adequate testing of the order levels, such data as were available tended to confirm the validity of the model. However, the firm described in this study had more than 100 major departments and only about a dozen of these were studied in any detail. The specific model in fact deals with only one department, but Cyert and March believed that the decision processes of that department were representative of the merchandising group as a whole and, further, since department stores tend to be similar in operation, it was argued that the model represents many aspects of decision making in that type of business. The simulations reported elsewhere in Cyert and March's book also give support to their approach: for example, the duopoly model described in Chapter 5 produced results for profit and market shares which were regarded as a 'surprisingly good' fit to the real world data. Further, the study of portfolio selection by G.P.E. Clarkson, reproduced in Chapter 10 of *The Behavioural Theory*, yielded results very close to the portfolios actually selected by the trust officer whose behaviour was simulated. Results such as these, however, are highly specific to the cases under investigation. General predictions about the behaviour of firms in a given market environment are not forthcoming except in the sense that if organisational slack exists, we can predict that a firm will generally make attempts to remove this slack when an impending crisis brings pressure to bear. We argued earlier, in discussing the theory of organisational goals, that the presence of organisational slack can be readily demonstrated in many instances. While a profit maximising firm would have no alternative but to accept a lower profit when confronted with an increase in fixed outlays, for example, local government rates (equivalent to a lump-sum tax), or in other fixed overheads, one can predict that a satisficing firm will respond by removing slack in order to maintain profits at an acceptable level. A knowledge of the more conspicuous alternatives open to the firm would then permit a reasonable assessment of the firm's most likely response. Despite the apparent simplicity of such a deductive process, the result is by no means trivial. Traditional theory, whilst offering general predictions, does so by assuming that, within a given market environment, all firms will respond to any given set of stimuli in the same manner. *The Behavioural Theory* has at least opened up an approach which permits an analysis of the decision alternatives open to firms whose behaviour is not governed by the market alone but also by their internal structure and mechanisms.

(b) *Normative Implications.* The fact that firms only seek workable solutions to problems which are tackled sequentially as they arise, frequently in the department responsible for the particular kind of activity with which the problem is apparently concerned, that response to feedback is preferred to forecasts in an uncertain world and that firms use rules of thumb rather than optimisation techniques, is of great significance for practising economists and corporate planners in industry.

Admittedly in the past decade, great advances have been made by many firms, for example in the use of operations research methods, the adoption of management accounting systems and even in the development of corporate planning capabilities. Such changes will have a bearing on both positive and normative implications of *The Behavioural Theory*. However, it is our belief that firms, particularly in the UK, are still represented more accurately by a satisficing model than by an optimising model.

A defeatist approach would be to argue that, since satisficing behaviour has been explained in a formal theory of the firm, it is both inevitable and respectable. Our interpretation, however, is that since firms do exist with organisational slack, there are steps which can be taken to improve performance of firms, industries, and ultimately the national economy. Few commentators would deny the importance of pursuing this end and corporate planning can bring change in the following ways:

(1)   by ensuring that mechanisms exist for identifying and specifying the nature of strategic, administrative and operating problems;
(2)   by anticipating problems sufficiently far in advance of their occurrence to enable corrective action to be taken, particularly where strategic decisions are concerned and where there is a long time lag between action and effect;
(3)   by fostering a systems approach to decision making, in particular by examining the totality of a problem rather than its impact on an isolated subunit; also to encourage more widespread search for decision alternatives;
(4)   by using methods of managerial economics, management accounting and operations research to replace rules of thumb by management science, and here should be included the use of forecasting techniques to facilitate anticipatory behaviour and remove the need to rely on short-run feedback data.

In formulating corporate planning advice, it must be recognised that the classical model of an omnisciently rational firm does not depict the business organisation of the real world. Cyert and March point to two difficulties in generating and implementing management science recommendations. Firstly, organisations do not have well-defined preference orderings and secondly, full implementation of proposals is often confounded by the failure to understand the wider implications of those proposals. Both of these difficulties, suggest Cyert and March, are typical manifestations of an adaptive, multiple goal system.

In conclusion, we regard *The Behavioural Theory* as having made a useful contribution to the literature of business behaviour, not for providing a model of the firm which organisations should aim to replicate, but rather for the insight it gives into satisficing behaviour and the problems which hinder the introduction of optimising techniques. Most importantly it demonstrates the gulf which exists between actual behaviour and the corporate planning ideal.

2.4 Baumol's Sales Revenue Maximisation Hypothesis[6]

The Sales Revenue Maximisation Hypothesis, henceforth SRM hypothesis, does not adopt the behavioural approach of Cyert and March but follows the tradition of classical theory by focusing on the market constraints which circumscribe the behaviour of the firm. W.J. Baumol's model incorporates the managerial objective of sales revenue maximisation, although profit does enter as a constraint which is in part exogenously determined by the need to satisfy shareholders, but it is also determined partially by the company's internal financing requirements.

Baumol has attempted to bring greater realism into oligopoly theory and claims to have provided a determinate solution for oligopoly without deviating from classical methodology. This approach has the virtue of tractability, unlike that of the behavioural theory which probes deeper into the firm by focusing on decision processes and internal resource allocation, but at the cost of being analytically evasive.

The determinacy of Baumol's model depends on the belief that oligopolistic interdependence is not a particularly important consideration in price and output decisions, otherwise, as W.G. Shepherd (142) and C.J. Hawkins (65) have shown, it is difficult to draw any firm conclusions concerning the behaviour of firms in an oligopolistic market from Baumol's SRM hypothesis. Baumol argues that the aggressive countermoves of competitors, normally postulated in theories of oligopoly, may not appear in practice unless the status quo in terms of market shares is threatened by the actions of one or more parties. The decision making apparatus of a large organisation is regarded as too clumsy for the effective interplay of strategy and counter strategy. Instead, firms use widely understood rules of thumb when changing prices and outputs, so that behaviour is not seen as predatory. This ensures predictability of behaviour and enables executives to enjoy the quiet life, security and respectability in the eyes of their competitors.

Sales may become a more important objective than profit in big business (particularly when ownership and control are separated) on account of the use of sales as a yardstick of success and also because power, influence and prestige are often associated with size measured in terms of sales. It is a more readily available yardstick of performance than profit, which is in many cases largely arbitrary, particularly in a multi-product firm. Baumol admits that the evidence to support his objective function is largely 'impressionistic' based on 'spotty observations' but a couple of studies[7] which we cite below, are suggestive of sales being a better explanatory variable than profit in accounting for variations in executive salaries. Baumol does not, however, neglect the importance of profit in business activity. As in all theories of the firm, it has a part to play, but in Baumol's model it becomes subservient to sales once the minimum level of profit has been assured. The sales drive does not become satiated in this model and, although the assumption of sales *maximisation* is clearly unrealistic in an uncertain world, it is a justifiable simplification given the terms of reference of this model. The profit constraint may or may not be invoked when the firm sets its price and output. In the absence of advertising it may be that when sales revenue meets its absolute maximum value, the firm is making profits over and above the minimum necessary, in which case the constraint would not be invoked. On the other hand, if predatory conduct is avoided by oligopolists, they will avoid price competition, which is regarded as against the joint interests of the participants and, in consequence, use advertising and other forms of non-price competition instead. Since advertising almost inevitably increases sales, although no evidence is cited by Baumol to this effect, it is likely that the expansion of sales and output will only be checked by profit considerations, thus resulting in a constrained sales maximum. By deducing that the profit constraint is always operative we arrive at the conclusion that the firm never makes more than an acceptable profit and, consequently, any crisis which impairs the profit position will necessitate corrective action to restore it to an acceptable level. Conversely, when cost or market conditions improve, the firm finds that the profit constraint is relaxed, permitting an increase in sales up to that level where the constraint is once again effective. It is therefore possible to predict the effects of demand shifts, changes in fixed costs and taxes and these predictions are the same whether the Baumol single period or multi-period model are used.[8]

(a) Demand Shifts

If the demand curve shifts upwards, without a corresponding increase
in costs, the firm's profit will improve, profit will then be greater than
the minimum necessary and sales can be increased until the profit
constraint again becomes operative. Conversely, a fall in demand will
bring a contraction in sales, with the firm forced to recover the potential
profits which had been sacrificed in favour of sales.

(b) Changes in Fixed Costs

'Fixed' in this context refers to insensitivity to output, to include such
costs as rents, insurance, and elements of managerial and supervisory
salaries and even some wage costs which, in the short run at least, do
not change as output changes. Such costs can and do change as a result
of other pressures and, as higher costs become payable, the firm's
profits will be reduced to an unacceptable level if, prior to the increase,
the constraint was operative.

Figure 2.2: Response of the Sales Revenue Maximiser to Fixed Cost
Increases

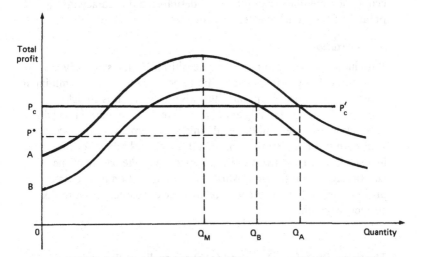

In Figure 2.2, A represents the original profit function. An increase
in fixed costs depresses this curve uniformly to B. The profit maximising output remains unchanged at $0Q_M$ but the constrained sales revenue
maximising output must be reduced from its former quantity $0Q_A$ to
$0Q_B$ otherwise profits will fall from the acceptable level of $0P_c$ to $0P^*$.

The new equilibrium could be attained by increasing price to reduce quantity demanded to the lower output now being achieved or, alternatively, advertising could be diminished to reduce demand to the required level. A mix of raising price and reducing advertising (or other promotional expenditures) is also possible. The likelihood of some increase in price is an interesting prediction given that firms who use a cost-based pricing rule will tend to raise prices in response to any kind of cost increase. Competing firms experiencing similar cost increases will do likewise even if open collusion or price leadership is not practised, simply as a result of revising their cost calculations and applying the customary percentage markup. In practice, oligopolistic firms do tend to raise prices in response to increases in costs be they of the fixed or variable variety. Traditional theory predicts no change for fixed costs and according to the Kinked Demand Curve Theorem,[9] variable costs can also move within certain limits without causing changes in price or output. Such predictions of price stability in oligopoly are at odds with every day experience, whereas Baumol's theory offers more plausible predictions even if the underlying hypothesis remains unproven. From the standpoint of positive economics, credible assumptions are desirable, but accuracy in prediction is of much greater consequence.

(c)   Taxation

Both lump-sum and pro-rata taxes are 'shifted' in the same way as fixed costs. The profit constraint has to be set in terms of the minimum acceptable after-tax profit, but otherwise the analysis is straightforward. Output and selling expenses will tend to be reduced, as will production expenses and those administrative expenses which vary with output. In general the same results as were obtained for the increase in fixed costs will apply, irrespective of the nature of the tax, the significant factor at work being the reduction in after-tax profit to below the acceptable level and the consequent need to take corrective action.

The three situations (a), (b) and (c) above spell out the positive implications. In general, the firm is seen to create organisational slack in terms of sales revenues pursued beyond the level which would be consistent with maximum profits. Thus, output is higher, and prices and profit lower than in the profit-maximising firm. Advertising and other promotional expenditures are explicitly introduced into this model and they too are higher than would be required if profit maximisation were the objective.

Casual empiricism seems to support the model both in terms of its predictions and the original hypothesis that sales revenue is a highly regarded objective in many organisations. It is also probably true to a certain extent that the use of conventions, for example full-cost pricing, permits tacit collusion to take place and thereby removes inter-dependence from the calculations of the firm. There are no grounds, however, to suggest that interdependence can be ignored where *strategic* matters are concerned. This argument only applies to those operating decisions which are not designed to bring about any radical changes in market shares and a major sales expansion drive would probably be met by retaliatory measures from competitors. Even if these competitors were profit maximisers producing a differentiated product,[10] at some point the price differential would cause them to react to a sales revenue maximiser by cutting price and expanding output − thus becoming sales revenue maximisers themselves. Unless the market is an exploding one, increasing output would lead to excess capacity in the industry so that the SRM firm would not be able to ignore the actions of its competitors.[11] In addition the existence of profit-maximising firms in an industry might appear to impose some market constraint on the SRM by virtue of price earnings ratio of the shares of the profit maximisers. This may be only temporary − for if the profit maximisers are forced to react to the policies of the SRM they may, if they cut price without increasing output, leave themselves open to a potential take-over from the SRM firm which would then lead to increased concentration in the industry.

Formal testing of the model in terms of its predictive power for prices and outputs is problematical since firms often raise prices when production costs in general (and not fixed costs alone) are rising and also because there is an alternative response in the form of reductions in advertising expenditure. In an attempt to circumvent these difficulties two kinds of indirect approach have been used:

(1) identifying profits sacrificed in favour of sales up to the point of the profit constraints;
(2) testing the assumption that the decision makers will prefer sales to profits.

The study by M. Hall (60) is an illustration of the first approach. This was conducted using data for the largest 400 US industrial manufacturing firms and he confined the sample to industries with concentration ratios of 50 per cent or over and to firms with a fairly assignable industrial classification. Hall felt that he had selected a group of firms whose market structural characteristics were not unfavourable to the practice of revenue maximisation with a profit constraint. The hypothesis was that current variations in sales can be explained by prior departures from the minimum profit constraint so that a positive correlation between 'surplus' profits in period $t-1$ and sales increases between $t-1$ and t would lend support to the model. In fact the test for the period 1960-2 produced negative correlations thus refuting Hall's hypothesis and running contrary to the conclusions derived from the SRM hypothesis. The main problem with Hall's test[12] lies in the determination of the minimum profit constraint. Hall used average profit rates for the industry as a proxy, but these can hardly be regarded as valid measures. Moreover, even if positive correlations had been obtained these might simply have reflected booming demand conditions, simultaneously increasing sales-revenue and profits.

The second type of empirical study is one which has received considerable attention particularly in the USA though there is a more recent study for the UK by A. Cosh (36). The study for the USA which we cite here is that of J.W. McGuire *et al.* (102),[13] and it is a useful one on which to focus since it provoked further work within this area – notably a study by R.T. Masson (100). McGuire's study used data on executive income (the salary of the chief executive and allowance for stock options) and sales profits for 45 of the 100 largest (as given by *Fortune*) US industrial corporations for the period 1953-9. For each year, profit, sales revenue and executive incomes were inter-correlated. Direct relationships, lagged relationships and relationships between increments of the three variables were obtained. One would suspect substantial multi-collinearity between the variables, making it difficult to isolate the separate influences of the independent variables. Notwithstanding this difficulty, more of the variation in income was explained by sales than by profit. In five out of the seven years, the relationship between average income and average revenue yielded a positive, significant partial correlation coefficient, whereas the corresponding relationship between income and profit was significant in none of the years. But R.T. Masson (100) has argued that the McGuire study and those conducted earlier did not correctly specify executive compensation and in fact omitted a large element of their income. He conducted a revised version of the study and found from his sample of industries that

. . . the firms in these industries do not pay their executives for
sales maximisation, that the financial incentives of the executives
do indeed affect stock market performance, and that the
coincidence of executive financial return with the stock performance of the firm benefits the stockholders. [p. 1290] [14]

A more recent study by A. Cosh (36) used cross-sectional data for
over one thousand UK companies for the period 1969-71.

It was shown that size alone explains on average 49% of the
observed variance of the natural logarithm of the chief executive
renumeration and that the inclusion of profitability as an
additional explanatory variables does little to improve the degree
of explanation, since size and profitability together explain only
54%. [p. 89]

In this test, company size, was measured by the natural logarithm
of net assets rather than sales revenue. The results are, however, in
keeping with the view that attributes concerned with the company's
size, such as turn-over or net assets, are more important determinants
of executive salaries than profitability.

Although the formal evidence is somewhat divergent in its
conclusions, Baumol's SRM hypothesis has achieved a degree of
respectability among economists and management scientists and one
must be alive to the possibility that sales expansion may take place
in large firms at the expense of profit. Organisational slack may then
be present in the form of enlarged output, higher advertising and
promotional expenditures, and lower prices as compared with those
which would prevail under profit maximisation. The decision maker's
attention can therefore be directed to these parameters when profits
are no longer satisfactory.

Although Baumol's model follows traditional methodology in so
far as the firm's decision processes remain at a highly abstract level, a
non-profit-maximising objective is assumed and the ability of the
firm to influence the environment through advertising is recognised.
No longer is the demand function given, and the firm is thus no longer
subservient to the wants of the consumer. This is an important break-
through in the theory of the firm particularly since it provides a
mechanism for sales expansion and the growth of the whole firm, and
Baumol's multi-period model develops this theme as we shall see in
Section 2.6. As such it forms a link between conventional theory and

the theory of managerial capitalism propounded by Marris (93). However, in the latter, it is product diversification, supported by appropriate advertising, which is the engine for growth and the model is rather richer in implications for strategic decision making than is Baumol's.

2.5 Williamson's Utility Maximisation Hypothesis[15]

Baumol's theory can be clearly distinguished from Cyert's and March's behavioural theory since the former is essentially market oriented. There is no treatment of decision processes beyond the level of marginal analysis, and internal resource allocation only enters in the shape of advertising expenditure. In short, the term 'managerial theory' is more appropriate when discussing sales-revenue maximisation. The theory of O.E. Williamson is often grouped with those of Baumol and Marris, since all three have in common managerial rather than shareholder objectives for their objective functions.

Despite having that much in common, there are subtle differences in methodology between these managerial theories and Williamson's does tie in rather neatly with the behavioural approach without being regarded as a behavioural theory itself. The link occurs through Williamson's use of the concept 'preferred expenditure' which is, in fact, organisational slack in another guise. As we have seen, there may be some scope in the typical large firm, for managers to pursue their own interests so long as profits remain acceptable. Although the firm is a coalition of conflicting interest groups, Williamson argues that managers are the dominant members and, as long as survival is not a pressing problem, it is their interests which will be represented in greatest force when coalition agreements are made. The literature on management and business organisation reveals managerial objectives which include salary, status, power, prestige, security, and professional excellence,[16] and these are incorporated into Williamson's managerial utility function by translating them into preferred expenditures. Managerial salaries and emoluments[17] fall, not surprisingly, into this category as do expenditures on staffing and investment expenditures incurred at the discretion of management, i.e. other than those necessary for the firm's continued survival. The objective function is then derived by observing that:

(1)   increasing the numbers of staff can indirectly bring salary increases as compensation for the additional responsibility borne by management following the enlargement of their departments; status,

power, prestige and security are also enhanced by this means;
(2)   certain of the firm's investments will be for replacement of worn
out, or obsolescent, assets and some of the new investments will be
regarded as desirable by other coalition members for their contribution
to profitability and growth. If production costs are defined so as to
include the amortisation of assets which are replaced periodically,
and a minimum after-tax profit constraint is set at a level which provides for the internal financing of new investment as well as shareholders' dividends, then the profit available for discretionary investment
spending will be the difference between the company's reported profit
and the minimum acceptable profit, having deducted taxes.

We shall use the following symbols and definitions in our exposition
of Williamson's model:

π is the actual profit of the firm which is calculated as $\pi = R - C - S$
where:

R is the total revenue earned,

C is the total production cost, including depreciation and the non-
discretionary elements of managerial salaries,

S is staffing expenditure, which is part of the firm's administrative
expenditure,

M stands for the Managerial emoluments paid by the organisation
and can be regarded as a form of economic rent − i.e. payments
above those necessary to keep managers in their present
employment, including 'slack' in the form of perquisites of office,

π_R is the profit reported by the company after managerial emoluments have been absorbed as cost out of the actual profit. Thus
$\pi_R = \pi - M$.

The reported profits are then subject to taxation (T) and, after satisfying the minimum profit constraint (π_0) the remainder will be profit
available for discretionary investment spending (P).

So, $P = \pi_R - T - \pi_0$.

Williamson's managerial utility function consists of three terms: staff,
managerial emoluments and discretionary profit. The utility function

$$U = U(S, M, \pi_R - T - \pi_0)$$

is to be maximised subject to the constraint,

$$\pi_R - T \geqslant \pi_0 \;.$$

Unlike Baumol's SRM hypothesis, where sales are always preferred to profit once the constraint is satisfied, Williamson recognises the positive utility managers enjoy from discretionary spending. As the term $\pi_R - T - \pi_0$ is part of the maximand, profit will generally be above the minimum acceptable level and the condition $\pi_R - T \geqslant \pi_0$ is unlikely to restrain the maximisation of managerial utility. The maximisation of the objective function supposes rational behaviour, a supposition which is open to the usual criticisms. Indeed, the utility maximising firm must equate marginal production costs to marginal revenue in order to provide as big a fund as possible out of which the preferred expenditures can be met, so the production decision is essentially the same as in the classical model.[18] The latter can be regarded as a special case of the utility maximising model under competition which is so severe that managerial discretion is not possible since the profit constraint is always operative. However, it is only for the production decision that the models always coincide. Under normal conditions, staff will be employed by the managerial firm beyond the level justified by marginal productivity on account of their contribution to managerial utility in the form of salary, status and prestige. A profit-maximising firm would cease to employ staff once the marginal value product was equal to the marginal cost of employment. Managerial emoluments absorbed as cost would not feature in a profit-maximising model, but in this managerial model, profits will be foregone as long as the marginal utility from emoluments is greater than the marginal utility of discretionary profit foregone, the tax rate influencing the marginal rate of substitution.

We may write the following equilibrium conditions for utility maximisation, where X is output:

1. $\dfrac{\partial R}{\partial X} = \dfrac{\partial C}{\partial X}$ (i.e. marginal cost = marginal revenue)

2. $\dfrac{\partial R}{\partial S} = 1 - \dfrac{\partial U/\partial S}{(\partial U/\partial P)\,(1-t)}$ [note 19]

3. $\dfrac{\partial U}{\partial M} = \dfrac{\partial U}{\partial P}\,(1-t)$ (where t is the tax rate)

Equation (2) shows that $\partial R/\partial S < 1$, meaning that the marginal value product of staff is less than its marginal cost, with staff being employed beyond the profit maximising level. (See Figure 2.3a).[20]

The system of equations can exhibit responses to changes in demand, and in taxation both of the lump-sum and pro-rata variety.

(a) Demand Shifts

An upward shift will cause output, and both S and M to increase. This follows because it becomes profitable for the firm to expand output, and the enlarged pool of resources enables organisational slack to be increased. The result for a fall in demand is obvious.

(b) Lump-sum Taxes

The imposition of a lump-sum tax, or addition to an existing one, has an 'income effect' on the firm reducing after-tax profits. Utility can then be increased by transferring resources from S and M to profit as we show in Figure 2.3b[20] where staff expenditure falls from S_1 to S_2. Reduction in a lump-sum tax would enlarge after-tax profits but part of the benefit would be absorbed by S and M in a utility-maximising firm. Output changes would come about indirectly in response to staffing variations and in the same direction, so long as the marginal value product of staff does not become negative.

(c) Corporation Taxes

The 'income effect', observed above, also comes into play when the rate of corporation tax rises. This encourages the transfer of resources from S and M to discretionary profit, but this tendency is normally more than offset by a 'substitution effect' which occurs because the cost of taking satisfaction in the form of profit increases with the tax rate and, consequently, S and M become relatively attractive and tend to be substituted for profit. The net effect in prosperous times tends to be in favour of slack expansion, staff expenditure being increased from S_1 to S_2 in Figure 2.3c, but in less favourable circumstances, when pressure comes to bear on the profit constraint, the firm could be forced to reduce organisational slack of both varieties in order to ensure survival.

We can compare these responses with those predicted by traditional theory and the conclusions of Baumol. If staff, in Williamson's model, is subsumed under total selling and administrative expenditure, and the advertising expenditure, in Baumol's model, is treated likewise, then we can display the direction of the responses to external parameter

Figure 2.3: The Maximisation of Utility

(a)   Firm not subject to tax

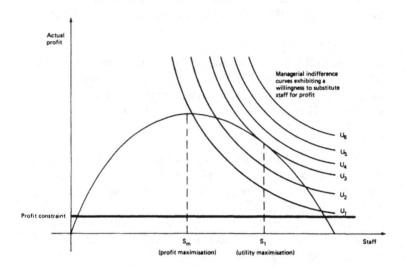

(b)   Firm subject to a lump-sum tax

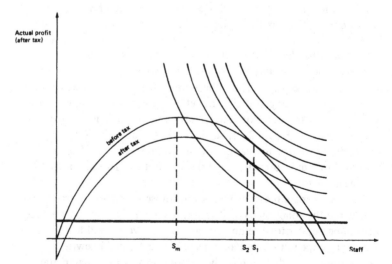

Figure 2.3 (cont.)

(c)   Firm subject to corporation tax

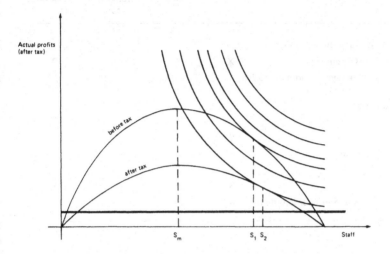

changes as shown in Table 2.1.

Baumol and Williamson offer different predictions for a change in the tax rate. Baumol predicts a reduction in S when t, the tax rate, rises since profits would be only just acceptable before the change and therefore unacceptable after the payment of extra tax. Williamson, by including profits in his utility function, deduces that the constraint will be operative only in times of adversity and that S and M will generally be expanded as the cost (in terms of tax) of reporting profits increases.

A.A. Alchian (4) regards this as a weakness in the SRM hypothesis, where sales are always expanded in favour of profit when the opportunity presents itself, regardless of the amount of profit which has to be foregone to improve sales. Alchian regards Williamson's approach as superior because it is capable of analysing the impact of managerial discretion without relegating profit to the status of a constraint. However, the SRM hypothesis is not seen as being entirely inconsistent with utility maximisation, since the pursuit of sales revenue can be rationalised in terms of its probable impact on salary and the latter is seen as a factor which contributes to managerial utility by Williamson.

In testing Williamson's predictions, the crucial parameters are tax

Table 2.1: Direction of Responses to External Parameter Changes

		E (Demand)	T (Lump sum tax)	t (Tax rate)
Traditional theory				
Output	X	+	0	0
Selling and administrative expenditure	S	+	0	0
Baumol				
	X	+	–	–
	S	+	–	–
Williamson				
	X	+	–	+ ?
	S	+	–	+ ?
Managerial emoluments	M	+	–	+ ?

changes but unfortunately lump-sum taxes are not generally levied (although other outlays may approximate them in their impact).[21] Even though changes in corporation taxes are fairly common, no satisfactory statistical test capable of detecting the response to corporation tax alone has emerged. Williamson offered an alternative test for his theory by attempting to show that firms did in fact respond to opportunities for discretion. For his test, twenty-six industries in the USA were selected and the largest two firms, ranked by sales, were included in his sample. The salary of the chief executive was correlated with staffing expenditures and indices of competitive pressure and managerial taste. The first index comprised concentration ratios and J.S. Bain's (14) entry-barrier measures, which should serve as a good guide to the strength of discretionary power. The second index, measuring managerial taste, was determined by the degree of internal representation on the board of directors, but Williamson accepted that this could only serve as a rough approximation. Cross-section data for the years 1953, 1957 and 1961 were analysed with the following results: all parameters were positively correlated with executive salaries. Coefficients were significant at the 2.5 per cent level and, in some cases, at the 1.0 per cent level, except for the taste index which did not yield correlations which were significant, even at the 2.5 per cent level. The most interesting of these results is that the absence of competitive pressure does seem to be reflected in executive salaries, suggesting that the opportunity for discretion implicit in that state is used to the advantage of management. Further support was given to the theory following field studies by Williamson in which reports of the trimming of staff expenses and emoluments in times of crisis were widespread. Similar responses were also reported by departments of firms suffering from increased departmental overhead allocations which can be regarded as akin to lump sum taxes.

The internal representation measure used unsuccessfully by Williamson in his empirical tests, gives some indication of control type and of whether managerial interests are likely to be dominant. There has been a number of other studies concerned with control type, for example, P. Holl's (72) study of its effect on the performance of UK firms. Holl relied on ownership data originally compiled by P.S. Florence (48) for 1951 and financial data from the Department of Applied Economics, Cambridge for the period 1948-60,[22] but found that control type had no apparent effect on the performance of the firm as measured by pre-tax profitability and the growth rate of net assets. He recognised the possibility that this result could be due to a 'corporate control mechanism'[23] and that it did not necessarily reflect an absence of conflict between managerial and shareholder interests. Another study by H.K. Radice (133) (on which we comment more full fully in Chapter 3) which was concerned specifically with the Marris growth theory, did find that 'owner' controlled firms in the UK had higher profit rates and higher growth rates than those under managerial control but the studies in the USA by D.R. Kamerschen (75), J. Palmer (122), K.J. Boudreaux (23) and R. Larner (81) have found no general agreement on the effect of control type on average profitability or variation of profitability. Other work which relates to Williamson's theory[24] includes H. Leibenstein's (83) 'X-inefficiency' hypothesis, which is that market power may be a source of *internal* inefficiency as well as allocative inefficiency in the economic system. The X-inefficiency argument is that dominant firms, free from strong competitive pressures, will allow costs to rise above the minimum possible levels as the objectives of both managers and employees are accommodated. The evidence which Leibenstein collected covered a wide range of economies, industries and types of firms so that it is difficult to relate it to Williamson's evidence specifically, but the existence of X-inefficiency was demonstrated thus lending some support to the theory of Williamson.

Williamson's work has reinforced the impression that staffs have a tendency to grow in the absence of close monitoring of employee numbers and if one relates this tendency to the observation of the behavioural theory concerning the failure of departments to ensure consistency between their objectives and those of the organisation as a whole, one can envisage an expansion of subunit staff numbers to serve the needs of their departmental heads rather than for their contribution to the organisation's performance. In organisations whose survival does not depend on profit this danger cannot be over-emphasised and in any corporate appraisal of staffing requirements, attention should be directed towards this element of organisational slack. The need to make profits by business organisation in the private sector may be suggestive of at least periodic elimination of excessive staffs and managerial perquisites. However, Williamson shows forcibly that corporation tax increases may act as a disincentive to the reporting of profits, possibly encouraging managers to take more utility in the form of staff and perquisites.

Possibly of greatest significance for corporate planning is Williamson's assertion that profits are sought as a means of financing projects favoured by management, including investments which would not have been chosen according to profitability criteria. Certainly internally generated finance is a convenient source of investment funds and, as issuing costs are absent, it is cheaper than other equity sources. It cannot, however, be regarded as a costless form of finance, since all capital resources have an opportunity cost. Planners must, in consequence, use their influence to ensure that profits are ploughed back into projects which will satisfy long-term corporate objectives rather than managerial objectives. If no opportunities can be discovered within the firm's current business activities, then the possibility of diversification should be considered.

The role of internal financing is given further consideration in Chapter 5, and the diversification issue is explored in Chapter 4, where we also take a look at a more recent contribution of Williamson's in connection with the impact of organisational structure on efficiency.

2.6 Dynamic Consideration in Decision Making

Although the models discussed elsewhere in the present chapter have implications for corporate planning, none of them explicitly examines the part played by forward plans in business activity, except for the behavioural theory which does examine the role of budgeting. Traditional theory, the SRM hypothesis, and Williamson's theory all assume a certain world in which a single course of action with known consequences is chosen from the available alternatives. The entrepreneur or management group is alleged in these theories to choose that alternative which is most conducive to the attainment of his or its goal, given a static environment. The responses which we deduced were of a comparative static nature where the environment shifts from one set of parameter values to another set. This implies one-way causality with the firm responding to various environmental parameters. However, in reality, the actions of the firm can influence the world about it and thus change the circumstances in which future decisions will be made for the real world is dynamic. One would expect theories concerned with growth to be dynamic in nature, but the use of this term needs qualification. J.R. Hicks (67) makes the distinction between static and dynamic conditions as follows:

> In mechanics, statics is concerned with rest, dynamics with motion; but no economic system is ever at rest in anything like the mechanical sense. Production is itself a process; by its very nature it is a process of change. All we can do is to define a static condition as one in which certain key variables are unchanging. A dynamic condition is then one in which they are changing. And dynamic theory is the analysis of the processes by which they change. [p. 6]

A dynamic theory to Hicks is thus not a theory of how the world changes as firms and their environments interact, but rather a theory of how economic agents make decisions in a changing world. His dynamic model amounts to a modification of the static theory of the firm to incorporate a pay-off function which depends upon both the future and the current actions of the firm. The dynamic problem is seen as the selection of a certain *production plan* from the available alternatives. However, the Hicksian model assumes complete information and it has been proposed by K.J. Cohen and R.M. Cyert (34)[25] that the model can be made more useful for the analysis of anticipatory and planning behaviour by incorporating a number of minor modifications: that expectations are not entirely reliable, that information absorbs scarce resources but the cost decreases as the future draws nearer and that since problem solving, decision making and planning are all costly activities, they should be avoided unless the expected return from them is greater than the cost.

A change of viewpoint incorporated in this revision is that it is not so much the selection of a complete plan as the selection of the best first move, broadly defined to include any failure to act, which is most crucial since it is non-postponable. The decision problem confronting the entrepreneur at a given point in time is then the selection of the immediate move rather than selection of an entire plan. The significance of this change in viewpoint is that although present actions will influence some aspects of the future and thereby constrain the options open to the firm, there are other aspects of the firm's future environment which will not be influenced by its present moves. In other words, the firm has to make anticipations about some but not all aspects of the future in order to choose the first move optimally. There are thus relevant and irrelevant parameters as of date zero, where a parameter is irrelevant if the optimum value of the first move is the same, regardless of the value of that parameter. An irrelevant anticipation is then one which is concerned with irrelevant parameters and, given the cost of obtaining information about the future, the firm should not make irrelevant anticipations.

In the analysis presented by Cohen and Cyert, it is argued that some parameters may be relevant over a span of time but, beyond that period, the parameter becomes irrelevant. Thus, in scheduling the production of a commodity in such a way that the quantity demanded in each of T periods is provided at the lowest possible cost over the horizon, there will be some date, t, at which the actual demand beyond t is irrelevant, except in the improbable situation of a perpetually increasing trend in demand. For products whose demands are subject to seasonal variations it is deduced that the relevant horizon within a given cycle extends to the peak of that cycle or shortly beyond it, with all future seasonal cycles being irrelevant. As a general proposition, it is argued that the length of the relevant horizon may tend to grow during periods where economic activity is high and expected to rise. This proposition, however, seems applicable only to restricted types of planning, notably production scheduling. Strategic planning, in particular requires that the company takes action, outside its existing product-market scope if necessary, in order to take advantage of lucrative opportunities, but also to avoid undesirable futures. In theory there is no limit to the time horizon which may be contemplated in strategic planning, but we take the point that the cost of acquiring information and difficulty in forecasting remote happenings imposes a finite planning period on the firm. We also accept that the firm's scarce and costly planning resources should not be absorbed in making irrelevant anticipations. What is envisaged by Cohen and Cyert is that

those components of future moves which are relevant as of date zero
be determined and the optimal first move selected, in the light of the
inter-relationships which exist between present and future moves —
possibly expressed in a system of simultaneous equations. It is quite
likely that the solution for the optimal first move will follow from a
solution for certain components of future moves. The development of
a plan may therefore assist in demonstrating the actions which need
to be taken in the present. Indeed one of the principal arguments for
national economic (indicative) planning[26] is that the various sectors of
the economy are able to see, through the plan, which actions they are
expected to take in order to achieve the desired future. The same is
true for a company: planning can facilitate communication and
co-ordination between the various subunits of the organisation.

The variables which decision makers can manipulate to influence
their futures have not been explicitly introduced into the models
we have discussed so far, but to provide a link between the present
chapter and the next we shall say a few words about a dynamic version
of Baumol's model.[27] In this dynamic version the profit requirement
is endogenously determined and the firm attempts to maximise the
rate of growth of sales revenue over the life span of the company.
Instead of acting merely as a constraint, the profits become an instru-
mental variable as the main source of company finance, though access
to external finance is not denied. Baumol argues that beyond a
particular point profits will compete with sales since too low a level
of profits will inhibit growth so he incorporates into this version an
optimal profit rate which is consistent with the rate of growth of
output (sales) over the lifetime of the firm. Baumol does not spell out
his model in any great detail but in recognising the importance of
retained earnings and thus dividend policy in financing expansion, the
model stands as a useful development in the formulation of a growth
theory. The Marris model is rather more sophisticated and we shall
see in the next chapter that the variables which are alleged to
determine the firm's growth rate are the profit margin, the rate of
diversification and the company's financial policy. The profit margin
(m) and the rate of diversification (d) chosen by the firm determines
the rate of growth in demand, and the same variables together with
the company's financial policy determine the rate of growth in supply.
For maximum balanced growth subject to a security constraint, m and
d have to be consistent with one another so that supply and demand
grow at the same rate. Thus, in terms of the dynamic framework
suggested above, the relevant parameters are those concerned with

future supply and demand and these are influenced by m, d and financial policy. Marris describes his approach as 'comparative dynamics' in which equilibrium conditions are deduced and then compared with new equilibrium conditions which arise in response to changes in exogenous variables, for example government monetary policy. In many ways Marris's contribution stands apart from the other managerial theories and it warrants treatment as a theory in its own right, consequently it will receive extensive coverage in the next chapter.

Notes

1. The 'peak coordinator' concept is used by A. Papandreou (124).
2. This is similar to H. Leibenstein's (83) X-inefficiency concept which refers to slack at both management and shop-floor level.
3. Marris has built a security constraint into his model, in part reflecting a need to provide a reasonable rate of return on capital. See Chapter 3.
4. For an empirical study for the UK which examines 'satisfactory' levels of profits see M. Panic and R.E. Close (123).
5. Our italics.
6. The references to Baumol in this section include his 1958 article (18), and his book *Business Behaviour, Value and Growth* (19).
7. For a case study approach to the SRM hypothesis see C.L. Lackman and J.L. Craycraft (80).
8. Brief reference is made to this multi-period model below in Section 2.6.
9. We have described this fairly extensively elsewhere (26). See also P.M. Sweezy (155) for one of the original papers.
10. If the product were homogeneous the competitors would be forced out of the industry if they were not prepared to follow the SRM firm as it became the price leader.
11. The diversified SRM firm would be less vulnerable to excess capacity in supply for any one market than his single product counterpart.
12. See L. Waverman (164) for further coverage of criticisms directed against Hall's test.
13. This study followed claims by P. Patton (126) and D.R. Roberts (135) that managerial income was directly related to company size.
14. A finding consistent with W.G. Lewellen's (85) conclusions – see Chapter 1.
15. We refer here to O.E. Williamson's 1963 article (170) and his book *The Economics of Discretionary Behaviour* (171).
16. For example, C.I. Barnard (17), H.A. Simon (143) and R.A. Gordon (55).
17. Williamson's usage of the term 'emoluments' is restricted to the portion of managerial salaries and perquisites which is discretionary.
18. The final output of the utility maximising firm will, however, be higher if one assumes that the additional administrative staff acquired will not be entirely non-productive.
19. This follows from the relationship between profit and staff, in which the net change in pre-tax profit is the difference between the marginal revenue product of staff and its marginal cost.
20. The diagrams only being in two dimensions, ignore the impact of M.
21. For example, rates on business premises levied by the local authority, and

any increase in fixed overheads.
22. See, for example, A. Singh (145).
23. See Chapter 3.
24. And to Cyert and March's behavioural theory.
25. Drawing on an earlier work by F. Modigliani and K.J. Cohen (110).
26. See Chapter 6.
27. See Baumol (20).

3 THE GROWTH OF THE FIRM

3.1 Introduction

We have seen in the previous chapters that the firm may have several
objectives, some of which may be competing, but one objective which
may dominate the management of the firm is growth — expansion
of the firm through time. Once we engage in a discussion of growth
then we are involved in rather more than just the making of profits
and the raising of finance for investment. We become involved in a
process of *change* and *adaptation* which occurs in an uncertain world.
This is well illustrated by J. Downie (41):

> The most fundamental characteristic of a capitalist economy is
> growth and change . . . [it] is characterised by a restless urge to do
> better, to change the conditions lest, through inactivity, they are
> changed against you. [p. 29]

The firm is therefore always in a state of flux and the changes which
the firm must go through in the growth process either come from
management itself (through the planning process) and/or from
external pressures on the management team. The process of adaptation
to change is examined in the behavioural theory of the firm in which
various goals are specified. Recall that failure to meet one of these
goals be it sales, market share, profit, or some other, sets into motion
a search process to determine the appropriate corrective action.
Although these goals are seen to change over time as aspiration levels
change within the coalition, the behavioural theory does not examine
a planning process directed towards long-term goals.

A firm which seeks growth is unlikely to meet with success if search
is only induced when the firm is under direct pressure; it really needs
a scanning process to anticipate changes in its environment and
mechanisms for identifying and exploring the avenues of growth. A
separate department or group, such as a corporate planning team may
be able to serve these needs, but such a department is not to be seen
as either a necessary or a sufficient condition for the achievement of
growth, despite its usefulness in performing the basic intelligence
activities of planning as it seeks and draws on information from a
variety of sources both inside and outside the firm.

74

Growth may involve internal expansion, possibly through innovations[1] developed by the firm's research and development department and/or external expansion through acquisition. Either way management occupies a key position, both in instigating change and in adapting[2] to its repercussions, so that the capacity of the management team may impose a constraint on the firm's ability to expand.[3] The knowledge, skills, and experience of managerial personnel will also influence the type of expansion undertaken by the firm, and its success, a view taken by E.T. Penrose (127) who has accorded a central role to management in her theory of the growth of the firm. This view has been supported by T. Barna (16) who found from his study on the growth performance of firms that the general characteristics and attitude of management were important variables in determining the need to precipitate change and to plan ahead — talents which were reflected in the relative growth performance of firms in his sample.

The development of a theory of the growth of the firm requires a conceptual framework which can handle the broad spectrum of parameters that the growth process involves. In the main[4] we will concentrate attention on the model formulated by R.L. Marris (92, 93, 94) but inevitably his approach has been influenced by the work of others particularly Professor Edith Penrose (127) whom we have already mentioned *en passant* and J. Downie (41), although the latter's contribution to the theory of the growth of the firm is a by-product of his work on how differing market structures may influence business behaviour in terms of differing business efficiency and rates of technical progress. We shall summarise both the Downie and Penrose models in a few paragraphs though we shall see continually in our discussion of Marris how influential Mrs Penrose has been in promoting an understanding of the growth process.

The main contribution of Downie's work in this context is the interdependence he sees between the creation of demand conditions necessary to achieve growth and the supply of funds to provide the productive capacity. The Downie firm finds itself within an industry in which the more efficient firms are expanding their market share at the expense of less efficient firms. This transfer from less to more efficient firms may lead to the less efficient either dying completely or being forced to innovate, which can reverse the transfer process as they then recover market share and profitability. By stressing the link between growth and profitability where the growth of capacity is directly related to the rate of profit (supply of finance), and the rate of profit is at least initially positively related to the growth of demand,

Downie provided a solid base on which others could build. His other contribution in terms of the market structure within which firms themselves and the impact this may have on business behaviour has not been followed through, as we shall observe in this chapter.

The Penrose firm has an objective of increasing long-run total profits and since 'total profits will increase with every increment of investment that yields a positive return, regardless of what happens to the marginal *rate* of return in investment', then it follows that 'firms will want to expand as fast as they can take advantage of opportunities for expansion that they consider profitable' (p. 29). Mrs Penrose does not provide a formal model of the growth of the firm but a verbal description and the centre-piece of this is the notion of the receding 'managerial limit' on the rate of growth of the firm. This limit is imposed by the amount of managerial time which is, and can be, devoted to the strategic decisions of the firm and the period required for new recruits to be absorbed into the management team. Even if appropriate changes in the administrative structure are made to facilitate the integration of the new staff, the experience of the newly expanded team working together is something which Penrose argues cannot be fully forecast and determined – particularly as she places great emphasis on the personal characteristics and attitudes of managers:

> If a firm deliberately or inadvertently expands its organisation more rapidly than the individuals in the expanding organisation can obtain the experience with each other and with the firm that is necessary for the effective operation of the group, the efficiency of the firm will suffer, even if optimum adjustments are made in the administrative structure. [p. 47]

However, she argues that through time the team will evolve (learning by doing) and be in a position to oversee expansion, which will be determined by both internal and external factors. Externally the firm may find that changes in demand and technology offer the firm opportunities to grow, but there are limits here in terms of barriers to entry into new markets and industries. Internally the main obstacle, as we have seen, is the managerial limit, but the firm may have a pool of unused productive services which can be used and these Penrose sees as:

> a challenge to innovate, an incentive to expand, and a source of

competitive advantage. They facilitate the introduction of new combinations of resources – innovation – within the firm. The new combinations may be combinations of services for the production of new products, new processes for the production of old products, new organisation of administrative functions. [p. 187]

The tenor of the statement above is that expansion will be related to the nature of the existing operations of the firm but the movement to entirely new spheres of business activity with or without acquisition is not precluded. Indeed we shall argue in Chapter 4 that diversification can proceed with rather tenuous links between the original and the new activities, although in practice there is generally some common thread either in production or marketing.

3.2 The Marris Model

We now turn to the managerial model of R.L. Marris, and we feel that its adoption here as the corner-stone of our analysis of the growth of firms is justified, since Marris has incorporated the critical features of managerial control (and capacity), finance and demand into a formal model. The Marris model has been seminal as is evidenced by the conference in 1971 (98) where many other dimensions of the questions of the growth of the firm were analysed. Let us in the first instance take the basic model of Marris which starts with three considerations:

(1)   The management team may subject corporate policy decisions to a utility function of its own, a utility function which may (though not necessarily) differ from that of the shareholders.

The treatment of shareholder objectives varies as between the managerial models of Baumol, Williamson and Marris. Baumol's SRM[5] hypothesis treats profit purely as a constraint whereas Williamson's model also recognises its role in promoting managerial utility. We shall see that the managerial growth objective in Marris's model may be reconcilable with shareholder objectives, certainly the two are not diametrically opposed. Marris's model is however essentially one of the firm within a system of 'Managerial Capitalism' where explicit recognition is given to the influence and power of the management team.

(2)   Given the institutional environment within which decisions are

taken in the execution of the management function, Marris sets out
to examine the probable nature of the resulting preference system.

He does not consider the kind of internal bargaining process,
described by Cyert and March, or the resolution of conflict between
competing goals within the coalition, but these issues are the
prerogative of the behavioural theory and their omission by Marris
does not warrant criticism. Furthermore, following Galbraith, we
may note that growth can satisfy many of the needs of the 'technostructure' and it thus serves as a unifying force.

(3)   Additionally he seeks to explore the extent to which the
'environment' will permit these preferences to count particularly
in terms of the constraints which will limit freedom of managerial
choice.

In specifying an objective function of 'balanced' growth
maximisation Marris stresses that the firm must *simultaneously*
maximise the rate of growth of the demand for the products of the
firm and the growth of capital supply to finance the growth process.
otherwise growth will not be sustainable. We have already outlined
Marris's reasoning in adopting growth for his objective function in
Chapter 1, but have yet to discuss the implications of this for the
shareholders. As we are no longer dealing with single period
considerations, it is necessary to view the stream of returns to the
owners over time, and consider the possibility that a growth
objective can satisfy both shareholder and managerial requirements.
Moreover the nature and composition of the shareholding body has
changed (as we have indicated in Chapter 1) with institutional shareholders now accounting for nearly 50 per cent of holdings and
trading in the market. These are, of course, interested in the long-run
survival of the firm, and they can be knowledgeable, powerful and
active. That is not to say that they necessarily buy to hold, but that
they are motivated by long-run as well as short-run considerations
particularly if they are using the asset to meet a contingent liability
at some distant time period, as in the case of superannuation funds and
life insurance offices. The economic theory of corporate finance
assumes that the share price is the discounted present value of the
future earnings stream of dividend and capital gain/loss thus implying
a long-term view. In fact, in practice we know that for some investors
the dividend consideration may outweigh that of capital gain and

vice-versa. This divergence of view is difficult to handle[6] and the presumption is made in the Marris model that investors receive utility from both dividends and earnings from retained capital, and that the growth of the earnings stream over time is of prime concern (although valuation may be sensitive to the payout ratio).

The Marris model thus does integrate both shareholder and management considerations by postulating that they are both interested in the rate of growth of the firm (not simply its size) and whilst we might not be fully satisfied with the rationale for shareholders, let us take the hypothesis at its face value and proceed to examine the implications of growth.[7] Before proceeding further, the measurement issue needs to be tackled: does Marris mean growth in output, revenue or capital? In fact, it does not matter in the Marris model because he is dealing with a specified type of growth profile – a steady rate of growth through time so that, because these indicators are likely to change in the same way, 'maximising the long-run growth rate of any indicator can reasonably be assumed to be equivalent to maximising the long-run rate of most others' (92). The firm in this situation chooses a constant rate of growth within a constant environment and maintains set financial ratios internally (as we see demonstrated in Figure 3.1 on page 83).

Constraints in the Marris Model

We have already argued that the single continuous objective to which decision makers are working is subject to constraints which are both internal and external. So whilst management may have considerable freedom of action, it is in fact still bounded, and although the modern firm can influence and shape the environment in planning its own growth it cannot *determine* the environment.

The first constraint to be considered is that of the organisational structure of the firm and more specifically of the management team. In this Marris is following Penrose who argued that a firm can grow through time by hiring new staff members to the managerial team and by absorbing these into the team. This team concept indicates that decisions are made on a group basis but no conflict is allowed for (unlike in the behavioural model which we discussed earlier) so that this group basis implies cohesion and a unitary objective. The constraint comes from the time taken to absorb new staff members into the team (recognising that extra numbers *per se* will not of themselves increase the *effective* capacity of the team). The planning and execution of expansion can be undertaken only by the existing

management team, so that whilst, over time, the management team may
expand continuously, at any moment in time the management team
is a fixed factor which sets an effective constraint or ceiling on the
growth of the firm. Similarly in each department of the firm, the mere
addition of extra employees will not necessarily increase its effective
capacity immediately and one key area is the research and
development department from which many, though not all, of the new
ideas for future expansion will come. Here again Marris and Penrose
are in agreement in that both recognise a limited capacity for
instigating and digesting change, but the Marris model does not include
growth by merger so that he is referring to the organisational problems
of handling a higher rate of internal expansion through diversification.
Mrs Penrose, however, also recognises the digestive problems
encountered by firms which have merged.

The second constraint on growth is financial in nature. It is
significant that the Baumol, Williamson and the behavioural models
all recognised the importance of profit as a source of shareholders'
utility and as provision for a sufficient flow of funds to finance
future development. This was expressed as we have seen in the profit
constraint, or the profit target of the firm, often expressed very
loosely in terms of a satisfactory level or as a target rate of return.
Marris, however, considers these two aspects separately. On the one
hand, the financing of expansion is treated as part of the balanced
growth equation and on the other, the need to provide a return to
investors enters the model in the form of a security constraint. So far
as management is concerned, job security is safeguarded if the firm
follows a prudent financial policy which avoids financial failure and the
removal of the firm as an identity which would occur if the firm were
taken over or if it went into liquidation. In this respect the firm has to
avoid excessively risky[8] projects and excessive contractual borrowing
(expressed in terms of the gearing ratio) and this desire for security,
if carried to the extreme, may thus lead to competition with the
growth objective. Perhaps the greatest threat is that of a firm being
taken over, in which event the management team is unlikely to be left
intact — managers may be fired or have their status and privileges
diminished. In neo-classical theory any firm which refused to maximise
the welfare of its stockholders would not survive as an entity but in
the world to which Marris is referring, such an event can be prevented
or its likelihood at least minimised. The key lies in stock market
valuation *vis-à-vis* book value — what Marris refers to as the valuation
ratio. Marris argues that the management will leave themselves open to

take-over raids if they do not maintain a sufficiently high valuation ratio. In other words he is specifying a direct relationship between the valuation ratio for the firm and the risk of being taken over. We can illustrate this in two quotations from Marris (93):

> We suppose that managers set some value of the ratio below which either fear of take-over or the sense of guilt becomes intolerable. [p. 45]

and

> ... for managers are assumed to include the valuation ratio in their utility functions for two reasons, to avoid pain from fear of take-over, and to gain pleasure from stock-market approval. [p. 262]

The first quotation implies that the valuation ratio is simply a constraint, while the second describes it as part of the utility function. The two can be reconciled by assuming that a saturation level of security exists, beyond which management will prefer growth to security when a choice has to be made.

The threat of take-overs has been seen as a 'corporate control' mechanism by some authors who regard it as a sufficiently potent force to counteract managerial discretion. For example H. Manne (90) writes:

> ... the take-over scheme provides some assurance of competitive efficiency among corporate managers and thereby affords strong protection to the interests of vast numbers of small, non-controlling shareholders. [p. 113]

and R. Sorensen (150):

> ... the existence of a strong market for corporate control forces management to take more than a casual interest in profits and stock price if it desires to remain in office. Since this market is external to the firm, even executives in management-controlled firms must attempt to achieve maximum profits. Consequently no difference in firms' behaviour should arise due to separation of ownership and control. [pp. 40-1]

Marris does not go so far as to suggest that the take-over threat eliminates managerial discretion, but he clearly accepts the view that it does impose a constraint in the form of a minimum valuation ratio.

Managers cannot completely control the valuation ratio but respect for financial conventions and skill in conducting public relations can influence it. The question of valuation of a company for take-over is a problem within the general theory of stock valuation, but Marris does not attempt to treat it as such. Instead he simply catalogues the various incentives which may lead a take-over raider[9] to strike and then *inter alia* the action an unwilling victim can take to avoid the take-over. The first incentive to a raider is where he sees a firm utilising its assets less profitably than it could do. In other words the internal rate of return on productive assets could increase with a change in management. This problem can be compounded by the second incentive − an excessive retention ratio within the firm, so that not only is it not using what capital it has borrowed and retained previously as efficiently as it could, but it is also retaining more for unprofitable purposes than other firms. The two factors taken together mean both low earnings and low dividends and, in consequence, a low share price. The third incentive comes when firms have excess liquidity to which a take-over raider can gain access and utilise. This may in fact also be coupled with the second incentive of an excessive retention ratio. For instance, in the United Kingdom in the 1950s when retention was effectively forced on firms in the form of dividend restraint and capital issues were controlled, liquid assets were often built up and this, coupled with out-of-date valuation of fixed assets particularly property, led to many spectacular chain take-overs where the capital released from one successful raid could be used for the next raid.

A firm however cannot reduce liquidity too far since this carries the danger of insolvency. Consequently a balance has to be struck in the holding of liquid assets since both too high and too low levels invite take-over. As the firm grows there may be economies of scale in the holding of liquid assets but this point is not covered in the Marris model. The safeguards against take-over are therefore: (1) to avoid projects with a low rate of return; (2) to maintain dividend payments at a level which will meet with market approval, but at the same time ensure that sufficient funds are available for profitable re-investment; and (3) to monitor liquidity to guard against insolvency, but avoid excess liquidity which represents capital tied up in an unprofitable form.

Despite the importance attached to take-over in this model (it is essentially the 'hidden hand') it remains as a threat to the firm as it pursues organic growth through diversification. It is therefore, a paradox that the crucial role given to take-overs in the model is not carried through to allow growth by take-over. Of course, the exclusion is for ease of exposition and in the final analysis it does not detract from the argument, though we shall return to growth by take-over in Chapters 4 and 5.

Decision Variables in the Marris Model

In the pursuit of growth, managers have a number of controllable variables at their disposal. The achievement of steady-state growth[10] requires a once and for all choice of growth rate and a consistent choice of variables such as sales, research and development, marketing outlays and financial variables. Marris (94) identifies steady state ratios for

> profits/assets, sales/assets, dividends/profits (or typically, r, the retention ratio), debt/assets, market value/assets (the so-called valuation ratio) and development expenditure/assets/ (or/sales). [p. 14]

Figure 3.1: Steady-State Growth Path

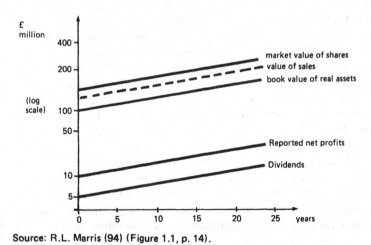

Source: R.L. Marris (94) (Figure 1.1, p. 14).

We illustrate in Figure 3.1 the Marris steady state path of a company growing at 5 per cent per annum with an average reported profit rate of 10 per cent and a retention ratio of 50 per cent and a valuation ratio of 2.0. This is where he brings an element of risk into the model, arguing that company policy can affect or determine a probability distribution of growth rates. These growth rates may have high variances and the firm will strive for an *expected* rate of long-run growth, although period by period it will not necessarily achieve this rate. Of course the illustration refers to only one feasible and sustainable growth rate and it is possible that with a higher growth rate, the rate of return might be lower, retention ratio higher and the valuation ratio lower (which may impose a security threat). Accordingly a solution to the problem requires simultaneous analysis of the multiple relationships at work. In particular, we note that if supply and demand are to grow at the same rate, the rate of diversification will not be chosen just in terms of its contribution to demand growth but also in recognition of the impact it will have on profits and thence the supply of finance.

The Growth of Demand

Although we have just agreed that a simultaneous consideration of supply and demand is necessary, it is convenient for purposes of exposition to look at the two dimensions separately. Looking at demand first, we consider the relationship between the firm and its environment. Marris in 1971 (94) distinguished two types of environment which face the firm: an immediate one which the firm can change continuously by influencing the demand curve (a point we take up later) and the wider environment referred to as the 'super' environment which limits the ability of the firm to change events. So that

> . . . if the super environment is constant, a constant policy will produce for the firm a steady state . . . the steady state will be sustained until either the super environment changes or the policy changes or both. Analysis takes the form of comparative dynamics, that is, the comparing of alternative steady state values. [p. 13]

The firm has to make successive increases in the volume of operations if it is to achieve continuous growth, but is it difficult to do this with a static product line since continuous penetration would be required in existing markets. This would imply sustained expansion in market demand or increasing market share at the expense of other firms if demand were static. Over the long term both are unlikely to be achieved. Fundamental change has to be made and the vehicle for this is diversification into new products and markets.[11] Both Galbraith and Penrose take similar viewpoints but the type of diversification in the Marris model concentrates on internally generated diversification, in particular that originating in research and development departments which is by implication 'science based'. This concentration on internal diversification follows from the fact that it is organic growth which features in the model. Marris's analysis of demand growth through diversification is directed initially towards what he describes as *differentiated* diversification which consists of entirely new product creations whose sales grow at the expense of total demand in the economy at large rather than at the expense of competing products. Accordingly the problem of interdependence is not raised in this context, but in extending his analysis to cover *imitative* diversification where sales expand at the expense of competitor's products, the problem is treated, albeit superficially.[12]

Both avenues of diversification are open to large firms and it should be possible to adopt a mixture of these in order to bring about continuous diversification and continuously expanding sales revenue and profit. The rate of growth of demand for the firm using differentiated diversification will depend upon the rate at which new products are tried, and the proportion of successes. The rate of diversification (d) (i.e. the number of attempts to introduce new products per period as a proportion of the number of items already catalogued) might at first sight seem to influence the rate of growth in demand directly, with a higher rate of diversification bringing a higher rate of demand growth. However, in the Marris model, an indirect effect is also postulated with an increasing rate of diversification reducing the proportion of successes, and thereby causing a fall in the rate of demand growth. The reasoning which Marris employs at this juncture runs along the following lines: for products to be successful they must possess 'intrinsic utility'[13] and this attribute will depend upon the quality of new product ideas and the amount of resources directed to their development. Within a particular development department, both of these will suffer as the rate of diversification increases, imposing dynamic limitations on expansion and so too high a rate of attempted growth will reduce the proportion of successes. *Ceteris paribus* the rate of growth in successful products will then be a rising but flattening function of the rate of diversification (d).

The other variable included in the demand growth function is m, the profit margin measured as the ratio of profits to sales. It is essentially a proxy variable for prices, advertising, promotions, research and development expenditures, etc. In his 1963 article (92) Marris writes:

> Thus policies of charging moderate prices, of spending large sums on advertising, and of maintaining relatively large development departments will all tend to raise the average proportion of successes. Given the production functions . . . they are all also associated with the average profit margin. Therefore we can conveniently represent the whole collection of policies in movements of a single variable, the profit margin itself. [p. 195]

The demand growth function is written using the notation of Marris:

$$D^{\cdot} = D(m,d) \qquad\qquad 3.2.1.$$

where $D^{\cdot}$ is the rate of growth of total demand.

Figure 3.2: Demand Growth Curves

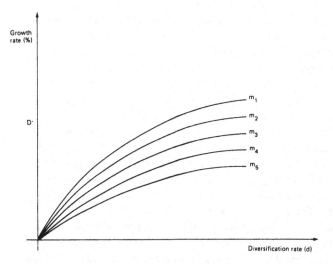

The function is represented in Figure 3.2 as a family of curves, each of which exhibits demand growth as a rising but flattening function of the rate of diversification; m_1, m_2, m_3 etc. represent successively higher profit margins, and thus are associated with declining success rates.

The analysis of demand growth so far pertains to differentiated diversification, but Marris believes that the same kind of functions can be used to represent imitative diversification, and combinations of the two varieties. Success in imitation is more likely to result when oligopolistic markets are exploding rather than saturated, but either way retaliatory moves are likely. The bargaining position of the imitator is related to his power to inflict damage or his 'threat' strength, and it is the latter for which m serves as a proxy variable in this instance

> the lower the profit margin he is prepared to accept, the stronger his threat strength and therefore the better the general prospects of the imitation: more precisely the better the chance of obtaining a peaceful settlement with a reasonable share of the market. [p. 198]

The rate of imitative diversification is also alleged to have a similar impact on the growth of demand as that described for the differentiated type. Now the dynamic limitations take the form of limited decision making capacity in the context of planning a campaign of imitative attacks, and it is postulated once again that the proportion of successes will decline as the rate of diversification increases. Function 3.2.1. therefore applies to both types of diversification, and to programmes consisting of combinations of the two strategy types. The possibility of an optimum combination is recognised with the mix for a particular firm depending on such factors as its productive efficiency *vis-à-vis* its innovative capacities.

The Growth of Supply

The supply aspects of the theory of the growth of the firm stem from financing considerations. In order to grow a firm must of course have the necessary funds and the sources of these can be internal and/or external. The internal funds come from the retention of profits, and the external funds can be raised by a variety of methods, for instance by issuing debentures, additional ordinary shares typically through a rights issue and borrowing from banks and other financial institutions. The financial policy of the firm involves the making of an optimal choice[14] not only between internal and external funds but also in relation to the form the borrowing will take and the effect it will have on the ratio of debt to total assets. Marris assumes that if the firm in question is already well established, further new issue finance will be rarely used or considered. This is clearly not always the case in practice[15] as many firms frequently resort to rights issues of ordinary shares (though often not for cash, but share exchange to support take-overs) as well as issues of debentures when stock market conditions are favourable. However, taking the Marris model as it stands, the major source of finance is internal and it is here that the financial security constraint enters. In fact Marris splits this into three ratios: liquidity, leverage and retention.

The *liquidity* ratio is liquid assets/total assets and, as we have seen earlier, too high or too low a liquidity ratio is dangerous to a firm from the point of view of take-overs and liquidation respectively. We can portray the relationship between security and the liquidity ratio diagrammatically (Figure 3.3). The Marris model assumes that the chosen ratio will lie in the area of positive slope of the liquidity/security curve rather than at L^* − the turning point. The reason for this appears to be the importance attached to the take-over threat in the Marris model, and its implication that the firm will err on the low side rather than the high. Presumably the chosen ratio L^D would not lie too far to the left of L^* since this would carry the danger of insolvency, the classic case of which remains the failure of Rolls Royce in 1971 following severe cash flow problems, despite its better long-term prospects.

Figure 3.3: Choice of Liquidity Ratio

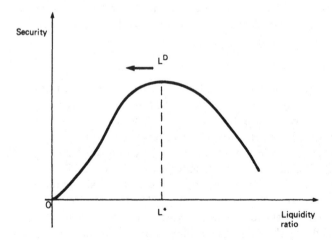

The *leverage* ratio — value of debt/total assets — is an indicator of the extent of the firm's contractual obligations, notably interest charges, and what it deemed an acceptable level will often be determined by external pressures. This level can become an absolute limit following the refusal of institutions and others to lend or underwrite issues.

The *retention* ratio — retained profits/total profits — is also determined effectively by pressures on the management team. It is not entirely free to choose the level of retention since there is a need to distribute some profits to shareholders in order to satisfy their aspirations[16] and, more particularly, to maintain the share price in line with the value of the assets. Whilst the share price would reflect the present value of future earnings from re-invested profits in a perfect market, there are many occasions in practice when this is not the case; market capitalisation fails to reflect the economic value of assets and a potential take-over is then created. However, firms do need retained profits for investment and the Marris model places particular emphasis on these as a source of finance for growth. The Galbraithian view that retained profits give the firm autonomy, provided that an adequate distribution is made to shareholders, is pertinent here. In other words, once the firm has achieved a size where it can and does generate profits for retention, it is not subject to detailed analysis in its investment strategy, as would tend to be the case if funds were sought externally.[17] Whether management would be inclined to choose projects widely different from those preferred by investors depends upon the relationship between profitability[18] and growth, which we explore more fully below. Suffice it to say that a reliance on retained earnings for expansion dictates that the profitability of investments will be significant to management even if the firm is somewhat insulated from the scrutiny of the capital market.[19] The three critical ratios of liquidity, leverage and retention are combined in a single financial security measure which we shall label ā. The value of the latter is inversely related to the liquidity ratio, and positively related to the other two ratios of leverage and retention. A high value for ā could therefore be indicative of a low liquidity ratio, high leverage or retention ratios, or some combination of these, such that security would be low but, on the other hand, finance supply would be favourable and conducive to expansion. Quite how ā is determined is left vague but the indication is that managerial attitudes to risk are important and also market conventions and constraints with respect to dividend policy and leverage. Firms willing to accept low levels of security in order to provide more funds for investment may be referred to as 'go-go' firms. Others which want a relatively easy and risk-free life can set a lower ā but not so low that liquidity becomes excessive. Both types are still constrained by the bounds on ā which can materially affect the prospects of the firm as a viable entity. Marris defines an upper limit, ā*, where liquidity is at its minimum level and the leverage and retention ratios are at their maximum levels. All the constraints are then operative, and the firm is unable to choose a higher value without endangering its survival prospects. Thus although management has to temper its growth ambitions with the competing desire for security, the latter may become satisfied once survival is assured and take the form of a constraint with ā = ā*. The company is then adopting a combination of financial policies which is 'growth maximising', but if it so desired, financial policies offering greater security may be pursued, so that in general

$$\bar{a} \leqslant \bar{a}^* \qquad\qquad 3.2.2.$$

Let us assume for the moment that ā is set at a definite value, possibly at its maximum value, ā*. The growth of corporate capital will then be determined by the firm's ability to generate profits if we continue to exclude the possibility of new equity issues. As in the demand growth function, Marris adopts m (the profit margin) and d (the rate of diversification) as the independent variables. The explanation he offers for specifying a function in which the rate of profit depends, in part, on the rate of diversification, draws heavily on the arguments which Mrs Penrose has put forward in favour of the existence of a limit on the rate of efficient managerial expansion. Given this limit, Marris supposes that if the rate of diversification is pushed beyond a certain point in the pursuit of expansion, the higher-level decision taking capacities will become stretched, resources will be misdirected, the efficiency of capital utilisation will be reduced,[20] and the capital/output ratio will rise as shown in Figure 3.4. Essentially d becomes a proxy variable for the capital/output ratio, and for a given value of the latter, a higher average profit margin (m) will result in a larger rate of profit. The profit function then becomes

$$p = p\,(m, d) \qquad\qquad 3.2.3.$$

where p is the rate of profit on productive assets, after depreciation and tax.

We can now incorporate financial policy to give a function in which

Figure 3.4: Internal Efficiency Relation

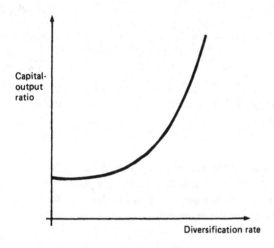

Figure 3.5: Supply of Finance Curves

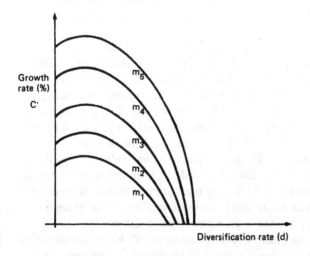

the growth of corporate capital C˙ depends upon both the rate of profit (p) and ā

$$C˙ = ā.p \qquad\qquad 3.2.4.$$

or

$$C˙ = ā.p(m,d) \qquad\qquad 3.2.5.$$

with a given ā, the supply of finance, or growth of corporate capital curves appear as in Figure 3.5.

Completion

So we have presented the two separate but interrelated sides of the growth process in the Marris model and we are now in a position to draw the threads together so as to complete the overall model. We can usefully do this by setting out the arguments discussed so far.

$D˙ = D(m,d)$	demand growth equation	
$C˙ = ā.p$	supply of finance equation	(1)
$p = p(m,d)$	profit rate equation	
$C˙ = ā.p(m,d)$	supply of finance equation	(2)
$ā ≤ ā^*$	security constraint	
$D˙ = C˙$	balanced growth equation	

Once ā is determined, the policy variables m and d can be set, but once a value is chosen for one variable then this is sufficient to determine the whole system. This is illustrated in Figure 3.6 where we have brought together the family of supply of finance curves of Figure 3.5 and the family of demand growth curves of Figure 3.2. The two sets of curves intersect at the given profit margins and if we join up all these points of intersection we arrive at the balanced growth curve with its maximum point at 'Z'. This represents the highest balanced growth rate and indicates optimum values of d* and m*. With this type of formulation there would appear to be only one optimal solution. However, it is possible to draw the D˙ and C˙ curves in such a way that there are several optimal solutions as the balanced curve flattens out.

So with a given financial security constraint ā*, having chosen either d or m the firm can then determine its equilibrium growth rate. As we have argued previously, profit is endogenous in the model and the

Figure 3.6: The Balanced Growth Curve

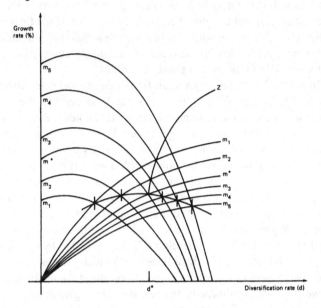

Figure 3.7: Changes in Financial Policy

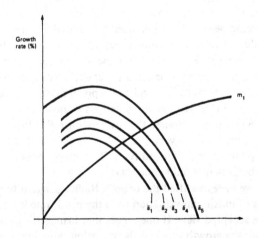

presumption is that the level will be sufficient to satify shareholders, but clearly if it is not, then ā has to change (e.g. by means of a lower retention ratio) and the model can then be resolved. If the financial policy does change, for whatever reason, a new balanced growth curve will result. A reduction in ā displaces all the supply curves downwards and a new set of intersection points will result.

In Figure 3.7 we take a given profit margin m_1 and demonstrate the effect of reducing ā from $ā_5$ to $ā_1$ in steps. If we consider the effect of a lower ā for all values of m, we can see that a new balanced growth curve with a lower peak will be generated. It follows that a company wishing to attain the maximum rate of balanced growth must pursue a growth maximising financial policy with $ā = ā^*$. If the value of ā is kept constant then maximising the growth rate means maximising the profit rate, but once ā is allowed to vary, it is likely that management would choose different combinations of growth and security from those preferred by investors, in which case there would be a conflict of interest. We can develop this theme further by utilising the simplified framework of H.K. Radice (133) which focuses on the essential features of the Marris model. It examines the relationships between growth, profitability and valuation. In Figure 3.8 we can see the combinations of growth and profit rates of the Marris type firm. The shape of the 'demand growth' curve follows from the arguments we considered earlier. Briefly it shows that as the firm tries to increase the rate of growth of demand for its products, it can initially enjoy a higher rate of profit but eventually the profit rate will decline as diminishing returns in the development and introduction of new products are experienced. The 'supply of capital' curve shows the maximum growth rate of capacity which is sustainable at each value of the profit rate, with the security constraint fully operative and new issues excluded (although the possibilities for new issues would depend on the profit rate in any case).

The feasible set of profit-growth combinations is shown in the shaded area of Figure 3.8 and Radice argued that owner-controlled firms would choose a combination lying between P and G, if we assume that both dividends and capital growth offer utility, while management-controlled firms motivated by growth would choose G.

In Figure 3.9 we have modified the original Radice diagram to show that at this point of maximum valuation ratio the profit rate is rising, which is now the accepted view. If one argues that managerial utility is a function of both the growth rate and the valuation ratio, managerial utility is maximised at the point Y where tangency occurs with the series of indifference curves J_1, J_2, etc. The choices of management and

Figure 3.8: Simplified Growth Model

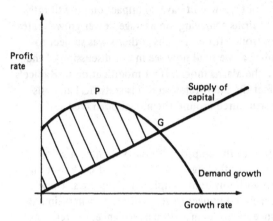

Source: H.K. Radice (133) (p. 549).

Figure 3.9: Valuation and the Managerial Utility Function

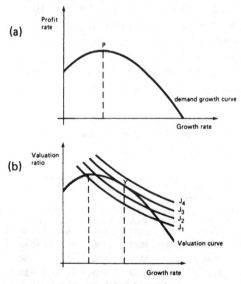

Source: H.K. Radice (133) (p. 548).

owners would only coincide at maximum valuation if management is completely constrained by the capital market. One would then hypothesise that control type would have an impact on growth rates with owner-controlled firms achieving, on average, lower growth rates than management-controlled firms. This hypothesis was subject to empirical test by Radice as we shall now see in our discussion of the studies which feature the Marris model. (Our modification to Radice's diagram does not affect the interpretation of his statistical analysis which was not itself structured around the model portrayed.)

3.3 Empirical Work

In turning our attention to the empirical findings we have a whole series of studies — many conflicting — for the UK and USA over many different time periods with different samples of companies. These studies cover the behavioural impact of separation of ownership and control, the importance of size in growth performance, the relationship between profitability and growth, and the financing implications of these relationships. They give some insight into the growth process but illustrate the difficulty of generalising about the growth of firms.[21]

Radice's study, which we have just mentioned, covered 86 firms (with net assest of £5 million or over) in three industry groups of food, electricial engineering and textiles for the period 1957-67. He recognised the initial problem of attempting to isolate the type of 'control' from other factors which could affect performance and it is fair to say that these were taken into account as far as was feasible. We reproduce one of the tables from his study of mean values of the profit rates and growth rates averaged over 10 years.

Table 3.1: Average Ten-Year Growth and Profit Rates, by Industry and Control Type

	Food		Electrical engineering		Textiles		All firms	
	Profit rate	Growth rate	Profit rate	Growth rate	Profit rate	Growth rate	Profit rate	Growth rate
Owner-control	14.58	9.44	19.68	12.14	16.98	10.05	16.81	10.42
Management-control	16.49	8.44	12.46	8.18	10.31	5.00	12.40	6.84
Transitional	13.22	11.60	16.82	13.79	11.61	3.95	13.41	9.33
All firms	14.93	9.59	15.29	10.12	12.24	6.13	14.02	8.45

Source: H. Radice (133), p. 555.

This would appear to indicate that whilst owner-controlled firms did feature a higher profit rate, they also had a higher growth rate. He did perform a lot of econometric work on the basic data particularly to test for other factors influencing profit rates as well as growth, for example opening size, industry structure, but whilst there were differences in performance in profitability between the two types of 'control' as Table 3.1 illustrates, the prediction of the Marris model is not confirmed. However, because the sample of companies has been chosen to fall in line with the Marris concept of the large firm, this may have caused a bias in the results in favour of the owner-controlled firms since the attainment of such a size while maintaining owner-control (and thereby sacrificing the benefits of access to the capital market) implies managerial performance of a high quality.

The findings of a number of other studies for the UK concerned primarily with size, profitability and growth are summarised in Table 3.2. The evidence on *profitability* and *size*[22] points to the conclusion that larger firms are less profitable, possibly because of managerial discretion, but they seem to enjoy greater stability of their earnings – a finding which has implications for financing, especially through the medium of debentures. This stability may result from the large firm being more diversified or prepared (through planning) in some other way for ups and downs in the markets which it serves or intends to serve.

The findings concerning the growth-profitability relationship are not consistent, with Singh and Whittington proposing a curvi-linear positive relationship between growth and post-tax rate of profit, and Meeks and Whittington arguing that the 'giants' feature faster growth and lower profitability. But even if the Singh and Whittington result holds, what is the direction of causation? Is it that growth depends on profit,[23] or, the inverse of this, that profits depend on growth? Clearly this is a difficult area in which to make definite propositions although Marris (96) did carry out a further test on part of the original British data of Singh and Whittington. He used an amended[24] sample of 265 quoted UK companies for the period 1948-54 and 1954-60 with a mean growth rate of 7.1 per cent and a mean post-tax return on equity assets of 11.5 per cent and found a high correlation of $R^2 = 0.78$ for the regression of growth on profitability. The Marris selection of data may have imparted some bias to the results, nevertheless it is an interesting finding even though it does not involve the question of the direction of causation. A further study investigating the inverse relationships between profit rates and firm size detected by Samuels and Smyth has

Table 3.2: Summary of Empirical Findings for the UK

Variables Study: time period sample used	Size/Growth	Variability of growth and size	Profitability/size	Variability of profitability and size	Growth/profitability	Significance of mergers in growth	Finance
SAMUELS (137) 1951-60 400 quoted companies in 4 size groupings across all industries	Large firms grow (as measured by issued capital) significantly proportionately faster and doubled their size between 1951-60	No significant variability				Dominant vehicle internal growth but larger firms relied more heavily on mergers	
SAMUELS and SMYTH (138) 1954-63 100 continuing companies in manufacturing, distribution, mining			Negative relationship between rate of profits and size of firms	Negative relationship of profit rates within given size class and size of firms			
SINGH and WHITTINGTON (146) 1948-60 (1948-54, 1954-60) 364 continuing companies (3 industry groupings and aggregate)	For aggregate data a tendency for growth to increase with size – less pronounced for the three industry groupings but not a systematic relationship	Large firms more consistency in growth	No systematic relationship between average profitability (pre-tax R of R on net assets or post-tax R of R on equity) and size	Negative relationship	Propose a curvi-linear relationship with strong positive relationship. For large firms no significant inter-industry differences		
MEEKS and WHITTINGTON (104) 1948-64 – 58 giants and other quoted 1964-69 75 giants and other quoted	'Giant' firms grew faster than the rest for 1964-69 but not 1948-64 and there was equality for 1948-69		Pre-tax rate of return on net assets lower for giants than rest for both periods	Greater stability for giants for 1948-69	Faster growth of giants 1964-69 and equality in growth overall achieved despite lower profitability than the rest	High rate of take-over by giants	Greater reliance of giants on external funds for 1964-69 – 70 per cent of long-term finance – greater gearing ratio
MEEKS and WHITTINGTON (105) 1948-64 quoted companies – 3 size groupings (1281 companies) 1964-71 (1070 companies)	'Small' firms achieved higher growth rate of net assets and 'large' a higher growth rate than medium		'Small' firms highest rate of return (and higher dividend payment rate as a percentage of net assets)	Large firms greater stability of earnings	The faster growers had a higher profit rate	Large firms relatively greater reliance on take-overs – often by share exchange	Internal source dominates financing but small firms highest rate of growth by equity finance – gearing a more important source of finance for large firms but small firms had the highest rate of growth by gearing issues for the period 1964-71

been conducted by G.D. Newbould, S.J. Stray and K.W. Wilson (117). In this study, the implications of company size for shareholders were examined but, although the rate of profit has been found by Samuels and Smyth to have an inverse relationship with company size, no corresponding relationship was found for rate of return or capital appreciation to shareholders in this later study. On the question of variability of earnings and capital appreciation, there was some correspondence in the results of the two studies, since the largest sized group appeared to offer a lower variability of return to shareholders and a less variable capital appreciation.

A rather different feature of the Marris model which has been subject to empirical investigation has been the take-over threat. D.A. Kuehn (78) in a study of 1961 data for UK companies found that the probability of take-over did depend, in part, on the valuation ratio. For the US, B. Hindley (68) has provided evidence which supports the view that the take-over threat does serve as a corporate control mechanism. On the other hand the implication of the Marris model that firms vulnerable to the take-over predator would be those which had a low valuation ratio was not substantiated by the study of G.D. Newbould (116) into mergers of firms in the period 1967/8. Moreover, A. Singh's (144) empirical work for the period 1955-60 and his later study (145) for the years 1967-70 both fail to find a strong inverse relationship between the valuation ratio and the probability of take-over. Even a relatively high valuation ratio would not seem to guarantee a firm's survival, and it might not even reduce the probability of its being acquired.

Kuehn (79) has extended his earlier study to cover UK data for the period 1957-69 and his results tend to support his earlier findings. However, Singh points out that when Kuehn's variables are normalised to make the groups of taken-over and surviving firms more comparable, the relationship between the valuation ratio and probability of acquisition is a very weak one. Consequently, there is little concrete evidence to support the proposition about the take-over threat in the Marris model.

Singh's evidence however gives some credence to the motivational aspect of the Marris model. The former argues that

> as a survival strategy, attempting to increase relative profitability may well be inferior to attempting to increase relative size, particularly so for larger unprofitable firms. [(145) p. 510]

3.4 Conclusion

The empirical studies referred to in the previous section lend some support to the Marris model but, because a consensus has failed to emerge, our comments are directed more towards the application of Marris's theoretical framework to business practice. Given its restrictive assumptions, the model's internal consistency is impeccable but there are a number of analytical problems in relating it to the firm in practice, even the large modern corporation of 'managerial capitalism'.

A deficiency which is immediately apparent is the scant attention given to risk and uncertainty which are crucial problems in business planning in the real world. This weakness extends to Marris's treatment of oligopolistic interdependence and his whole analysis of market structure and pricing. From our point of view, however, with attention focused primarily on strategic decisions in this book, we find the relegation of such matters to be justified as a means of clarifying the role of such issues as the objectives and decision making capacities of the management team. The concept of balanced growth, with supply and demand expanding together, does have implications for corporate planning. Firms must ensure that finance is available to sustain growth in demand which is generated through product-market strategies, otherwise the research and development and marketing effort will have been to no avail. In other words Marris's model points to a corporate, or systems, approach to strategic decision.

It is apparent, though, that more needs to be said about the role and scope of diversification in corporate planning and the nature of the financing decision, given that external sources are used for expansion in practice. We shall explore these issues further in Chapters 4 and 5 respectively and, in the former, consider the implications of acquisition as a means of diversification rather than as a take-over threat. Nevertheless, in viewing corporate planning from the standpoints of diversification and financing we are demonstrating our belief in the relevance of the Marris model to the world of business enterprise.

Notes

1.   E. Mansfield (91) found that in the case of the steel and petroleum industries in the United States of America small firms in particular were beneficiaries of growth from innovation and successful innovators grew twice as fast as unsuccessful innovators of the same initial size.
2.   For a useful coverage some of the problems of organisational adaptation

see T. Burns and G. Stalker (30).

3.   Although this viewpoint is to be found in biological theories of the firm and in particular that of E.T. Penrose (127), her concept of a 'managerial limit' on the long-run growth of the firm can be traced back to A. Marshall's *Principles* (99).

4.   Reference has already been made to W.J. Baumol's (20) attempt to link his sales revenue maximations hypothesis to the theory of growth, and we shall also cite frequently the work of J.K. Galbraith (49), although he did not develop a formal model of growth. Also significant is the contribution of J.H. Williamson (169) who did provide a theoretical framework.

5.   Sales revenue maximisation. See Chapter 2 for coverage of both Baumol and Williamson.

6.   Though we shall cover this later in this chapter and also in Chapter 5 when we discuss the question of retention versus distribution of profits.

7.   Investors would not necessarily choose the *same* rate of growth as management, but both parties would appear to value growth to a greater or lesser degree.

8.   There is no extensive treatment of risk or uncertainty in the Marris model.

9.   G.D. Newbould (116) indicates from his sample of mergers for the period 1967/8 in the UK that 'a theory of a *merger activity* rather *take-over activity*' was more applicable to the phenomenon. The idea that large numbers of predators might be waiting to strike is thus seen as a misrepresentation of reality.

10.   Steady state models of the growth of the firm have also been developed by J.H. Williamson (169) and R.M. Solow (149).

11.   In practice a firm can expand sales for an extended period without true diversification, by seeking new markets overseas for its existing products, by improving existing products, and by segmenting existing markets — see Chapter 4.

12.   Marris did not see his model as a contribution to the theory of oligopolistic interdependence. Clearly retaliation of some type could be expected from a policy of imitative diversification depending particularly on how close a substitute, or copy, it was for existing products. All one can assume is that there is some uncertainty as to how competitors will react, but that the firm can in essence take account of the various forms of retaliation, viz. price competition, advertising, product variation, etc. In this respect elements of game theory are employed by Marris in his basic model and he does give further consideration to the subject in his writings of 1971 (95).

13.   This rather nebulous concept implies that new products must have some attributes which consumers will value, and consequently it stands in opposition to the Galbraithian view of the modern corporation's complete domination of the consumer through the medium of persuasive advertising.

14.   The question of optimal financing is raised in Chapter 5, particularly in the context of the debate on gearing in which Modigliani and Miller (111) have been so prominent.

15.   See, for example, the study of B. Tew and R.F. Henderson (156) for the period 1949-53; also a limited coverage of the issue by H.K. Radice (133) who for the period 1957-67 produced figures of 30 per cent external finance, on average, for his sample of 86 firms in food, electrical engineering, and textiles, with the faster growing companies averaging 45 per cent external finance; in addition a more comprehensive survey by G. Meeks and G. Whittington (105) which does point to the significance of internal funds. (The latter is covered more fully in Chapter 5.)

16.   And we shall see in Chapter 5 that the maintenance of dividends may be

an important goal which makes the retention ratio a residual.

17. Some commentators would argue that there should be a policy of 100 per cent distribution to force a competitive market in borrowed funds.

18. For a detailed discussion of the profitability of retained earnings see G. Whittington (167).

19. We shall explain in Chapter 4 that the diversified firm may adopt a divisionalised structure ('M' form) within which the separate activities may compete for company funds. There then exists a kind of internal capital market with the firm.

20. Marris assumes that with a given capital stock the relationship between diversification and output is initially positive and that the Penrose effect does not operate immediately.

21. The study of P. Holl (72) revealed no systematic relationship between control type and profitability or growth. See Chapter 2.

22. For a summary of the evidence prior to 1970 see J. Eatwell (46).

23. A causal relationship identified by T. Barna (16) for 1949-59 and by J.E.S. Parker (125).

24. The original sample was for 690 firms but it was reduced to 295 by eliminating no growth, no profit firms and excluding all but internally financed companies.

4 THE DIVERSIFICATION PROCESS

4.1 Forms of Development and Diversification

The diversification of the product line is seen by Marris as the prime
means by which growth in demand is sustained. In fact diversification
may involve changes in the relationship between the firm and its
markets as well as changes involving the product line itself. The firm's
choice of strategies can be represented in two dimensions. First, in
H.I. Ansoff's (9, 10) terminology, is the classification according to
'product mission' which is a description of the job which the product
is supposed to perform. Second is the product line which can be
described in terms of the physical attributes of the products and
their performance characteristics. Ansoff prefers to use the concept of
a mission rather than that of a customer since the latter has many
different needs to be satisfied, each of which may require a different
product.

Businesses can achieve growth without diversification, using *market
penetration, market development* and *product development* strategies.
Market penetration is brought about through increasing the volume of
sales to the firm's present customers, or by finding new customers
with the same mission requirement. Market development involves the
seeking of new mission requirements which can be served by the
present production line, albeit frequently with some minor modifications in the products' characteristics. Product development is an
attempt to improve the performance of the mission by introducing new
characteristics to the product line, but without seeking to serve a
different mission. Although the term 'product diversification' is often
applied loosely to product developments thus described, we shall
henceforth, following Ansoff, only refer to a change in product-
market strategy as 'diversification' when there is a simultaneous
departure from the present product line and the present missions.

The diversification alternatives described by Ansoff in Chapter 7
of his book *Corporate Strategy* (10) comprise horizontal, vertical,
concentric, and conglomerate varieties. (1) Horizontal diversification
occurs when new products are introduced but where a link exists in
the shape of technical, financial or marketing experience which can
be applied to the new activities. In other words, although the product
line is changed, the new missions lie within the existing industry of

103

which the firm is a member. (2) Vertical diversification (or more usually vertical integration) involves an extension of the company's activities into the provision of materials, the manufacture of components (backward), or the distribution and retailing of the final product (forward). (3) Concentric diversification is in effect a more extreme form of horizontal diversification where the link between the old and new is somewhat tenuous. Typically the firm is able to draw on its existing skills, either in marketing or technology but it is no longer appropriate to regard the firm's new activities as being within the same industry as its existing ones. (4) Conglomerate diversification, as its name implies, occurs when a number of disparate activities are undertaken within one firm.[1] This form of diversification is thus the most extreme with no link whatsoever between the individual products or markets.

The above classification with its subtle differences between the various types of diversification is rather more elaborate than Marris's categorisation which consists of 'differentiated' and 'imitative' diversification. To recapitulate on this aspect of Marris's work, differentiated diversification takes place when the products are new to both the firm and the public, whereas with imitative diversification they are new only to the firm, having entered the field only when the product has gained acceptance.

Differentiated diversification involves sensing the existence of 'latent needs' and converting these into wants (backed by purchasing intentions) by marketing and advertising appropriate products. In the creation of wants, pioneering customers must be initially attracted in order to begin a chain reaction which proceeds as they stimulate their contacts who, in turn, stimulate other contacts and so on. New products, having passed through an initial phase of gestation, then pass through an unstable process called 'explosion' before reaching saturation. Profitability is alleged to rise at an early stage, then flatten out and gradually decline. A high proportion of young products in the catalogue at any one time is therefore conducive to a high average profit rate, but if a firm makes too many diversification attempts in a particular period, it is argued that the proportion of successes will fall as the inventive resources of the firm become stretched and successive ventures have falling consumer appeal or 'declining intrinsic utility'. Consequently the average profit rate among new products eventually fails.

Imitative diversification is inevitably accompanied by competition with other firms. Marris distinguishes between entry into *exploding markets* and entry into *static markets*. Entry into exploding markets, or 'bandwaggoning', has the advantage that the chain reaction has been instigated by another firm at its own expense and yet, since the market is expanding, there is a relatively high probability that the invader can be accommodated without a commercial war. Imitative diversification in static markets, on the other hand, is likely to provoke retaliation and conflict may ensue. With either form of imitative diversification the firm will opt for the more conspicuous opportunities likely to meet with a successful outcome, but as the rate of diversification increases, the opportunities subsequently taken will offer a smaller probability of success and the average profit rate will fall. In fact, Marris proposes a demand growth function for imitative diversification which has characteristics similar to those for differentiated diversification. Which of the two varieties is preponderant in any given firm will depend upon its innovatory capacities, its ability to withstand oligopolistic competition, and its technological virtuosity. The central feature of Marris's theory of demand growth is the departure from the neo-classical tradition of static, stable demand functions, and the ability of the large corporation to manage consumer demand is a theme which also runs through much of Galbraith's work.

Demand management does not always require diversification as defined above and Galbraith's analysis of the modern corporation's product-market strategies in fact refers more often than not to product developments backed by advertising rather than the creation and marketing of entirely new products. Galbraith argues that the consumer can be persuaded to buy the products of the modern corporation after their creation (development), but clearly the discussion revolves around product development rather than diversification in many instances. Demand management, as he calls it, encompasses not only the advertising industry but the media, merchandising and selling organisations together with research, training and a multitude of other establishments. If one accepts the need for planning, Galbraith argues, one must recognise the need to control consumer behaviour. This control is brought about through a sales strategy for each of the products emanating from the industrial system, but equally important is the creation of products around which sales strategies can be formulated. In this context Galbraith (49 (1969)) suggests that model change is a key component of product development:

   . . . in a culture which places a high value on technological change, there will be a natural presumption that any 'new' product is inherently superior to an old one . . . — a great many changes in product and packaging will be merely for the sake of having something to be called new. [p. 208, n. 4]

One reference to diversification, in the sense defined earlier, is made in the same chapter: 'The size and product diversification of the mature corporation allow the firm to accept an occasional . . . failure without undue hazard' (p. 211) — a statement which emphasises the risk-spreading quality of diversification rather than its use in demand management by the corporation. Earlier in *The Affluent Society*, Galbraith (50) discussed the influence of modern advertising and salesmanship in bringing into being wants which 'previously did not exist'. This implies something rather more radical than the improvement of an existing product. Moreover, it implies an even greater susceptibility on the part of the consumer to demand management than is posited in Marris's model, in which it is assumed that 'latent needs' exist and that new ventures must have 'intrinsic utility'.

Galbraith does not deny that certain kinds of expansion can be risky, and in a later volume[2] he discusses the conglomerate explosion of the late 1960s which usually took the form of acquisition or merger and which did involve high-risk growth with a high failure rate, especially among the smaller firms which attempted growth by this means. It would seem in fact that risks increase as one moves from product development through vertical and horizontal diversification to concentric and conglomerate diversification.

4.2 Causes of Diversification

Diversification may be horizontal in which case there is some complementarity either of a technical or marketing nature. However, Galbraith (51) emphasises that complementarity in diversification is not essential, as he explains in discussing the mix of goods produced by the modern corporation: '. . . its primary concern is not with technical complementarity or whether similar markets are served. Its primary concern is with growth' (p. 103).

It is clear, then, that the form of diversification chosen by the firm depends upon its goals. The more drastic forms of diversification cannot be explained in terms of profit maximising behaviour, but once growth is accepted as an important end it is easy to understand the widespread adoption of concentric and even conglomerate[3] diversification strategies. Even if one accepts that growth is the overriding goal of

managerial capitalism one must be wary of neglecting other important
goals, and Marris indeed tempers his objective function of balanced
growth maximisation with a security constraint. Ansoff believes that a
basic economic objective of return on investment is essential to
ensure efficiency of the resource-conversion process and also includes
stability and flexibility in his hierarchy of objectives. The inclusion of
stability implies that profitability and growth objectives will be set
not only as target magnitudes but also in terms of their variations.
Flexibility reflects the firm's ability to survive through unpredictable
events, by minimising the impact of catastrophies on the one hand
and by taking maximum advantage of any opportunities which may
come its way on the other.

Planning for balanced growth over a long time period is one
source of diversification strategies, but in our economic system we find
many firms which are diversified yet which have apparently reached
this state without formal planning or consideration of long-term
objectives. It is convenient to distinguish between *ultimate* and
proximate[4] causes of diversification in this context. Ultimate causes
lie in the identification of gaps between desired performance in the
long-term and anticipated performance which can only be plugged by
a change in product-market strategy which involves a simultaneous
departure from the existing product line and the existing missions
served by it. Once the need for diversification has been recognised, the
form which it will take depends upon the immediate pressures and the
range of alternatives which are generated. This will reflect the kind of
search process undertaken by the organisation, but whether search is
limited or wide-ranging, there will be some possibilities open to the
firm which are relatively conspicuous,[5] at the point in time when
search takes place. The sets of immediate opportunities open to the
firm are then to be seen as the proximate causes of diversification.
Thus the availability of by-products for development, production
opportunities which can fill unused capacity, the presence of other
organisations ripe for take-over,[6] requests by important customers for
products which are complementary to the firm's operations, and the
emergence of new products from research and development activities
are all examples of proximate causes of diversification (although the
presence of an innovative R and D department is indicative of a conscious diversification policy, so that the firm is not just responding to
favourable opportunities, when it exploits the fruits of its research).

Both T.A. Staudt (151) for the US and L.R. Amey (6) for the
UK have noted the impact of the second world war on diversification,

for example motor car companies on both sides of the Atlantic entered into the production of military vehicles and aircraft engines. The opportunities open to industry were therefore proximate causes of their diversification experiences, but Amey argues that a successful war-time extension of activities encouraged management to deploy its expertise and capacities in other kinds of business during the post-war period as well. Consequently, with confidence in their own versatility, managements have tended to be more ambitious in the forms of diversification undertaken and the conglomerate enterprise has become more common (although the extent of conglomeration is sometimes exaggerated as we shall explain in surveying the empirical work).

4.3 Potential of the Various Product-Market Strategies

Before examining the forms of diversification in detail and their potential, let us consider the more conservative strategies which fall short of diversification such as: market penetration, market develop-ment and product development. Market penetration can be achieved by persuading customers to increase purchases through the medium of advertising alone, or through promoting the product with special offers, prizes or bonuses and an advertising campaign to inform, as well as persuade, the consumer. If new customers are sought, the company may segment the market to exploit variations in demand intensity or elasticity between different socio-economic groups. Segmentation often involves the multiplication of varieties, each of which has its own minor packaging, quality or performance difference and ear-marked for a particular segment and price band of the market. A good illustration of penetration through segmentation can be seen in the market for gramophone records, where long-playing records are sold in three broad bands: full-price, budget-price, and the mid-price band. A feature of segmentation is that it is usually difficult to isolate completely any one segment from another, and 'cannibalism' occurs, for example although sales of gramophone records increased when budget-priced recordings became available, some customers who would normally have paid the full price preferred to save their money by choosing an alternative lower-priced recording.

　　Market development involves the adaptation of the existing product line (generally with some modification in the product characteristics) to new missions, for example an aircraft manufacturer may adapt and sell its passenger transport for the mission of cargo transportation. There is no cannibalism problem with market development unless the company already makes other products which serve the new mission, but clearly a product designed for a specific purpose is unlikely to be capable of serving more than a few different missions.

Product development is the modification of existing products to incorporate new or different characteristics and many of the so-called 'new' products of the automobile industry are essentially product developments, which in many cases merely incorporate minor styling changes or insignificant mechanical improvements. The British Leyland 'Mini', for example, has been in production for nearly twenty years and although the latest version has many refinements which make it a much more attractive vehicle than earlier models, it is still basically the same concept in motoring. Although there are obvious advantages to be gained from a long association with a particular range of products, many companies have had cause to regret their over-dependence on traditional lines.

The common advantages of these conservative product-market strategies, which do not go as far as diversification, lie in their consistency with the principle of achieving cost reductions through economies of scale, the allegedly prudent management practice of staying within the kind of business for which the company 'has a feel', and the avoidance of the extensive re-organisation often required to pursue a diversification strategy, especially where merger is concerned. The scale effects can accrue through aggregate size and the length of production run (or size of the batch). Expansion through market penetration, market development or product development will probably bring lower costs through scale in general purpose equipment even if the production of multiple varieties accompanies the strategy. However, as M. Howe (73) has argued, multiplication may mean short production runs for each variety and the time and cost of resetting can counteract the advantages of scale. Another off-setting factor is that in addition to the general purpose equipment from which economies might be enjoyed, each product variety tends to require some specialised equipment.

There are other advantages of conservative expansion strategies associated with the use of human resources since new technical skills will generally not be called for, neither will new managerial skills, and furthermore the existing sales organisation may well suffice. Certainly a firm already in existence can sell to new customers or cater for new missions with a head's start over firms setting up in a new kind of business from scratch.

There are limits to expansion if the firm refuses to adopt diversification strategies. For one thing, markets have a tendency to become saturated even if the product or the market itself undergoes development. Actual decline may however be prevented if the product's life cycle can be anticipated and strategies introduced at the appropriate moment. The life of a product can be broken down into four consecutive stages: product introduction, market growth, market maturity and sales decline (see Figure 4.1).

Figure 4.1: Life Cycle of a Typical Product

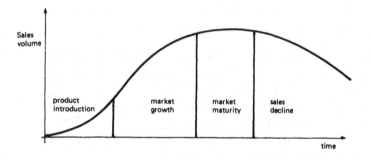

When the product is introduced, the demand for it is yet to be proved, sales are frequently low and creep along slowly while the firm is promoting the product in an attempt to attract 'pioneering' customers. If the product survives as far as the market growth stage, the innovator will begin to make profits but, following Marris, one must recognise that a success may attract imitative diversifiers, though these may well be accommodated if the market is exploding. Eventually most customers that were likely sales prospects will actually be using the product and the market is then saturated. The advent of saturation is indicative of market maturity by which stage a number of competitors may have entered the market and competition may become aggressive as market shares come under pressure. The market maturity stage may continue for many years if appropriate product-market strategies are adopted. Thus household appliances like washing machines and vacuum cleaners, and consumer goods like tobacco products and breakfast goods are in the market maturity stage.

Competition between rival manufacturers usually takes the form of product development backed by persuasive advertising but, as Baumol emphasises, seldom through the medium of price.

On the fourth and final stage of the life cycle, not all companies are able to weather the storm. Over-capacity becomes apparent and, as firms go to the wall, production becomes concentrated in fewer hands. Those surviving may be able to revive demand by re-styling and promoting, but the process of decline is hard to arrest and even harder to reverse. The probable length of the cycle will be an important factor in strategic planning, but demand forecasting is not such a highly developed art that complete life cycles can be mapped out. However, the onset of maturity can often be anticipated even if refined forecasting techniques are not used and the company relies on feedback. Obviously though such a reliance leaves less time for adjustment when the need for change becomes apparent.

An illustration of a successful attempt to stretch out the life of a product is given by T. Levitt (84) and it relates to the life history of nylon. This product, manufactured by Du Pont, was originally used mainly for military purposes in the form of parachutes, thread and rope, followed by its entry into the women's hosiery market where substantial market growth was enjoyed. Before market maturity, Du Pont developed measures designed to re-vitalise sales and profits. These measures involved most of the basic product-market strategies open to a company and comprised:

(1)   promoting more frequent usage of the product among current users;
(2)   developing more varied usage of the product among current users;
(3)   creating new users for the product by expanding the market;
(4)   finding new uses for the basic material.

As a result, the life cycle of nylon took on the form exhibited in Figure 4.2.

The fourth strategy listed above does imply diversification in a limited (horizontal) sense, but the success of Du Pont in extending the life cycle of nylon does indicate that the more drastic option of diversification is not always necessary in pursuing an objective of growth. Ultimately, though, sustainable growth usually does depend upon diversification to a greater or lesser degree, and in this regard the firm needs to be searching out opportunities which match the strengths

Figure 4.2: General Form of the Extended Life-Cycle

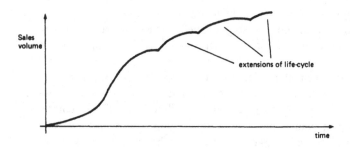

of the company in marketing capabilities, management skills or financial standing. Such a policy, which will be part of the strategic planning activities of firms can produce an optimisation of synergistic effects.

Looking now at each of the diversification alternatives in turn, it can be seen that there are significant differences in their potential contributions to the objectives of the firm. Horizontal diversification, which consists of moves with the same industry or market type, permits a substantial transfer of skills and experience in technical, financial or marketing activities. From this standpoint, there may well be some scale economies which result from horizontal diversification, although it is unlikely that these will arise to any great extent in the manufacturing costs since general purpose equipment will typically only be used in a restricted number of stages of production, with the number of types of specialised equipment increasing as the firm becomes more diversified. Horizontal opportunities will seldom improve to any great extent the flexibility of the company or its internal stability since a single technical base or a common marketing thread leaves the firm vulnerable to sudden changes in fortune, for example, strikes of production workers, or irregular variations in market demand. The strategy will generally, however, offer synergy particularly if the common link is in the market giving the company an opportunity to create a product range with interrelated demands. Even if the new products require new or different manufacturing facilities, the established company with a well organised marketing organisation can trade on its reputation in the market and diversification into dissimilar but complementary lines may bring a more widespread recognition of the brand name.

Horizontal diversification which involves technically related production will be preferred by companies which have specialised knowledge or skills in production. Specialised machinery and equiment is seldom an advantage unless there is a large minimum efficient scale in one or more stages of production, in which case the established firm would be at an advantage compared with firms starting from a different technical base. In general, however, it is only in the short term that plant capacity and even specialised production knowledge will be a source of competitive strength. In the longer term, productive facilities and skills can be acquired by potential competitors, but market reputations and established brand names are much more difficult to cultivate. A most important source of technical know-how in diversifying firms is research and development, and strong research and development capability enables the company not only to develop established products and to innovate, i.e. create products which are new to the firm and the consumer, but also to imitate successfully. We shall refer to other aspects of the empirical evidence of M. Gort (57) in Section 4.6 below, but it is appropriate to mention here that in his study of diversification in a sample of US manufacturing firms, the proportion of technical personnel employed by the firm appeared to be related to the extent of diversification, although the direction of causality is difficult to detect.

If the company can diversify into a product-market situation in which both production and marketing skills can be employed, economies and synergy can be exploited to the maximum permitted by horizontal diversification. On the other hand the company will be enjoying minimal benefits from the strategy in terms of stability and maybe flexibility too, although the internal strength of a company which has not over-stretched its resources may enable it to weather a storm better than a company which has diversified into an alien industry or market.

Vertical integration may occur backwards in which case the firm becomes engaged in operations previously undertaken by suppliers, for example, the manufacture of basic materials or components, or forwards, which involves the extension of operations towards the consumer, that is in distribution or retailing. The strategy offers limited opportunities for growth, but clearly there are only a finite number of operations between extraction of basic materials and sale of the final product. Vertical integration may offer greater security, a motive stressed by E.A.G. Robinson (136):

> Vertical integration is sometimes the consequence of a reuniting of separated processes of production. It is more often the consequence of a search for security. [p. 110]

The security results from regularity of supply or the guarantee of a retail outlet, but, despite this kind of advantage, the firm's dependence on a particular segment of economic demand leaves it sensitive to variations in the market and less able to respond to change. The same technology may run through several stages of the total operation, in which case the firm may benefit from synergy, but frequently the technology will differ (motor-vehicle manufacture and assembly involves an entirely different technology from the manufacture of electrical components for vehicles). Certainly a firm which enters retailing activities from a manufacturing base is unlikely to possess the managerial skills within its existing organisation, although typically this type of forward integration would be accomplished by taking over an existing concern. An associated disadvantage in connection with integration by acquisition is that the subsidiary may itself be diversified and consequently be engaged in types of production which have no natural relationship to the activities of the parent.

Profit advantages may accrue through integration if the rates of return in the other stages of production are higher than in the original stage. There may also be cost savings which result from being able to avoid certain market transactions and associated selling costs. The assured supplies and orders which follow vertical integration also enable contingency stocks to be run down with a consequent release of working capital which can be re-invested profitably elsewhere in the business. It is not always true, however, that avoiding the market (for intermediate products) enables costs to be reduced, since administrative procedures do not necessarily provide a more efficient means of co-ordinating producer and user than the mechanism of the market. Furthermore, the effects which vertical integration may have on competition may be detrimental to the efficiency of the resource allocation process in the economy as a whole.

An excellent example of a vertically integrated company is that of Unilever.[7] The company which Lord Leverhulme created was built on a vertical structure in which the company owned (and still does) plantations which produced part of the basic raw materials. These were shipped in the company's own fleet to the factories where they were processed and packaged. The products were subsequently transported to retail outlets and promoted through the company's own advertising agency. Unilever today is also a highly diversified company in which horizontal, conglomerate, and especially concentric forms are all represented. Much of this has been accomplished through acquisition, and in Britain the Unilever Empire include around forty companies amongst which figure Lever Brothers, Birds Eye, Batchelors, Wall's, Gibbs Proprietaries, MacFisheries and Thames Board Mills.

In 1973 the sales breakdown[8] was as follows:

Foods	£2,670m	(53%)
Detergents and toilet preparations	£ 985m	(19%)
Paper, plastics and packaging, chemicals,		
transport and other interests	£ 607m	(12%)
Animal feeds	£ 334m	(7%)
Merchandise and other activities of the		
United Africa Co. and plantations	£ 472m	(9%)

Before turning to the role of acquisition in corporate strategy brief mention will be made of concentric and conglomerate diversification, but since these frequently proceed by means of acquisition, a fuller discussion will follow in the next section. It is argued that concentric diversification can offer synergy and that it will usually be more profitable and less risky than a conglomerate strategy which is equivalent in its economic prospects and flexibility. Ansoff (10 (1968)) argues, however, that a well planned conglomerate strategy can be justified so long as it has 'a sense of direction expressed through competitive advantage, product-market scope, and objectives' (p. 119). It can confer greater profitability and stability if industries with better economic characteristics are sought and leave the firm relatively free from catastrophic declines in particular markets. The size of the conglomerate may also bring with it a more favourable relationship with capital markets and greater security from take-over threats, but conglomerate diversification can bring with it particular risks. H.I. Ansoff and J.F. Weston (12) have found that in the USA conglomerate firms under abnormal conditions, such as a sharp recession, have less staying power than concentric ones, particularly where organisational over-centralisation occurs. In consequence there are both advantages and pitfalls associated with conglomerate diversification, and the latter tend to be magnified when the route chosen for this strategy is through acquisition.

4.4. Diversification by Acquisition

Economic analysis has traditionally regarded merger or take-over activity as a means of reducing competition, or establishing mono-polistic dominance. Penrose (127) regards this tendency in economic thinking as 'placing the wrong emphasis on one of the most significant characteristics of the firm in the modern economy' (p. 155). The fact is that acquisition or merger may be the best means of achieving growth, profit, and other objectives of the firm, by the avoidance of entry barriers and the purchase of assets in the form of a going concern.

The role accorded to take-overs in the growth of the firm is unusual in Marris's model in that they are seen as a threat to the security of the company rather than as a means of diversification. Take-overs, as we have seen in our analysis of that model, are viewed therefore very much from the stance of the company which might be taken over rather than that of the company which might be considering acquisition as a diversification strategy. In practice diversification frequently does involve acquisition, almost certainly when conglomerate diversification is planned, but it is also highly likely for the concentric variety, vertical integration and even horizontal diversification. In this section we shall be examining the role of acquisition in corporate strategy as a means of achieving growth rather than as a constraint or threat.

W.G. Lewellen (86) lists the 'operating' advantages to be gained from the merging of companies as: opportunities for economies of scale or other direct efficiencies in manufacturing; the enhancement of competitive sales positions through augmented monopoly power or the appeal of a more complete product line; a complementarity in research and basic technological expertise relating to new products; and a convenient fit of scarce managerial skills leading to greater administrative efficiency. In theory, if one or more of these conditions is present, the new company should enjoy a higher profitability and higher market value than its constituent parts did prior to merging. These advantages are most likely to arise when the merging companies are engaged in similar business activities, that is, where there is at most only diversification of the concentric type. So far as conglomerate mergers are concerned, Lewellen argues that although these 'operating' advantages may be negligible, there are 'financial' benefits which may accrue: taking advantage of transient errors in the market valuation of acquisition candidates; utilising the unused debt capacity of an acquired firm subsequent to a merger; or obtaining a diminished variability of total corporate earnings through the portfolio diversifica-tion implied by conglomeration.[9] These financial factors may have an important bearing on the security, flexibility and stability of the combined enterprise in addition to the possible creation of share-holders' wealth and contribution to corporate growth.

The stability effect resulting from reduced variability of corporate earnings is fairly obvious. Quite simply, over-all market risk is reduced through the diversification into unrelated spheres of activity. Risks resulting from economic activity in general cannot, however, be diversified away and conglomerates have found it as difficult to adjust to the recession of the 1970s as have companies operating in a more restricted range of business activities. The external flexibility of the conglomerate enterprise arises from the diverse aptitudes, experience and skills it possesses which enable it to respond to a wider range of opportunities than firms with a narrower technical or marketing base. Internal flexibility may also be enhanced if the merger makes the new company more self sufficient financially, that is if internally generated finance is stable and of a sufficiently high volume to enable the firm to adjust to changing circumstances without relying on external funds. Increased security (in Marris's sense) may follow from conglomeration if it enables the firm to realise a high valuation ratio (and thereby become less vulnerable to take-over by some other company) and this may be facilitated if the conglomerate can survive with a reduced liquidity ratio following the diminished market risks. There will also be a beneficial effect on security if the more successful components of the organisation provide a sound basis for contractual obligations so that the less successful components are insulated from creditor interference. The diminished relative variability of earnings may also enable the company to negotiate higher limits on debt-finance and so long as this does not in itself encourage the company to take on higher financial risks than it otherwise would have done, the security of the firm will be improved in consequence, as will the supply of finance for growth.

The use of the take-over bid in business strategy became more common in Britain after 1945. Before the war, amalgamations normally took place either by mutual agreement or gentle persuasion by the proposing company which had often previously acquired substantial shareholdings of the other company. Another characteristic of the post-war scene has been that mergers have been motivated by a rather wider range of considerations than those most prominent in the early years of the century and in the inter-war period, which were notably the need to achieve scale economies to compete efficiently against foreign (usually American and German) companies and the need to eliminate spare capacity in the face of market decline. Admittedly, many of the mergers of recent years have been justified in similar terms, particularly those which came about in the years following the creation of the Industrial Re-organisation Corporation in 1966. (The IRC, now disbanded, can be credited with the merger between Leyland and British Motor Holdings, a dubious achievement in the light of recent experience, besides a number of more successful amalgamations.) Many other factors, however, have been at work leading to a number of take-over booms. For example, the take-over movement in the 1950s[10] grew out of a 'curious combination of circumstances' which included undervaluation of companies' assets by an uninformed capital market and diminished expectations on the part of investors. Share prices often failed to reflect the large cash reserves held by companies or the freehold properties which they owned. These discrepancies enabled the more astute businessman to make a vast fortune overnight. The share values of the leaders in the take-over movement were enhanced following their initial successes, thus strengthening their position for the next round of conquests. Charles Clore (Sears (Holdings) Ltd) was buying up primarily shoe-store chains but a natural consequence of some of his later acquisitions was diversification. Other entrepreneurs who pioneered this movement were Harold Samuel, Isaac Wolfson (Great Universal Stores Ltd) and Hugh Fraser.

By the following decade, companies were more realistically valued and the motivation for take-over changed from bargain seeking to an aim of long-term strengthening of the business, which frequently involved diversification. There were some operators in the market who managed to enjoy the best of both worlds, notably Jim Slater whose strategy was to take over a company, re-organise its human, physical and financial assets and its trading activities, sell off some of its assets and then recoup benefits in the form of realised monetary profits and enhanced share value. At the same time his acquisitions were over a very broad industrial base and Slater Walker, as the company became, was among the first conglomerates of this era in the UK.[11]

The holding company method[12] of merging businesses has been widely adopted and is particularly favoured where a consequence (or indeed the purpose) of the merger is diversification. The holding company may be formed as a non-trading company which controls the activities of the various businesses, or alternatively one of the constituent companies is designated the holding company and acts in the dual capacity of trading-cum-holding company. The holding company will acquire the whole of, or at least a controlling interest in, the equity of the various trading companies and the legal and organisational entities composing the merger may remain undisturbed.

If a new holding company is formed, it will be able to negotiate its own arrangements for the raising of capital, including debt, and this will facilitate expansion. The holding company will typically be responsible for over-all strategic planning and the raising of long-term finance while the trading companies will be responsible for operating decisions and the planning of small capital schemes. The use of an existing company which continues trading will avoid the preliminary expenditures, such as stamp duties, which might be payable on the formation of an entirely new entity, but there are disadvantages associated with this method in connection with its financial flexibility, notably debt-raising potential in the case of an existing company which is already highly geared. On the other hand, there are financing advantages over a newly formed holding company in that the reserves of the holding-cum-trading company can be freely used whereas those of operating companies owned by a holding company will be largely frozen and immobilised.

An alternative to the holding company structure is complete amalgamation or absorption which involves the full integration of the various undertakings within the legal framework of a limited company. The new company, which often retains the names of the major enterprises from which it was formed, controls all the assets and assumes responsibility for all liabilities. There is again a choice as to whether an entirely new business should be formed, or an existing company used to absorb the others. Generally the use of an existing company seems preferable, since expenses and legal proceedings involved in the formation of a new company are avoided. An existing company which takes over other businesses can finance the operation either by cash payment out of liquid resources, or out of the proceeds of a new capital issue; alternatively it can offer its own shares and debentures directly, in which case the value of these securities has to be valued in relation to those of the company being taken over. Another possible means of merging businesses is the pooling arrangement. Such arrangements were more common before the war and they involved the formation of some common organisation to serve part of the activities of the various firms, for example a research establishment, but the companies continued to operate as separate units with their own boards of directors. The demise of pooling arrangements in the UK followed the post-war Monopolies and Restrictive Practices legislation, since it would now be very difficult to prove that such arrangements were in the public interest. An example of pooling in Europe is the new group Societé Franco-Suedoise des Moteurs PRV, which is an arrangement whereby Peugeot, Renault and Volvo collaborate in the manufacture of power units for their motor vehicles. Clearly, though, the potential of this means of merging interests is severely limited so far as diversification is concerned.

The organisational structure adopted in the diversified firm, if accomplished by merger, is strongly influenced by the merger process itself. Thus a holding company operation will often leave the internal organisation of individual components undisturbed, apart from the strategic decision making capacity, whereas a complete amalgamation will usually require a measure of re-organisation or a dovetailing of existing management structures. If the newly formed company comprises clearly demarcated product-market capabilities, there may be a minimum of disturbance if a divisionalised management structure is adopted, but even this will generally require a degree of re-organisation within the original components of the new enterprise. Indeed, unless some re-grouping and rationalisation of activities takes place following merger, it is highly unlikely that any synergistic benefits will be enjoyed.

4.5 Organisational Structure and Efficiency

At this stage it is appropriate to return to the work of O.E. Williamson whose managerial theory was discussed earlier in Chapter 2. In his book *The Economics of Discretionary Behaviour* (171) Williamson alluded to the possibility that a divisionalised structure might warrant rather different analysis from that applied to a conventional departmentalised structure (unitary form), but this theme was not developed within his managerial theory at that time. The analysis which we put forward here is based on Williamson's paper 'Managerial Discretion, Organisation Form, and the Multi-Division Hypothesis' (173) and a fuller exposition of Williamson's research is given in his own book on this subject (172).

In the traditional, unitary form of enterprise (henceforth U-form) there are the principal functional divisions of sales, finance, manu-facturing, etc. Williamson believes that this kind of structure is viable in a medium-sized firm, but that as the firm expands, more hierarchical levels will be added and the U-form structure becomes subject to cumulative control loss and the character of the strategic decision process is altered, with a resultant shift away from the major objectives

of the enterprise in favour of partisan interests. Departments press
their own claim on resources, especially for staff expenditures, and a
permissive attitude towards other elements of slack may also develop.
Admittedly the capital market, notably through the take-over threat,
does impose a constraint on non-profit pursuits but this tends only to
be invoked when the offence reaches 'egregious proportions'. Thus
Williamson has qualified his original hypothesis so that it is
reserved largely for U-form organisations and the multi-division form
(henceforth M-form) is then treated apart.

Figure 4.3: Multi-Division Form of Organisation

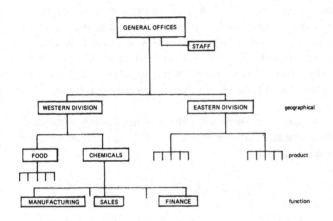

The M-form innovation, initially devised in the 1920s in the USA
independently by Du Pont and General Motors, can in theory solve
the problems characteristic of the U-form organisation by separating
activities into divisions which may be delineated on a product, brand
or geographical basis before the U-form functional structure appears
(see Figure 4.3). By scaling down the U-form structure to a manage-
able size in each division, the associated problems should diminish.
Williamson considers there to be a need for an 'élite staff' to assist the
general office in its strategic decision making and control activities,
but the creation of the M-form structure should in itself allow top
executives to spend more time on strategy, having delegated operations
to each of the operating divisions.

Galbraith in *The New Industrial State* (49) and again in *The Age of*

Uncertainty (52) refers to the organisational complex as the 'techno-structure' and he attaches particular importance to the specialist staff including corporate planners, management accountants, research scientists, engineers, economists, computer experts and so on. To Galbraith, organisation charts convey a false impression of power originating from the top of the hierarchy, ultimately from the shareholders. He believes that the reality is of concentric circles with power flowing between them, giving the corporation strength. Just how the M-form could be accommodated within one of Galbraith's circles is an interesting problem which we shall not tackle here, but one doubts that he would deny the problem of control-loss and the significance of multi-division forms of organisation in a modern industrial economy. Where he does seem to break with Williamson's modified hypothesis is that the technostructure's goal of growth is not recognised as being a consequence of control loss. Galbraith sees growth as a goal which has universal appeal within the organisation and he does not associate it solely with the U-form of organisation. Williamson (173), on the other hand, argues that the M-form organisation in the large enterprise,

> favours goal-pursuit and least-cost behaviour more nearly associated with the neo-classical profits-maximisation hypothesis than does the U-form organisational alternative. [p. 367]

Clearly this has implications for the diversified company, particularly the conglomerate in the form of a holding company. If the parent or holding company is highly profit-oriented and maintains tight control over the activities of the separate divisions or subsidiaries, the large corporation may be more effective than the external capital market in recognising where profitable opportunities exist and in channelling finance into them. The conglomerate is seen to act in this respect 'as a miniature capital market' (173, p. 375). Another argument put forward by Williamson in support of the conglomerate is that if horizontal and vertical mergers are hampered by governmental policy towards industry, the conglomerate merger can provide 'a vital route by which small U-form firms can quickly obtain the requisite size to support the M-form structure'. A further defence for the conglomerate propounded here is that since this kind of diversification is commonly brought about through acquisition, a permissive attitude towards conglomeration ensures that the take-over threat necessary to maintain an efficient capital market is maintained, even if mergers leading to an increase in concentration are suppressed.

On the debit side are a number of arguments put forward by Williamson as 'social costs of conglomeration' (p. 377). Here he lists: internal subsidisation of weakly performing divisions; the exploitation of tax or other legislative loopholes; the restriction of competition among a group of 'super-giants', if the conglomerate process is carried too far, out of their recognition of mutual dependence. K.D. George (53, 54) indicates a number of other associated dangers. Not only might there be internal subsidisation of weakly performing activities but also cross-subsidisation where monopoly power and high profits enjoyed in one market enable the firm to wage a price war in markets where competition is keener. Large firms may carry their mutual respect, as far as developing 'spheres of influence'. Furthermore, where a few large firms are involved in multiple activities, interdependencies will grow between them as customers and suppliers and the choice of supplier may then be made, not because of price or quality, but because the supplier is also an important customer for some of the firm's output. George also doubts that the M-form does act effectively as an internal capital market. So long as investment and financing decisions remain in the hands of top management, it is their expertise which governs efficiency and, given a limited availability of high quality management, large firms will vary in their collective skills and in the quality of decisions they make. So far as competition for funds between divisions of a company is concerned, George points out that the interests of the firm as a whole will generally not be served by genuine competition between affiliates.

M. Broke and G. Turner (28) have examined the reasons for the failure of companies to disinvest subsidiaries or activities which are not making a positive contribution to company performance. In the firms which this study covered, the failure of management to analyse opportunities for running down or disposing of activities casts doubt on the miniature capital market within a company thesis. Many of the obstacles to a rigorous analysis of such opportunities centred on interdependence. For example, where common facilities are used it is difficult to ascertain avoidable cost, and where subsidiaries trade with one another, the problem of setting an appropriate transfer price precludes an accurate calculation of the profit consequences of a decision. Ignorance of the relevant facts and fear that a closure will have repercussions on a wider scale result in a tendency to 'play safe'. It would seem a reasonable conclusion that, all other things being equal, the wider the range of activities and the larger the number of enterprises taken over, the more likely is an informational problem of this nature to persist.

4.6 Empirical Evidence

Although there is a wealth of empirical data on the profitability, size and growth of the enterprise, as discussed in Chapter 3 in the context of the Marris model, little evidence has been available until recently on the subject of diversification. Here we shall concentrate on evidence for the UK (mentioning that for the US *en passant*) and focus on attributes not covered in earlier chapters, for example relationships between diversification and research and development, and measures of the nature and extent of diversification.

At the time of writing, the most recent published study of diversification in the UK is that of M.A. Utton (160) who obtained data from the Business Statistics Office. This covered the two hundred largest enterprises in manufacturing industry but not the sectors outside the BSO's production register, a deficiency which omits some of the biggest and most diversified companies in the UK. The general industry headings are the Standard Industrial Classification (SIC) Orders, modified by amalgamating Orders IV and V and also XVI and XVII to give fourteen classes, into which the two hundred enterprises were initially classified. Each of the local units of these enterprises was then classified according to three-digit industries (Minimum List Headings) which were then ranked according to their importance in terms of employment for each enterprise.

Utton found that in 1974, about 57 per cent of the enterprises' total employment was in their primary three-digit industry. Below the third most important industry, shares of total employment were on average very small, but the largest firms seemed to have a long tail of insignificant activities spread through a number of different industries. A 'numbers equivalent' measure of diversification was adopted, result-ing in a finding that the largest two hundred enterprises were diversified to the equivalent of operating equally in just over four narrowly defined industries (including vertical integration). Utton suggests that the finding places 'a question mark' against the quantita-tive importance of conglomerate power. Indeed, the study as a whole tends to confirm the view that firms diversify into industries with close technical and marketing links, although there are a number of firms, especially those classified in Petroleum and Chemicals, Bricks and Timber, and some rubber companies, who take a more adventurous line.

M. Gort's (57) study of 721 firms in the USA and that of L.R. Amey (7) for the UK have shown a positive correlation between diversification and size of the enterprise for the manufacturing sector as a whole.[13] However, within Gort's sample of 111 large enterprises there was little clear association between these attributes, possibly indicating that once we enter the large firm group and thus reach a certain over-all size, there is no further inducement or scope for diversification. Utton's results did not follow precisely the same pattern but he too suggests that there is an 'apparent lack of a strong direct relationship between diversification and size within the *sample of the largest enterprises*' (p. 111, our italics).

Amey's study mentioned in the previous paragraph remains an important reference for diversification in the UK. Using data from the 1958 Census of Production he tested a number of hypothesised relationships and in part of this study he examined the significance of research activities using figures of scientific manpower as a surrogate for research expenditure. He concluded that there was a direct relationship between diversity of activity and the extent to which an industry is research based. The figures for scientific manpower were taken from *Industrial Research in Manufacturing Industry, 1959-60* (Federation of British Industries and the NIESR), and the regression equation of degree of diversification[14] per cent (Y) on scientific manpower (X) was found to be:

$$\log Y = 0.2872 + 0.2882 \log X$$
$$\quad\quad (0.1086) \quad (0.0422)$$

$\bar{r}^2$ (corrected for degrees of freedom) = 0.6556
and the value of F was significant at the one per cent level.

The relationship between diversification and size has already been mentioned and it held for most industries in Amey's study, the exception being in low diversification industry groups 4, 7, 17, 32, 44 and 51 which include some food products, tobacco, agricultural machinery, motor vehicles, footwear, printing and publishing. Five of these industries (4, 17, 32, 44 and 51) and two others (21, contractors' plant and 25, other mechanical engineering) also fell outside the general scatter for the regression of diversification on growth of markets 1948-58, using log scales as before. However, even after excluding these cases, there was 'no observable relationship between growth and diversification'. In fact the value of $\bar{r}^2$ was only 0.1275 and was not significantly different from zero with $F_{0.01} = 7.30$. This result appears at first sight to cast doubt on the assertion that companies diversify for growth, but on further consideration the result is less surprising. For one thing, diversification may be pursued for defensive reasons, and diversification may do no more than arrest decline; for another, diversification may not be as successful in promoting growth as the less drastic product-market strategies. The evidence does not refute the contention that diversification is necessary for sustained growth, since market saturation normally constrains growth in single-product firms even if high growth rates are initially possible through product or market development. Amey did not attempt to test the proposition that differing profitability between industries might stimulate diversification, with the data at his disposal. Gort's evidence for the US reveals little systematic relationship between profitability and diversification, but the same kind of interpretation as offered for the growth-diversification relationship is appropriate here.

Amey also analysed the degree of relatedness of secondary activities and showed that of 9,076 enterprises in 13 SIC Orders comprising 50 manufacturing industry groups, *together* operated in a total of 829 industry groups — 88 within the same order, 206 in other orders and 535 unidentified. Thus, on average, the enterprises of a given order operated in more than twice as many industry groups outside the order as within it. However, Amey did not weight the secondary activities to give an indication of their importance relative to an enterprise's primary activities, and the widespread diversification conveyed in these figures is largely an illusion. Thus, in Utton's study (160) discussed above, which is in any case more up-to-date, the bulk of firms' secondary activities only accounted for a small proportion of their total employment.

Finally, brief mention will be made of P.K. Gorecki's (56) inter-industry analysis of diversification in the UK manufacturing sector. Gorecki used census data for 1958 and 1963, reproducing his 1963 findings in the article, choosing to ignore the 1968 census which used a classification scheme that he regarded as 'too broad' for his purposes. He concluded that technological links formed the basis of diversification for many enterprises, and consequently it was unlikely that stability had been enhanced. He did not produce any evidence of his own concerning stability but referred back to an earlier study by Utton (159) for the UK in which a sample of diversified companies were found not to enjoy a statistically significant lower variability in profits than a sample of specialist enterprises in the same industry. Also cited was R.S. Bond's (22) study for the US in which data for 157 large corporations showed no significant relationship between the variability of profit and diversification.

The most general conclusion to emerge from the empirical work on diversification is that firms concentrate on closely related industries, suggesting that the popular image of diversification as being of a conglomerate nature is unfounded, that a thorough knowledge of the business is perhaps a more significant consideration than the stability which might be attained from broader-based diversification. The emphasis on manufacturing industry in most of the studies perhaps understates the importance of conglomerates, although A. Wood's review of empirical studies (174) points to conspicuous cases in the US of broad-spectrum diversification which 'has been associated with very high rates of sustained growth'. If, however, conglomerates are not as significant in the UK industry as is popularly believed, then the fears of diversification being accompanied by internal and external inefficiencies in resource allocation have perhaps been overstressed. Certainly, for the UK in particular, diversification is a comparatively under-researched topic and as it has such wide-ranging implications both for corporate planning and for government policy towards industry, further research on the issues explored in this chapter is desirable so as to provide a firmer foundation for the analysis of diversification as an element of strategy.

Notes

1. Conglomerate diversification frequently comes about through acquisition or merger, but the firms subsequently become a single concern possibly with separate divisions.
2. *Economics and the Public Purpose* (51).
3. Conglomerate diversification is rather more common in the US than in the UK.
4. For a fuller coverage of this issue see L.R. Amey (7).
5. These might include 'pet projects' of coalition members which are conspicuous simply because they are put forward with strong supporting arguments – see Cyert and March (38).
6. Thus recognising take-over as a positive strategy open to the growing firm and not just as a threat against it as in the Marris model.
7. An interesting account of this company's activities and historical background is to be found in G. Turner's book *Business in Britain* (158) (Chapter 5).
8. These figures are taken from Unilever's Report and Accounts for 1973.
9. K.V. Smith and J.C. Schreiner (148) have presented a portfolio analysis of conglomerate diversification including an empirical study for the US.
10. As described by Turner (158) (Chapter 3).
11. For an interesting account of Slater's activities in the 1960s see the first case 'How Jim Slater Bought Forestal' in A. Vice's book (161).
12. The various ways of accomplishing a merger are discussed in R.W. Moon (114) (Chapter 3).

13.   Gort's measure of diversification here is *number* of secondary products rather than their proportion of output, whereas Amey measures degree of diversification as a percentage.
14.   The degree of diversification of an industry is the ratio: (net output of enterprises in the industry group which consists of other than principal products of the group):(total net output of enterprises in the industry group).

5 THE FINANCING OF GROWTH

5.1 Introduction

The achievement of balanced growth depends upon the firm's ability
to match the growth in the demand for its products with the growth in
its productive capacity. The model of Marris rests on demand growth
through diversification, and capacity growth through re-investment of
profits. The subject of finance is explored in the present chapter with
an examination of the role of internal finance and the other associated
issues raised by Marris, namely the question of liquidity, the matter
of gearing (and access to external finance in general) and the idea of
maintaining a valuation ratio which will deter take-over raiders.

'Corporate' planning implies that decisions about investment are not
taken independently of decisions about financing. Indeed, in so far as
the company's cost of capital is influenced by its financial structure,
the latter will have an impact on expansion in terms of the number of
profitable investments open to the company. Nevertheless in order to
provide a framework for analysing the complex matters discussed here,
it is convenient to proceed as if the product-market strategy has been
determined, the investment plan formulated, and the total financing
requirements specified.

In keeping with the analysis presented so far in this book, our
discussion will revolve around the large company,[1] its environment
and internal structure. We begin in Section 5.2 by considering the
balance sheets, income and appropriation accounts, and sources and
use statements of UK industrial and commercial companies, with
some analysis of the variations between them. Section 5.3 is concerned with gearing and includes a discussion of the alternative views
on the question of optimal debt financing. In Section 5.4 we examine
the valuation of companies in connection with merger possibilities
and dividend policy is then discussed briefly in Section 5.5 before we
attempt to provide a model incorporating these various elements as a
synthesis in Section 5.6.

5.2 Balance Sheets and Sources and Uses of Funds

In this section we wish to analyse the balance sheets structure of
companies in the UK and then to examine the 'flow' elements in terms
of the sources and uses of funds. Our reason for proceeding in this

fashion is that whilst we must concentrate attention on the flow of
funds through companies, that is income and expenditure flows as
major determinants of financial behaviour, we have to take into
account the 'stock' position which expresses the portfolio of assets
and liabilities.

We commence by detailing in Table 5.1 the balance sheet structure
for UK-owned non-financial companies for selected years. We have
divided the assets into 'operating' (which included fixed assets, stocks
and work in progress, trade investment, trade and other debtors) and
liquid financial assets which include cash and various short-term
deposits with banks, local authorities, etc. What the table illustrates is
a fall in liquidity as a percentage over the period and, given that these
stock items are large in absolute values, this clearly represents a large
volume of funds. Whilst this structural change cannot be ascribed to
any single factor, there is some indication that liquidity levels were
abnormally high in the 1950s, but since then liquid balances have been
increasingly run down. On the liabilities side there would appear to be
a substantial degree of stability with long-term borrowing and equity
capital, particularly the latter, being the dominant item.

Balance sheet data are of limited value because they represent
historical snapshots of the firm at particular moments in time, but
they do give a clear indication of the inherited 'stock' position on
which the 'flow' elements will be based, and perception of any
imbalances in stock positions can then set in motion forces to reduce
them. The income and appropriation accounts of companies illustrate
the 'income' and 'saving' flows, and Figure 5.1 gives the data for
1971-6. From this, we can observe that gross trading profits were the
major source of income before tax (and before depreciation) even
allowing for stock appreciation.[2] This item of stock appreciation has
assumed major importance (nearly 27 per cent of income of 1975)
representing the impact of inflation[3] on the company sector.

The other forms of income are rent and non-trading income such as
interest payments (9 per cent in 1975) and net income from abroad.
In the allocation of this income we have detailed only those elements
which involve payments outside of the companies and, of these,
dividends and other interest payments are the major items (31 per cent
in 1975 with 21.3 per cent for interest payments on debt and 9.6 per
cent dividend payments on ordinary shares). The other two items are
UK taxes on income, which in 1975 was a relatively small item – 6
per cent (and a significant part was advance corporation tax), and
profits due abroad. The fact that companies retain a large share of

Figure 5.1:

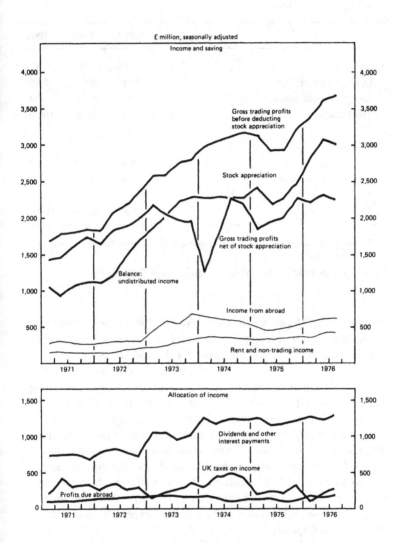

Source: *Economic Trends* (HMSO), February 1977.

Table 5.1: The Balance Sheet Structure of UK-Owned Non-Financial Companies* 1957-66

	1957	1962	1966
Assets	%	%	%
Operating assets	88.8	91.1	91.6
Liquid financial assets	11.2	8.9	8.4
Total assets	100.0	100.0	100.0
Liabilities			
Bank borrowing	6.6	6.4	7.2
Trade credit received	13.8	11.1	11.9
Long-term borrowing and equity capital	79.6	82.5	80.9
Total liabilities	100.0	100.0	100.0

* Excluding oil, shipping and property companies, co-operative societies and marketing boards.

Source: R. Stone and A. Roe (154), also quoted in A.D. Bain et al. (13).

their income, 60.5 per cent in 1975, and the observation that profits are the major form of income to firms, is indicative of the role profits can play in providing funds internally for the maintenance of operations (for replacing worn-out equipment) and/or for expansion. Such profits also serve to satisfy an important precondition for raising finance whether it be short- or long-term, namely the need to accept a future call on income by way of interest and dividend payments. This is particularly important at times of high interest rates, not only with regard to contractual obligations on debt finance, but also the expected returns on equity since, although dividend payments can be passed, the availability of additional share capital depends in part on a history of regular dividend payments and on the state of the stock market which itself is influenced by investors' expectations and the funds at their disposal.

Even though the absolute level of profits is important, profitability or rates of return on capital employed provide a more effective indicator of the profit performance of companies. We illustrate in Figure 5.2 three alternative measures of profitability and all three indicate a largely downward path for the period 1960-75. Faced with such figures it is understandable that there may be a reluctance on the part of

Figure 5.2: Rate of Return on Capital Employed 1960-75,
Industrial and Commercial Companies

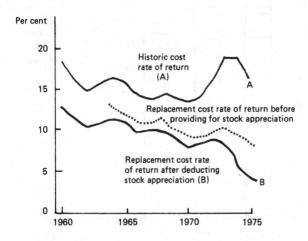

Source: *Trade and Industry* (24 Oct. 1975) and Treasury Economic Progress
Reports.

companies to contemplate future fixed-investment programmes,[4] and
they may use their retained earnings to reduce company debt or to
make financial investments from which they can derive relatively high
rates of return.

Having indicated (in Figure 5.1) the current income and saving
(appropriation) account of companies, we are now in a position to
examine the over-all sources and uses of funds of companies which we
give in Figure 5.3 for the period 1972-5.

They indicate the dominant, but variable, role of retained earnings
in the total sources of funds with the individual external sources
varying, even over this short period, quite markedly. Bank borrowing
for instance was very high in 1973 and 1974, reducing then
significantly in 1975, with the cause of this variability lying in the
'uses' to which funds are put. Investment in fixed assets for the
period under review has shown a steady increase in absolute terms[5]
although an examination of post-war data would indicate a more
marked cyclical path with expenditure tending to rise in the year
following the up turn in the profits cycle. Expenditure on stocks is an
unstable item and, whereas for the period 1964-72 additional financing

Figure 5.3: Sources and Uses of Funds

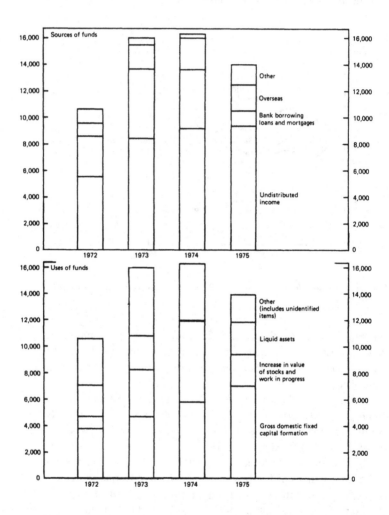

Source: *Economic Trends* (HMSO), February 1977.

of stocks absorbed on average 16 per cent of the total uses of funds (5 per cent for increased volume and 11 per cent for stock appreciation), with the increase in the rate of inflation, financing for stocks took 45 per cent in 1974 (of which 6½ per cent was for increased volume and 38½ per cent was a result of inflation). Cash expenditure on subsidiaries also fluctuated, although this is contained in the category 'other'. The liquid assets of companies would appear to act as a buffer to be run down and increased at will.

Whilst 'sources' and 'uses' statements are useful in that they summarise the flow elements, they do not in themselves bring out the full implications of the financing decision. In any time period a firm will have profits generated from past investment and, given a particular dividend pay-out ratio, the level of 'internal' financing from profits will be given. The firm will also have a given endowment of net liquid assets (i.e. net of short-term borrowing) which can be used, if positive. Against these internally financed sources the firm will have specific requirements for fixed capital – for projects which were agreed in previous time periods and requirements for working capital. If the total requirements exceed the capacity to finance from retained earnings and liquid assets, the cash deficit has to be financed by external sources: short-term typically through bank borrowing which may be particularly important in financing stocks and other working capital, and long-term which may include increased corporate debt and/or new issues of ordinary shares.

In general, the relative importance of both internal and external funds fluctuates over the cycle of economic activity, with external funds appearing to reach their peak in relation to internal funds in the year following the peak in the profits cycle. The use of external funds, whether they be short- or long-term inevitably brings us to the question of relationships with the capital market and ultimately to the flow of funds between companies and all other financial sectors. In Figure 5.4 we depict the respective surpluses and deficits of four sectors in the economic system for the period 1971-6. The public sector has had a deficit over most of this period but the company sector had deficits in 1974 and 1976 and these have had to be financed by the surplus units which have been the personal sector and overseas sector (since 1973). In periods when the public sector deficit is high this can draw away funds which would otherwise have been available to the company sector, and consequently this can have repercussions on the growth path of companies and of the whole economy. Although we have been considering data for the whole sector of industrial and commercial

Figure 5.4: Financial Surpluses/Deficits

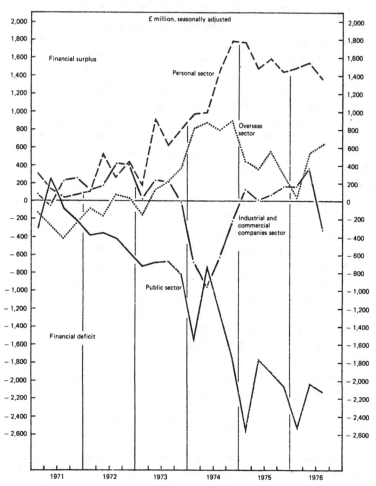

Source: *Economic Trends* (HMSO), February 1977.

companies, our interest in the larger companies warrants an examination of the differences in financing (both needs and sources) between companies of different sizes. Despite the difficulties encountered in conducting such an exercise, data are available from government sources (see J.L. Walker (162, 163)) and from empirical studies. We shall restrict our own coverage to the two studies of G. Meeks and G. Whittington (104, 105) (referred to earlier) and we summarise the findings of their 1948-71 study in Table 5.2. The arbitrary size distribution of low, middle and high reveals some interesting differences. Small firms had the highest rate of growth of equity issues in both periods and the highest rates of growth by 'gearing issues' (if we take the later period) and they featured the highest rate of return and dividend payout (with respect to net assets) so, in fact, their high rate of growth is from all sources. The large companies have the highest ratio of long-term external finance to retentions, and loan issues have a larger share of total sources of funds – probably owing to the greater stability of earnings and tax advantages. In addition, during the period 1964-71 when there was heavy reliance on external finance, there was also a high level of take-over activity often financed by share exchange; certainly large firms, it is argued, have a favourable relationship with the capital market in this respect.

The 'high' size-grouping does cover a large number of different-sized firms but we can disaggregate this in part by examining their earlier study which covered the 'giants' for the period 1964-9. Recall (from Chapter 3) that they found the giants to be faster growers than other firms but to have inferior profitability, with the vehicle for growth being mergers financed by share exchange (which involves a reallocation of control of existing assets rather than a growth of total assets *per se*). Given that the giants are included in a mixture of other firms in the size grouping 'high' it is not surprising that the results are not fully consistent. What they do show perhaps is that there are probably non-linear relationships between scale, finance and growth. To assist in a comparison we quote the results for the 'giants' in Table 5.3.

In conclusion we have attempted in this section to analyse some of the key aspects of the sources and uses of funds of companies both in total and for large firms in particular. Let us now summarise our findings both as they relate to the discussion in previous chapters and as they reveal the factors which need to be taken into account in the formulation of models of the financing decision.

(1)   There are substantial differences in capital structure between companies of different sizes as there are between companies from different industries (see A.D. Bain *et al.* (13)).
(2)   Internal funds are the dominant form of finance – this is broadly in agreement with Marris, Galbraith and others, but long-term external sources can be important and this has been detected in the fast-growing 'small' quoted companies and the larger companies

Table 5.2: Performance and Financing Ratios: Analysis by Size

	1948-64			1964-71		
	Low	Middle	High	Low	Middle	High
RATIOS (% p.a.)						
Growth of net assets[a]	10.2	8.2	8.5	14.7	9.9	10.9
Growth of physical assets[b]	13.8	10.5	10.8	16.5	11.9	11.4
Growth of equity[a]						
total	2.6	1.3	1.7	4.0	3.0	3.0
for cash	n.a.	n.a.	n.a.	1.3	0.9	0.6
in exchange	n.a.	n.a.	n.a.	2.7	2.2	2.4
Dividends[a]						
net	4.2	3.3	2.8	4.3	3.3	3.0
cost	5.0	3.9	3.4	6.8	5.3	4.8
Growth by gearing issues[a]						
total	0.7	0.7	1.1	2.6	2.0	2.2
for cash	n.a.	n.a.	n.a.	1.6	1.2	1.4
in exchange	n.a.	n.a.	n.a.	1.0	0.8	0.7
Pre-tax rate of return[c]	20.0	17.7	16.0	22.2	16.0	14.4
OTHER DATA						
Number of companies	417	416	417	322	322	322
Opening size (£ million)	0.273	0.732	6.644	0.994	2.816	32.958
SOURCES OF FUNDS (% of total)						
Equity issues; total	13.2	9.7	12.0	10.6	11.5	13.7
Gearing issues; total	3.9	4.2	7.3	8.5	8.3	12.4
Retained profits	46.4	47.3	41.6	41.6	33.5	28.0
Depreciation	36.2	38.7	39.0	39.3	46.5	45.6
APPROPRIATION OF INCOME (% of gross income)						
Depreciation	17.5	18.6	20.8	21.9	26.6	27.4
Loan interest, gross, plus cost of preference dividends	3.6	4.6	5.6	4.1	6.3	7.4
Ordinary dividends (net)	17.0	15.7	14.7	14.4	14.9	14.6
Retained profits	20.0	20.0	20.5	20.0	15.3	14.8

[a] Percentage of opening net assets
[b] Percentage of opening physical assets
[c] Percentage of average net assets
Source: G. Meeks and G. Whittington (105).

Table 5.3: The Finance of Growth: Giants and the Rest

	1948-69		1964-69	
	1948 Giants*	1948 Rest	1964 Giants	1964 Rest
Sources of funds (% of net assets)				
Retentions	4.2	4.9	2.9	3.4
Issues				
for cash	n.a.	n.a.	2.6	2.2
in exchange for subsidiaries	n.a.	n.a.	4.0	2.2
together	3.2	2.4	6.6	4.4
Pre-tax rate of return on net assets (% p.a.)	14.6	17.2	13.0	15.4
Proportion of pre-tax income retained (%)	24.0	23.7	19.3	20.7

The Stability of Performance, the Patterns of Financing, and the Rate of Returns on Equity Assets: Giants and the Rest

	1948-69		1964-69	
	1948 Giants	1948 Rest	1964 Giants	1964 Rest
Average inter-year standard deviation (% p.a.)				
Rate of return on net assets	4.6	8.0	2.1	5.2
Rate of growth of net assets	8.9	11.5	10.2	11.5
Pre-tax rate of return on equity assets	5.9	9.8	3.0	6.2
Average interval between years in which losses were made (years)	87	29	62	16
Loan issues; total net sources (%)	17.0	8.6	35.2	18.2
Loan issues; total issues (%)	44.3	32.7	58.8	50.3
Average pre-tax rate of return on equity assets (% p.a.)	16.5	18.6	14.5	16.2

* That is, members of top 100 companies in 1948.

Source: G. Meeks and G. Whittington (104) (Tables 3 and 4, pp. 832-3).

particularly the 'giants'.

(3)   Whilst the use of long-term external finance is often linked with the acquisition of fixed assets, the larger firms and, particularly, the giants use this finance to promote growth via take-overs using share-exchange. This means that take-overs, as we argued in Chapter 4, go beyond the trustee role ascribed to them by Marris, and if we add the argument of A. Singh (144) that *size* can provide a shield *against* bidders, then we see why the take-over appears as an approved policy instrument of 'large' firms.

5.3 Capital Structure

It would appear from the above discussion that the large companies are willing and able to accept gearing ratios higher than those of smaller companies. We illustrated that the Marris model assumed an optimum gearing ratio which firms needed to achieve, to within a small band of toleration. But how does the introduction of corporate debt affect the company both from the point of view of the cost of capital and ultimately the shareholder? A certain amount of contro-versy exists over this question. The traditional view is that the cost of capital is a function of the capital structure such that the cost can be reduced by a judicious use of debt finance. The use of debt will, however, tend to magnify fluctuations[6] in the earnings of equity so that there is a trade-off between debt finance with its lower cost,[7] and risk (in terms of variations in company earnings). A further aspect of the traditional view is that there exists some optimal level of gearing which will minimise the cost of capital. Any increase in gearing beyond this point would cause the average cost of capital to rise, because of increasing risk, giving rise to the 'U-shaped' cost of capital function illustrated in Figure 5.5. However the capital market might in practice set an upper limit for the firm and the 'U' would then be transformed somewhat with the curve rising steeply or even vertic-ally[8] beyond this limit.

The Modigliani-Miller (MM) (111) viewpoint (proposition I) which lies in opposition to the traditional argument is that the cost of capital to a firm is independent of its leverage (gearing) so that the cost of capital is a horizontal straight line as in Figure 5.6. Their argument is that although debt finance is a cheaper source than equity, its introduction into a company's financial structure immediately increases financial risk to shareholders who require a premium to compensate them for this risk (MM, proposition II). This premium offsets the apparently lower cost of debt and leaves the overall cost of

Figure 5.5: The Traditional View of Leverage

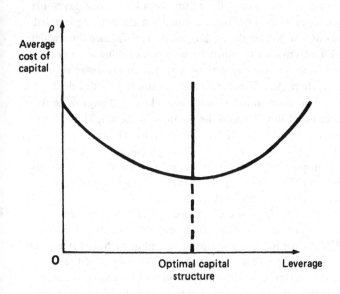

Figure 5.6: The Modigliani-Miller Theorem

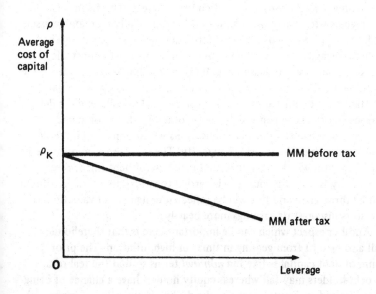

capital to the company unaltered. Their basic propositions change when corporation tax is brought into the picture because interest payments on debt qualify as an expense when corporation tax is being assessed.[9] In other words, the greater the proportion of debt finance the smaller the tax bill. Distributions to equity holders do not bring any tax relief, indeed they accelerate the payment of corporation tax under the imputation system. At a 50 per cent tax rate the real cost of debt is only half of the coupon rate (i.e. the annual interest payable to debt holders) because of the effect on the company's tax bill. This influences both propositions of the MM theorem (112) in that equity holders no longer require quite such a large premium for a given degree of leverage (proposition II) and that the reduction in the tax bill does effectively lower the cost of capital so that the latter is no longer independent of leverage (proposition I).

The MM after-tax view (also illustrated in Figure 5.6) is thus similar to the traditional view in that the cost of capital declines with leverage. MM do not recognise an optimal point as such, but stress that companies should increase debt as far as possible subject to the constraints of the financial world. Crude rules of thumb are found in such guidelines as 'the proportion of debt must not exceed one fifth of total financial assets' (measured either at book or current market value) or 'interest payments on debt must be covered four or five times by earnings'. Each case should, of course, be treated on its merits. Companies with stable profits, those who own highly marketable assets and those with sales covered by contractual agreements, can reach higher gearing levels than their counterparts operating in unstable markets or involved in lease obligations. For example, companies in the multiple retail business, breweries and restaurant chains, often have substantial freehold premises which can be used as collateral for debt finance (mortgage debentures). On the other hand, oil companies typically have substantial lease obligations which impair their credit status and reduce debt-raising capability. The traditional point of view is perhaps still worth heeding in that if the use of debt finance by a company is not judicious, but is carried to excess, its whole livelihood can be threatened and this will be reflected in its market valuation as investors discount its earnings more heavily.

Another aspect which can be important here is that shareholders will also benefit from gearing in times of high inflation. The prior claim of debt capital is fixed in *nominal* terms so that the real return to debt-holders may fall whereas equity holders have a chance of being compensated, at least in part, for the decline in the value of money,[10] particularly as the annual debt charge will, through the years, assume less and less importance and will be out of line with payments on recently negotiated debt if there has been a general rise in interest rates.

The empirical study of Meeks and Whittington gives an indication of the benefits which large companies have derived from debt financing. The 'giants' achieved their higher growth rates using external funds to a greater extent than the 'rest' and the capital market was thus willing to supply relatively more finance to the less profitable group. The explanation offered by Meeks and Whittington is that the giants achieved a more stable performance over time, made losses less frequently and were able to operate at higher gearing levels. The average rates of return on *equity capital* stood comparison with the rest rather better than the return on net assets (see Table 5.3). The giants' high gearing may thus have helped their equity performance, although MM would regard the benefit as compensation for financial risk, further-more if one considers the tax exemption of debt interest, it is apparent that these relatively highly geared companies have been able to derive direct benefits in the form of a lower proportion of income paid in tax. The advantages in this respect became apparent after the introduction of the corporation tax system in 1965 and the subsequent increase in the use of debt financing is illustrated in Table 5.4. Since 1970 however, the proportion has fallen steadily so that by 1976 it was only 8 per cent.

Table 5.4: Debt as a Proportion of Total Capital Issues

	Debt finance (£m)	Percentage of total
1961	148.1	26.5
1962	173.8	42.1
1963	271.5	60.3
1964	234.0	56.6
	Introduction of Corporation Tax System	
1965	454.6	90.3
1966	479.5	75.1
1967	343.5	81.5
1968	309.5	45.8
1969	397.4	67.1
1970	312.9	82.0
1971	370.9	53.4

Source: Midland Bank Review (February 1972).

5.4 Valuation and Take-Over Policy

The importance of take-overs in the growth process as discussed in our coverage of diversification and as revealed in our break-down of the uses of funds leads us to the question of company valuation. Our concern for this stems in part from the crucial role Marris placed on the valuation ratio to block take-over bids, but it extends beyond this as take-overs are to be viewed not just in defensive terms but as part of company policy for growth. In consequence the valuation of companies for take-over is clearly an important issue. Recall that in the Marris model security from the threat of take-over was seen to be related to the valuation ratio and, in particular, we argued in Chapter 3 that firms need to ensure that the retained earnings are used productively in order to maintain this ratio. The measures most frequently used in valuation are the *earnings per share* (EPS) and the *price-earnings* (P/E) ratio, which is the ratio of the current share price to the current earnings per share. Both are widely used in financial analysis and are simple to calculate although they answer rather different questions. The P/E ratio is an indicator of relative cheapness and serves as a measuring rod which can be used to compare the 'bidder' with the 'victim', and other alternative victims, whereas EPS focuses on the earnings per share of the existing share-holders and the expected increases which would result from merger. Both suffer from serious weaknesses despite their continued use by analysts and the financial press. They both ignore the growth of earnings after the current year (in their simplest forms) which is a severe drawback if we assume that there will be synergy. Indeed our argument is that this should be the case with mergers because if they are to be used to assist growth (particularly by diversification) and if the apparent signal to encourage the take-over is in Marris's terms an ineffective utilisation of existing resources, then the merger should produce economic benefits. It may produce some short-run costs (particularly if the policy of merger is carried out too rapidly) of the Penrose type discussed in Chapter 3, but net benefits are clearly to be expected if the outlay of funds *vis-à-vis* their use in some alternative scheme is to be justified. In other words, it is like any other investment decision and, in consequence, careful appraisal is required. To conduct such an appraisal the bidding firm requires information about the intended 'victim', particularly data on any surplus assets which the firm might have in the form of cash, property, land, etc.; the extent of gearing and the time profile of the debt with respect of its maturity; the replacement programme needs for the existing operating assets and of course an estimate of future profits. Whilst in the main the reason for taking over the firm may be to derive benefit from diversification and a return on financial resources by operating it as a going concern, it is quite feasible for a take-over to be instigated in order to realise the assets[11] in which case the replacement cycle of these assets would be less significant.

In consequence one must look beyond the present and take a longer view than is possible through examination of just P/E and EPS figures. The P/E ratio has the additional weakness of ignoring the financing of the merger, for example cash, share exchange, issue of debt capital, etc., whereas the EPS method implicitly takes this into account. In practice both kinds of indicator are still used in the evaluation of take-overs and we shall demonstrate the P/E approach using a simplified merger situation as an illustration.[12] The initial ground rules[13] laid down are that companies will not consider taking over any other firm whose shares stand at a higher P/E ratio since the current earnings per share of the bidder will be reduced in consequence.[14]

Table 5.5: Valuation and Take-Over

	Bidder	Victim
Earnings (net)	£4,000	£2,000
Issued shares	20,000	10,000
EPS	20p	20p
Price per share	£2.00	£2.60
P/E ratio	10	13

This is shown in the example based on the earnings and P/E ratios for bidder and victim given in Table 5.5. The bidding firm intends to finance the deal by share exchange (something which as we have seen in Section 5.2, is quite common in practice). The bidder offers £2.60 per share which is equivalent to 1.3 of its own shares for each one of the victim's. The earnings per share of the bidder will fall after the take-over to £6,000/(20,000 + 13,000) = 18.2p from the original figure of 20p. This would appear to be against the interests of the shareholders but a potentially profitable investment may be lost through a rigid concentration on current P/E ratios and those which will prevail immediately after the merger.

G.D. Newbould (116) examined pre- and post-merger P/E ratios for 86 mergers in the UK in the period 1967/8. Three types of P/E relationship were distinguished:

(1)   P/E ratio of victim exceeded that of bidder by 2.0 or more (19 mergers);
(2)   P/E ratio of victim and bidder were within 2.0 either way (19 mergers);
(3)   P/E ratio of the bidder exceeded that of the victim by 2.0 or more (48 mergers).

In a detailed analysis of the background to the mergers as well as the P/E ratios, Newbould found that the conventional wisdom 'was widespread, and was reinforced by the behaviour of investors in determining the P/E ratio immediately after the merger' (p. 84).

In consequence it would appear that a firm active in the take-over scene would only buy out those firms whose shares were at a lower P/E than its own. However, the Newbould findings would suggest that the apparent myopic viewpoint would 'be detrimental in anything other than current and immediate future earnings per share' and in consequence the firm would be 'diluting its own rate of growth' (p. 80).

However, if it is possible to assess the future earnings of the merged concern allowing for synergy, then the growth-oriented firm may take over firms offering a high growth potential but whose P/E ratios are higher than that of the bidder. However, the post-merger P/E ratio may fall below the weighted average pre-merger and even below the bidder's own initial P/E ratio.[15]

In the above example, net earnings of £2,000 per annum can be purchased for £26,000 and, given the bidder's present P/E ratio of 10 implying a capitalisation rate of 10 per cent, the acquisition might appear to be an unfavourable opportunity. If the two companies are subject to the same relative magnitude of fluctuations in earnings, but perhaps operating in different market environments, how can the bidder justify the investment to his shareholders? One possible justification could be that net earnings of the firm to be acquired are growing, rather than constant at £2,000 per annum. If the earnings were in fact growing at 2.14 per cent per annum ($g = 0.0214$) and the appropriate capitalisation rate was 10 per cent ($r = 0.1$) the present value of the growing stream would be

$$£2,000 \times \frac{1+g}{r-g} = £2,000 \times \frac{1.0214}{0.1-0.0214} = £25,989 . \quad \text{(n. 16)}$$

The bidder would therefore be prepared to pay £26,000 for the other company at the given capitalisation rate.

In the absence of growth, benefits may still accrue to the amalgamation through the portfolio effects of diversification. In other words if the firms are not operating in the same markets, fluctuations will, in part, offset each other and the combined enterprise would be subject to lower over-all risk.[17] The appropriate capitalisation rate would fall and the present value of the new company would then exceed the sum of the current present values based on a capitalisation rate of 10 per cent. The joint valuation could also rise because of synergy, for example through improved market performance or increased efficiency in production. Furthermore, liquidation of some assets might be feasible on merger without reducing the existing earning power of the two companies. Indeed, because of such benefits as we have discussed here, a particularly desirable take-over possibility may well increase in market value once the bidder makes his intentions known.

5.5 Dividend Policy[18]

So far we have not made any explicit references to the dividend policy of companies. We have referred to the role of retained earnings in financing growth and the need to make profitable use of these. In a perfect capital market dividend policy would not matter since shareholders[19] would be indifferent between retained earnings invested to increase the share price and dividend payments which they could invest in alternative investment schemes. If the investor needs income in some future time period he can sell some of his shares to realise the capital gain (less transactions' costs). In other words, the shareholders would regard dividend policy as irrelevant once the investment decision was known, assuming that the company adopts only those projects which offer a return above the cost of capital to the company. The decision for the company would then be to determine how much to retain and how much to distribute as a residual. In practice, however, there are complications and, indeed, the dividend policy of the firm often assumes primacy of place, leaving retained earnings as the residual. In consequence we need to examine the considerations which may bring this about.

The reasons fall into two broad headings, tax considerations[20] and the importance which shareholders attach to dividends. At first sight, it might appear, if we take account of tax (both corporate and personal), that there has been a built-in bias towards retention. Under the 1965 Finance Act retained earnings attracted less tax, but under the present imputation system there is no discrimination in terms of total tax paid even though the payment of dividends necessitates an advance payment of corporation tax. Additionally high marginal rates of personal taxes might encourage investors to wait for capital gains which are taxed at a lower rate. However, we need to look at the shareholding body and their preferences in more detail. In the first place they are likely to be averse to risk and payment of dividends now will be to many less risky than letting the foregone dividend be buried in the share price, particularly as the latter will suffer at times from extreme variability. Additionally, some shareholders do require regular and guaranteed income and it is not always practicable for them to sell shares, given the transactions' costs and variability of price, to raise the amounts of the dividends. Pension funds for instance require regular income payments from shares and the annuity and group pension business of life assurance companies[21] is often similarly dependent. These two groups of institutions are important holders and traders of shares, particularly the quoted shares of the larger companies, but many individual shareholders also rely on their holdings to produce a regular income. The Inland Revenue estimated for the period 1972-3 that 40 per cent of all recipients of dividends and taxed interest receipts were national insurance retirement, or widow, pensioners who would have some marked degree of liquidity preference. Whilst it is not possible to separate out the dividend payments of companies from such data it is indicative of income needs. If we also add the fact that elderly people receive the bulk of pensions and annuities paid out of the dividends received by pension funds and insurance companies, then perhaps the need for companies to have a dividend policy is clearer, as failure to pay regular and 'adequate' dividends may discourage some important investors. Thus low dividend payouts can affect the share price which, in turn, can limit the ability of a company to raise future finance either by way of rights issue or other external means. Companies can also leave themselves open to a potential take-over bid because of a low valuation ratio which a new management could raise by increasing the dividend payout. What one would therefore expect to find is companies stabilising dividends in the face of short-run fluctuations[22] in earnings so as to satisfy the clientele and impart confidence by

maintaining the implied contract. Whilst the payment ratio may
still fluctuate marginally in the short-run around a long-run target,[23]
the expectations of shareholders will be for a steady, gradually rising
future dividend stream. A sudden increase or decrease in dividends
can cause a sharp revision of expectations, so that even if a company
did cut dividends to increase investment in a very profitable project
the motive may be misconstrued and the share price may fall as a
result. The determination of the actual target raises complex issues
but the maintenance of a particular dividend, albeit with a rising
aspiration level, implies that it may become a business convention
or rule of thumb.

Some companies will consistently have a higher payout ratio than
others[24] and this diversity of policy can assist some shareholders who
may wish for more potential capital appreciation than income. The
different segments of the shareholding body can therefore be catered
for, but the ability of companies to raise dividends has been limited
at times in the UK, by government regulations, as part of an incomes
policy. These regulations do change over time and there are often
gateways to allow, subject to Treasury approval, increases above the
norms in force. However, Meeks and Whittington (105) in their
evidence to the Royal Commission on the Distribution of Income and
Wealth found that if dividend restraint ended and dividends rose in
consequence, firms would have to raise a large additional amount of
funds externally.

5.6 Portfolio Behaviour

Here we wish to draw together some of the threads of the earlier
sections in order to understand the over-all nature of the financing
decision. The firm must have both short- and long-term financing
plans so that it is aware of the expected month to month requirements for funds and the financing requirements over time. We
illustrate the requirement for funds in Figure 5.7.

What this figure demonstrates is that short- and long-run plans
intertwine. Investment decisions will dictate long-term fund
requirements from the range of alternative internal and external
sources. The latter can be short-run expedients (particularly bank
credit) or, more likely, liabilities to match the length of life of the
assets, for example corporate debt or permanent capital in the form
of ordinary shares. The decision to go to the capital market is,
however, taken only at discrete intervals of time so that short-term
financing may be used for a period, until an issue is made when

Figure 5.7: Financing Requirements

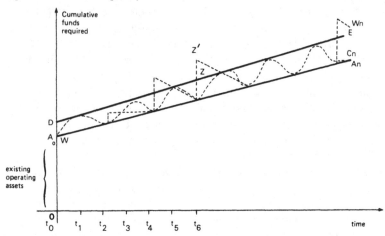

short-term borrowing can be reduced or even eliminated. This point is illustrated in the figure where the firm is presumed to have a cumulative financing requirement as measured on the vertical axis. The firm starts at point t_0 in time and has total operating assets of $0A_0$. At a minimum it assumes that to finance its growth it requires cumulative finance as represented by the line A_0A_n, but in addition it has short-term cash requirements which for the next time period t_1 are necessary for stockbuilding, etc. If we can presume that between t_1 and t_2 a similar pattern of short-term financing needs will materialise, and likewise to t_n, then we have a cyclical line A_0C_n in addition to the long-term needs. If only the funds to finance long-term growth were raised by retained earnings and/or external debt on equity issues then the short-term requirements would have to be met by short-term borrowing and/or reductions in any holdings of liquid assets.

If the firm could raise all its finance by retained earnings or long-term capital, then we would have a line DE and there would be no need for short-term financing. In practice, the need for finance will be met by a mixture of short- and long-term sources. If the latter are based on retained earnings, then since those fluctuate in cyclical fashion the gaps will have to be met by short-term finance or recourse to long-term external sources. The latter as we have already argued are only used at discrete intervals. In practice what we might have therefore is more of a stepped long-term sources line (WW_n) which represents the firm's ability to back the cumulative demands. The stepped path will represent both the impact of variability of retained earnings and long-term issues. The gaps, for example ZZ', between the stepped relationship and the sum of the short- and long-term financing requirements permit the building up of liquid assets to act as a buffer for future periods. Decisions concerning short- or long-term borrowing and the use of liquid assets as a buffer need to be analysed more fully and we shall do this later in this section.

Let us now assume that the firm has determined an optimum balance sheet[25] which specifies the desired relationships between the constituent parts of assets and liabilities. Adjustments towards this optimum take time because of frictional impediments so that at any given period, t, the firm may be in disequilibrium[26] but may still be presumed to take action in an attempt to restore the equilibrium. If we allow for the continual change which pervades the business and general environment, then the desired relationships will be subject to virtually constant reappraisal. Consequently instead of a long-run steady state optimum towards which firms adjust period by period in varying degrees, the dynamic nature of business will bring about continual changes so that, in fact, the firm may have a kaleidoscopic view of long-run relationships.

Concentration on the equilibrium of the balance sheet *per se* can neglect the flow influences which we discussed in Section 5.2. Various approaches to the incorporation of both stock and flow elements are possible and the first major econometric model was developed by W.M.L. Anderson (8) for USA manufacturing industry for the period 1948-60. The starting point was to assume that, in terms of the firms' present operations, plans for current production spending were fixed and so too were their capital spending plans for the next planning period. With these autonomously determined, the finance function had to provide an optimal mix of long-term external finance and net liquidity (liquid assets and short-term borrowing) within specified maximum and minimum safe levels of debt and liquidity (as specified by Marris). Thus if a company commenced operations in period t near to the upper limit of its debt ratio then the increased risk of further borrowing would tend to produce in practice an alternative form of financing, for example, running down liquid assets. The Anderson model appeared to indicate that these balance sheet constraints were effective with financing behaviour responding to them. Certainly our previous discussions have indicated that we need to take explicit account of liquidity, leverage and the utilisation of net income *vis-à-vis* dividends and retained earnings.

To develop a framework to incorporate these variables so that we

Table 5.6: Simplified Balance Sheet

Liabilities	Assets
Long-term capital	Operating assets
	Short-term assets (net)

have a consistent short- and long-term finance function we need to return to the stock, or balance sheet position. We can portray this in a more simplified form than Table 5.1 as Table 5.6. An examination of these positions over successive periods will enable us to derive flow of funds statements which indicate[27] the results of the company's expenditure and financing decisions. Recall that in Section 5.2 we argued that the cash surplus/deficit (C), the net difference between the current sources of funds and the uses to which these could be put were in a sense predetermined from current and past production decisions. We can represent the financing of this deficit (or use to which a surplus could be put) in the following identity:

$$C \equiv \Delta E + \Delta D + \Delta B + \Delta TC + \Delta LA .$$

This relationship indicates the over-all choice process which we can state as a series of alternatives some of which are mutually inclusive:

(1)   an increase in ordinary shares, for example by means of a rights issue (ΔE);
(2)   an increase or retiring of corporate debt (ΔD);
(3)   an increase/decrease in bank borrowing (ΔB);
(4)   an increase/decrease in trade credit (ΔTC);
(5)   a build up or reduction in short-term assets (ΔLA).

Apart from the constraints discussed above, which will feature as specified balance sheet ratios, there are others which are fully outside the control of companies. These are supply constraints caused by market imperfections and/or an unwillingness on the part of the lender to lend the amount required on the terms required. These blocks[28] or impediments can exist because of government policy, for example in controlling the level and direction of bank advances[29] as well as the 'cost' of this line of credit. In the case of long-term finance the ability to raise this is affected by the conditions in the capital market which themselves are affected by the economic climate. In bearish markets with prices of securities falling, conditions are not favourable for new issues of ordinary shares or debentures, whereas in bullish markets the funds available for investment may outstrip the various demands by the industrial sector. In consequence the timing of borrowing (particularly long-term borrowing) is important and whilst the firm may desire a particular structural change in the balance sheet, for example by raising additional long-term finance, it may have to resort to short-term accommodation. Additionally, with marked movements in interest rates which can cause quite significant differences in the cost of funds at particular times, a further dimension is added in that firms may delay borrowing long in the expectation of lower long-term rates of interest (although it is worth noting that periods of high interest rates generally coincide with bearish security markets).

Suppose that the firm in question has a cash deficit which is presently financed by running down liquid assets so that the firm's net liquidity (liquids assets – short-term liabilities) is negative. Reference back to the identity on page 152 indicates the choices open to the firm which, given the cash deficit, are essentially either short-term borrowing and/or long-term finance (of ordinary shares and/or corporate debt). The decision to go for these external sources may, as we have seen, be constrained by supply blocks, particularly in the case of long-term finance, and the decision to go for ordinary shares or corporate debt will depend on the safe leverage ratio of the firm which itself will be determined by past profitability (and variability of this), and the size of the firm. If the firm is near to the upper limit of this leverage ratio it will have to choose an equity issue if it wishes to raise further long-term finance or raise short-term finance. Equally the firm will not wish to borrow over-short as it could find that it is difficult to re-finance this by long-term capital in the future.

We can portray the choice process for net liquidity and long-term borrowing in Figure 5.8[30] where the opportunity line (45° line) is CC'. The firm is on this line in period t by virtue of its inherited portfolio and cash surplus/deficit, and let us assume that it is at point (A) which indicates that net liquidity is negative. The firm can remain at this point or it could move up its opportunity line[31] by raising more long-term finance which enables it to increase its net liquidity. Assuming that there are no supply constraints on this process, the choice it makes will be determined by its 'desired'[32] portfolio. We

Figure 5.8: Choice Between Long-Term Capital and Net Liquidity*

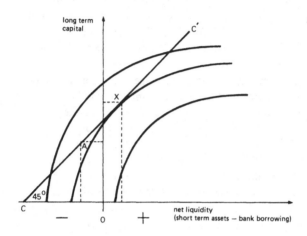

*   Adapted from A.D. Bain et al. (13) (Figure 3.1).

have already argued that this will take the form of liquidity and
leverage ratios and we can illustrate the liquidity considerations in
Figure 5.8 by assuming that there is some desired level of net liquidity
which represents a balance between short-term borrowing and holdings
of liquid assets. Too low a level of liquidity can lead to insolvency
or too high a level can bring with it a reduction in security
because of possibilities of take-overs. Furthermore the cost of raising
additional long-term capital is likely to be higher than that of short-
term borrowing — in other words there is a term structure problem
which may be due to the need to pay lenders a premium to cover their
increased illiquidity. If management can successfully anticipate
movements in the structure of interest rates, it may be able to raise
long-term finance more cheaply by timing its issue of corporate debt
to coincide with a trough in interest rates though, as we have already
suggested, in practice there may be few buyers at these low rates.
We can represent the preferences of the borrowing firm in terms of a
family of indifference curves which slope upwards from left to right
and are convex upwards. There is a trade-off to the company in that
to increase net liquidity by means of raising longer-term finance it has
to meet the increased service costs. The point (X) where one of these
indifference curves is tangential to the opportunity line represents the

Figure 5.9: Choice Between Liquid Assets and Bank Credit*

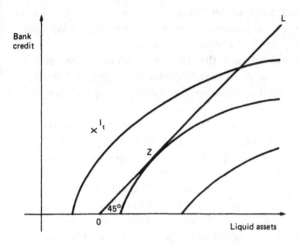

* Adapted from A.D. Bain et al. (13) (Figure 3.2).

optimum position. If there are market imperfections or the company cannot raise this finance[33] because of a perceived lack of credit worthiness then it must settle for a non-optimal position. There are transactions costs in raising long-term capital both in terms of management time and the costs of issue although there are economies of scale here. Given these considerations, companies raise their long-term finance in discrete amounts and this can cause further temporary disequilibrium in the balance sheets if, prior to the issue, companies have run down their liquid assets, have increased their short-term borrowing and then, with the issue, repay some of this short-term borrowing and build up liquid assets. Quite what final choice is made will depend on individual circumstances, but firms may be tempted to retain some bank borrowing (some may be for fixed terms) in order to establish good relations with their bank so that in future periods when they may need accommodation it is more readily forthcoming. We can in fact illustrate this decision as in Figure 5.9.

If the firm was at a position I_t prior to the new issue, the influx of funds gives it the choice of several mixes of net liquidity which we show as an opportunity line 0L, to which we can append our indifference mappings which have the same characteristics as in Figure 5.8. The firm will have, as we have argued, a minimum safe level of liquid assets and a maximum safe level for bank borrowing – a level which may be externally given. The optimum point Z may not however be reached, as adjustment to this can take time, so that the firm may well be at some other point on the line and may be assumed to be adjusting to point Z in a sequential manner.

Two questions still remain – the choice between corporate debt and ordinary shares, and the types of liquid asset purchased. Taking these *seriatim*, two factors would appear to determine this choice:

(1)   the purpose of the issue; if the issue is to enable the purchase of another company, equity finance (often by share exchange) will tend to be used and the wider joint equity base of permanent capital can then support debt capital in the future;

(2)   the existing gearing ratio and the future expectation of earnings (and their variability); the relative cost of the two types of issue will not in itself determine the choice, as debt finance is uniformly cheaper[34] than equity which therefore on strict economic criteria might appear to signal preference for debt over equity. However, debt capital often has a maturity date or a choice of conversion to equity which can militate against a strong preference for it, and, in addition, the market tends to set an upper limit to the level of gearing (built into the security constraint in the Marris model).

The choice of liquid assets will be determined by two considerations, which will in part be interrelated, namely the degree of liquidity and the return (and its variance). Companies will need to maintain assets of differing degrees of encashability to meet expected outcomes (for fixed capital, stocks, tax payments, etc.) and any unexpected contingency. Therefore, we might expect the asset mix to include cash and bank deposits extending to short-dated securities, which can often yield a relatively high return to compensate for the short-term loss of liquidity. The deposits are fixed in nominal values, but some of the securities which companies purchase can vary in their market price so that, if companies can anticipate future movements in security prices, they may be tempted into investment in these more illiquid assets.[35] The investment decision within the liquid asset set is thus a portfolio selection problem and the data we give in Table 5.7 suggest that year by year companies make quite substantial changes in their bank borrowing (and thus in net liquidity) and in the composition of their liquid assets.

Table 5.7: Net Acquisitions of Selected Capital Assets and Bank
Borrowing 1963-75; Industrial and Commercial Companies

	Notes and coin	Treasury bills	British Govt. securities	Local auth'ty debt	Bank deposits	Building society dep'ts	Bank borrowing Advances	Bills
1963	26	−30	NR	133	219	5	−391	78
1964	134	−82	NR	63	82	2	−630	−70
1965	118	−25	NR	−70	114	−6	−416	−81
1966	29	−16	NR	−81	138	−2	−204	−15
1967	63	−	NR	41	303	7	−218	−61
1968	−19	−38	NR	−31	242	2	−466	−65
1969	72	−12	NR	−84	−241	5	−504	−106
1970	205	9	NR	−65	127	−3	−896	−231
1971	166	−	−14	25	919	69	−551	−168
1972	255	−20	16	125	2039	48	−2820	−172
1973	70	−10	39	164	2430	−28	−4507	7
1974	355	43	−39	141	−263	−28	−3714	−703
1975	408	276	92	−46	1761	3	−995	282

NR: not recorded
Source: *Financial Statistics* (HMSO).

5.7 Conclusion

In this chapter we have attempted to analyse several aspects of the
finance function. What we have found is that internal sources provide
finance for four-fifths of gross capital expenditure, with issues of
equity contributing only 12 per cent although the relationship
has changed somewhat over the post-war years. There are also inter-
industry differences and variations according to size.

We have hypothesised that the firm has a preferred distribution of
assets and liabilities although adjustments towards this are unlikely
to be instantaneous and, in consequence, firms will generally be in permanent disequilibrium. The desired relationships are manifested in financial
ratios such as liquidity, gearing, retentions, dividends and, over-all,
a valuation ratio. In pursuing its aim of expansion the firm, whatever
its size, will be purchasing new capital equipment and acquiring
other companies in its policy of diversification. In doing so it
requires an information flow which permits the appraisal of its
investment decisions (of which take-overs are just a special case) and

also enables it, within the constraints set by capital markets, to decide on and work towards an optimal financing policy. Although reliance on internal sources apparently frees the firm from the strictures[36] of continuous competition for new capital, and semi-automatic short-term borrowing rights from banks are often available, there are occasions when a company has to resort to long-term finance either by equity and/or debt, particularly if it is pursuing an active take-over policy.

We focused attention on the need to combine short- and long-run financing decisions so that the firm knows in advance what its likely commitments are period by period. Advance warning can then be given to the need to go 'long' before the maximum, safe, net borrowing position is reached. The decision to go long will be a strategic decision in Ansoff's terms and will occupy a lot of managerial time — accordingly it is taken only at discrete intervals. Within this is the decision to go for equity or debt which may depend on the purpose of the investment and, more importantly, on the existing capital structure. The facts that external long-term financing does not play a major role in most companies[37] and that profits (and therefore retained earnings) follow a marked cyclical pattern throw a lot of the burden on to liquid assets (which can act as a buffer) and bank borrowing, all of which we examined in terms of desired portfolio relationships. The data we have presented in the net acquisition of bank borrowing and liquid assets does reveal marked fluctuations due, in the main, to the cyclical nature of retained earnings, but a contributory factor which may cause changes within the short-term asset set is the possibility of some investment behaviour by management to achieve the highest expected yield on their short-term assets.

Notes

1.　S.J. Prais (129) found that for the period 1948-53, differences between large firms and 'others' in relation to growth, profitability and financing were not marked, although in a later study (130) he did find differences between the process of evolution of large companies and the rest. A re-examination of Table 3.2 indicates the difficulties of drawing definite conclusions.

2.　Stock (raw materials, work in progress, and finished goods) appreciation is the difference between the original cost of stocks, in the basis used by companies in calculating their profits, and the current cost of replacing such stocks at the time the finished goods are sold. This financial gain is more apparent than real because it is offset by the financing requirement to maintain the physical volume of stocks to ensure future operations. In November 1974, tax relief on the increase in the cost of replacing stocks was given to larger companies and this was followed by giving the same consideration, in April 1975, to all smaller companies and unincorporated businesses.

3. The Sandilands Committee (HMSO, Cmnd 6225) reported on the question of inflation accounting in 1975 and recommended that Current Cost Accounting (CCA) should be introduced. The Morpeth Committee have produced detailed proposals for the new system with the hope that it will be introduced in 1978.

4. For a discussion of the recent profitability of British industry see M. Panic and R.E. Close (123).

5. Judgement of our national investment performance *vis-à-vis* the performances of other countries is normally based on investment as a proportion of GNP rather than its absolute value.

6. As measured by the coefficient of variation but not by the actual range.

7. Ignoring tax at this stage. Because there is a contractual obligation to repay the investor the full capital sum on maturity (unless it is a convertible stock) and intermediate interest payments, the investor has some security against default and protection from variability of earnings and the required rate of return will be lower than the expected return from equity (the risk-bearing part of the capital structure). The rate will approximate that on long-term government securities though there will usually be a premium to cover the investor for the possibility of default and for the lack of complete marketability of corporate debt as compared with government securities.

8. If the upper limit is absolute and made binding by the prime debt-holders.

9. Although modifications in 1973 under the imputation system of company taxation may have reduced the tax advantages of debt in the UK for the company sector as a whole.

10. See J. Wynn (176), A.J. Merrett and A. Sykes (106) for illustrations of nominal and real rates of return on securities in the UK.

11. Mergers can be investigated by the Monopolies Commission on the recommendation of the DTI. The decision to refer will most likely be conditioned by considerations of increased concentration and the possibilities of asset-stripping which goes beyond the normal rationalisation which a post-merger situation would cause.

12. Based on an illustration in G. Newbould (116).

13. See G.P.E. Clarkson and B.J. Elliott (31) for support of this consideration.

14. H.H. Lynch (89) has found for the USA that some conglomerates have grown by the chain letter effect, whereby the P/E ratio of the bidder is successively improved by its take-over activities such that the process becomes a continuing one.

15. This was found in 6 of the 19 cases examined.

16. See A.J. Merrett and A. Sykes (106) for the derivation of this formula.

17. See W.G. Lewellen (86) and K.V. Smith and J.C. Schreiner (148).

18. For a useful coverage of the practical aspects of dividend policy see A. Wood (175).

19. For a comprehensive coverage of the neo-classical viewpoint on dividend policy and refinements to it see M.H. Miller and F. Modigliani (108).

20. See M.A. King (76) for a model which examines the effect of changing the structure on dividend behaviour.

21. In addition some institutions, for example life companies with annuity funds, do receive more favourable tax treatment.

22.   G. Meeks and G. Whittington (105) found that the proportion of gross income paid out as net dividends on ordinary shares was relatively stable for the two periods 1948-64 and 1964-71 (14.7 per cent) but the taxation of dividends caused a large increase in the retentions foregone to pay for the dividends being 18.4 per cent in 1948-64 and 23.8 per cent for 1964-71.

23.   Evidence for this is to be found in J. Lintner (87).

24.   For example, Meeks and Whittington (105) found the smaller companies had to keep payout high to attract more external capital.

25.   The ability to rearrange the capital structure is limited by statute in the UK since companies cannot make an issue of corporate debt to replace the ordinary shares of its own company. It can however make an issue to buy the shares of *another* company.

26.   This is rather different from the K.E. Boulding (24) concept of homeostasis which would, in terms of the balance sheet structure, trigger off forces to restore equilibrium. We are arguing that whilst these forces may be at work it is unlikely that they can bring about complete adjustment period by period.

27.   The flow elements are thus first differences of stocks but in practice there are difficulties particularly due to revaluations so that a straight comparison of balance sheets period by period will not necessarily indicate *actual* flows.

28.   The other problems of satisfying credit worthiness to lenders both short- and long-term are contained in the balance sheet ratios already discussed. These other blocks are completely outside the scope of the individual firm, although in a rationing situation a pecking order will be established so that the internal operations of companies can indirectly assist.

29.   Direct control of advances was used up to September 1971 and thereafter, with the introduction of Competition and Credit Control, a similar effect could be produced by other instruments – specifically special and supplementary deposits, and the control of the growth of the interest earning deposits of banks.

30.   Ignoring the transactions costs of borrowing. Based on the study by A.D. Bain *et al.* (13).

31.   Theoretically it could re-finance long-term capital by borrowing more short-term finance which would move it down the line.

32.   Such portfolio dispositions may be partially determined by industry capital market norms.

33.   At various times attention is concentrated on gaps in financial markets which may impede this. This has been well-documented for small companies; see E.W. Davis and K.A. Yeomans (39).

34.   Because of the deductability of interest for tax computation purposes.

35.   Illiquid is a relative term. If assets are 1 or even up to 5-year stocks they can be held to maturity provided the funds are not required. They are all virtually default-free so any loss will be due to forced sale, typically when interest rates have risen in the meantime.

36.   Though not freed from the need to invest profitably to maintain a high valuation ratio.

37.   Although we detected its significance in the giants and some other smaller but fast-growing firms.

6 PLANNING IN THE PUBLIC SECTOR

6.1 Introduction

The focus of interest so far in this study has been the business firm, but in this chapter we shall demonstrate that the planning and decision making activities of public bodies are in many important respects similar to those of firms. Both types of organisation are purposive institutions transforming inputs of resources into goods and services, not necessarily for resale but to satisfy the 'wants' and perceived needs of the consumer. Given that all these organisations utilise scarce resources, they are justifiably a subject of interest for the economist, both in terms of the resources used internally in the pursuit of their objectives and in terms of the competition for resources externally — between the public and private sectors of the economy and between different agencies in either sector.

In previous chapters we have examined theories of business behaviour with an emphasis on the planning process with its diversification and financing dimensions. We now wish to broaden our discussion to include planning in the public sector at both 'micro' and 'macro' levels. The justification for this is not only that planning of one form or another is carried out in the public sector, but also that to understand the planning process in an economy, it is important to recognise the interdependence between private and public decisions particularly in the context of investment. Firms need an indication of the activities of the public sector and the future progress of the economy as parameters which influence their own plans and, likewise, projections of the private sector, in particular of business investment, are needed by the government in the determination of current and capital spending in the public sector. Thus, one set of decisions is dependent (in part at least) on another set which is itself dependent (again at least in part) on the previous set. The fact that these two sets of decisions are undertaken in mixed economies by different institutions complicates the problem and this reinforces the need for more explicit recognition of this interdependence. Clearly there are differences between the activities of business firms and public sector bodies (we cite defence and health) but the similarities are such that a study of these can usefully form part of this book — indeed the principles of defence planning have undoubted applicability to

161

business planning.

Although we have considered business planning in the context of 'growth' objective which may be inappropriate for public bodies, it is not necessarily so, given:

(1)   the macro-economic objective of growth; and
(2)   managerial discretion in the public sector.

The schema for the chapter is as follows: Section 6.2 briefly reviews and synthesises the ideas we have developed about planning systems in firms and in Section 6.3 we examine national economic planning. Sections 6.4 and 6.5 take examples of planning in the public sector – defence planning (6.4) and health service planning (6.5); in Section 6.6 we review and appraise the role of modern micro-economic theory to planning in the public sector.[1]

6.2 Corporate Planning in Business Firms

In drawing together the implications of earlier chapters for the corporate planning activities of firms, certain features need to be high-lighted. Planning, first and foremost, is anticipatory in nature; it involves continuous scanning and the making of decisions before events take place, rather than waiting for circumstances actually to change before the appropriate response is determined. Furthermore, the firm not only anticipates changes in its environment when planning, it also investigates change through its strategic decisions, particularly where innovative diversification is concerned. If planning is described as 'corporate', the implication is that the firm is viewed as a total system and that it is the whole unit's relationships with the environment which are analysed when strategy is under consideration.

Corporate planning should enhance a firm's survival prospects, and increases in performance measured in terms of growth and rate of profit are to be expected. The American studies of H.I. Ansoff (11) and S.S. Thane and R.J. House (157) support this view in demonstrating that firms which have adopted a corporate planning approach have produced significant increases in sales and earnings per share, and have done better in these respects than firms which have not followed this approach.

The managerial theory of R.L. Marris has been the focal point of this book and the need to harmonise expansion in terms of its market demand and finance supply dimensions has been stressed. Additionally, in the managerial theory of O.E. Williamson, and the behavioural theory of R.M. Cyert and J.G. March, the importance of internal organisation in the allocation of resources and co-ordination of subunit activities has been emphasised as a further dimension. In Figure 6.1 we offer a schematic representation of basic planning framework for business firms in which these various dimensions are incorporated.

Figure 6.1: Planning Framework of Business Firms

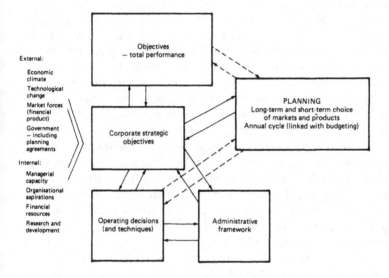

Environmental influences and constraints

External:

Economic climate

Technological change

Market forces (financial product)

Government – including planning agreements

Internal:

Managerial capacity

Organisational aspirations

Financial resources

Research and development

Objectives – total performance

Corporate strategic objectives

PLANNING
Long-term and short-term choice of markets and products
Annual cycle (linked with budgeting)

Operating decisions (and techniques)

Administrative framework

A word of explanation is perhaps warranted in connection with the annual cycle which features in this diagram. An annual cycle can provide a discipline to ensure that strategic matters receive their due attention, since the regular feedback from operations tends to focus the attention of management on immediate organisational needs rather than strategy. Additionally if the annual planning cycle is linked to budgeting, a means of co-ordinating long-, medium- and short-term plans and of relating strategy to operations, can be provided. We shall see that the annual cycle is a device which has been adopted widely in the various public sector planning systems which we discuss after our next section on National Economic Planning.

6.3 National Economic Planning

Planning should be seen as a means of reaching organisational objectives rather than as an end in itself. It embodies a rational approach to decision making and is essentially neutral, but in the context of national economic planning it has frequently been associated with communist systems and their ideologies. It is not difficult to see why – the actual term 'economic plan' dates from the USSR's first five-year plan of 1928 which featured centralisation of the control and direction of productive resources. Since World War II, however, it has become more widely appreciated that economic planning can be applied to any kind of economic system – to socialist, mixed, or developing economies, but that since no two countries will have identical economic systems, the planning styles adopted have to be tailored to the individual needs of the economy. The essential features of the planning process which we described in Chapter 1 will, however, be common to all: specifying objectives over appropriate time horizons, considering alternative programmes of action, etc. The differences will occur in the actual objectives set, the role of the state in the process and, linked to this, the actual execution and control of the plan.

The increased awareness and use of planning in Western Europe and other non-Eastern bloc countries can be explained by a series of factors which have been present since World War II. In the case of the newly emerging and developing countries there was the demonstration effect of a 'non-classical' industrial revolution of the socialist bloc – particularly the USSR. There was also the fact that the international aid agencies, for example, the World Bank,[2] required countries to establish their development plans so that they could assess financial and technical requirements. Indeed organisations such as the World Bank would lend only on projects which were part of an integrated plan rather than isolated developments. In the developed countries the desirability of economic forecasts and projections was evident from the need to harmonise developments in private and public sectors, reinforced by the requirements of the Marshall Plan of 1948 for a blueprint of aid needs to assist post-war reconstruction. The emergence of techniques like input-output analysis further stimulated these rather diverse interests in planning.

The planning experiences of different countries has varied widely with some that were apparently success stories and others which were clear failures. In Western Europe two distinguishable planning types have emerged:[3] *indicative planning*[4] and *forecast planning.* Both have their roots in the early post-war period, with France being credited as the originator in 1946 of the former type, and the Netherlands and Scandinavia as the pioneers of the latter.

The indicative planning of France[5] rests on three pillars: a strong public sector which accounts for over 50 per cent of investment, participation in the formulation of plans by government officials, industrialists, trade union representatives and academic experts, and an element of inducement and coercion of the private sector by the government. Instead of central direction and control the process works by the dynamic interaction of the parties to the plan. This is illustrated by reference to an extract from the first plan (1947-53) which is contained in J. Mitchell (109).

> For the first time, all elements interested in the progress of an industry or a production have found themselves assembled in order to carry out together a common task . . . The knowledge acquired in common in dealing with common problems greatly facilitates decisions and their understanding once they are taken. In many cases, action results from consultation alone . . . [p. 195]

Forecast planning differs from indicative planning in that the forecasts relate to macro-economic variables in the main, and these are often linked to the annual budget (though longer term forecasts are also used). Although forecast plans do indicate expected progress in the future they do not contain targets *per se* or commitments, rather they serve as a source of information on which plans could be prepared. In this sense they are only the first stage of the planning process.

In the UK, the growth of the public sector gave the state increasing control over a broad spectrum of economic activity, but despite the creation of an economic planning board in 1947, it was not until the 1960s that indicative planning was formally introduced. Prior to this 'forecasting'[6] had been used in various forms by the Treasury, and governments had worked towards various economic policy objectives which were spelled out in the Radcliffe Committte Report (on the working of the financial system) of 1959 (132). These included a commitment to full employment, balance of payments equilibrium, avoidance of inflation and the achievement of economic growth. These are still retained although at various times one or more of them appears more important in the eyes of the government of the day than the others.

Our progress in planning is often compared with other countries in

Western Europe in order to assess the causes for our poor economic performance. It was the 'low' growth record (even though it was good in relation to the pre-war years) compared with our overseas competitors which brought about the adoption of indicative planning[7] to chart the way to both a greater growth potential and the achievement of this. This was officially recognised in July 1961 with the announcement of the creation of the National Economic Development Council which was to act as a forum[8] to examine the economic prospects of the country and to link the resources of the country to the competing demands of consumption, government expenditure, and investment. The programme of work which it adopted was threefold:

(1)   to study the implications of a faster rate of growth on certain key indicators – foreign trade balance, investment, etc.;
(2)   to study this on an industry wide basis; and
(3)   to examine the constraints and obstacles to the growth process so as to establish preconditions for growth.

This was cast in terms of an over-all plan for 1961-6 with a growth objective of 4 per cent which in terms of our historical performance was extremely ambitious[9] though not when compared with that of our European counterparts.

A considerable amount of progress was achieved in providing fore-casts and illuminating the constraints in achieving the faster rate of growth specified, but in fact only a 3 per cent rate was achieved with recession in 1962-3. In 1964 the direction of planning was changed with the establishment of the Department of Economic Affairs. Planning became a key feature of policy and although the NEDC was maintained in a new form, the main thrust of purposive planning was to come from *within* government, and the DEA was charged with producing a national plan. This was finally published in 1965 covering the years 1964-70, indicating a growth path objective of 3.8 per cent per annum. This plan was all embracing giving a check-list for action and target expenditure plans for the public sector, including the nationalised industries, tied to the growth figure. By the summer of 1966, however, the plan was effectively a dead letter with the need for short-term action in the economy in the wake of a further crisis in the balance of payments, an event not fully allowed for in this particular planning process. But even without the balance of payments crisis it is debatable whether the growth target could have been achieved. A further but more limited attempt was made in 1969 with the publication of 'The Task Ahead' (70) which was an economic assessment to 1972 but the influence of the DEA was weakened and it was finally abolished.

This collapse of 'formal' planning has meant that planning of this type has become discredited, although the activities of the NEDC have continued and broadened with the further development of economic development committees for particular industries. In addition the government does produce plans for individual aspects of the system such as transport, energy, regional policy as well as its own public expenditure plans. Another important aspect of government involvement is in the process of forecasting and, in fact, the Treasury model used for its budget forecasts has been published so as to indicate the relationships specified in the model.

Table 6.1:

Objectives	Instruments	Constraints
Reductions in unemployment	Fiscal policy	Growth in productivity, balance of payments equilibrium[a]
Growth of GNP	Monetary policy	
Control of inflation	Exchange rate policy	
	Prices and incomes policy	

[a] Balance of payments equilibrium is often, as we have seen, referred to as a policy objective but it can also be seen as a constraint.

We can set out in a simple chart (Table 6.1) the objectives[10] of government policy, the instruments available and the constraints which may be in operation. Government control over the economy is still exercised in part through fiscal policy, but over the past decade or so the importance of the annual spring budget has lessened, with appropriate measures (including changes in taxation and in government spending) being taken when judged necessary. Monetary measures (influencing the target money supply and the cost and availability of credit) are again under continuous review. Other measures are sometimes reverted to, for example the imposition of import surcharges

or import deposit schemes, but these are normally in response to a
crisis as is usually the case too with prices and incomes policies. The
latter have also been tried as longer-term policy instruments in the
pursuit of high employment and faster growth without inflation, but
their success in this context is debatable.

The present Labour government (1977) feels that the policy
instruments indicated above cannot bring about the fundamental
restructuring and regeneration of British industry which is now
thought to be necessary for the restoration of economic growth.
Interest in a planning style which involves closer contact with industry
has resulted in a proposal for planning agreements. These are referred
to in the White Paper on 'The Regeneration of British Industry' (71).
Such agreements would involve consultations between the government and big companies and the drawing up of plans for three years
ahead, in which any needs for assistance in achieving the plans
would also be agreed.

A principal aim is to improve communication, not only between
government and large companies, but also between employers and
unions, management and the shop-floor. In part, the call for planning
agreements has followed from a desire of the political left to
constrain the power of board rooms[11] in the private sector, reinforced
by a more widely based effort to secure greater disclosure of information from big business. The White Paper initially met with an
unfavourable response from the President of the Confederation of
British Industry, possibly because of the political undertones underlying the justification for planning agreements but, for whatever reason,
even companies enlightened enough to operate their own corporate
planning systems have been reluctant to co-operate. Of course there
have been notable exceptions, for example Chrysler UK but, as
recipients of public rescue money, one feels that they had little
alternative but to make their strategy explicit in a formal agreement.

Initial reluctance among firms is natural when one considers the
additional burdens which planning agreements would impose — in the
shape of managerial time absorbed and higher staff costs, not to
mention a possible distaste for disclosure of more information. The
pay-off for companies may seem remote, whereas the costs would be
immediate, but on the other hand few kinds of planning activity
confer benefits in the short term. The possibility of ultimate rewards
in the form of a national strategy in which the sub-plans of the major
sectors of the economy were harmonised and some of the uncertainties
inherent in corporate planning were resolved, does seem to warrant a

more pragmatic approach to the whole subject of government-industry relationships.

6.4 Defence Planning

In the course of our discussion on this topic we shall focus our attention on the Planning-Programming-Budgeting System (PPBS) approach which lies at the heart of planning in this sector and assess the implications which the experiences of defence planning might have for other sectors. A system based on PPBS was initiated by the US Department of Defence in 1961 following its development by the Cost-Analysis Department of the RAND Corporation.[12] The methodology inherent in the system was that of planning and budgeting for the outputs of defence expenditures in terms of missions, forces, and weapon systems, rather than for the inputs classified according to the standard appropriation categories. So far as budgeting as an instrument of expenditure control is concerned, it is still necessary to classify outlays according to areas of responsibility within the Army, Air Force and Navy. But PPBS as an instrument of planning begins with the recognition that programmes designed to serve a particular mission requirement usually cut across the boundaries of the three military services, with the consequence that budgeting on a service by service basis is unhelpful in ascertaining cost-effectiveness. PPBS is entirely consistent with the views we have expressed elsewhere in this book, namely that planning activities must be geared to total system objectives and that individual subunits should be seen as part of the wider system rather than as isolated elements. Thus the long-range plans of the Department of Defence are rather more than an aggregation of separate service plans. In fact the process tends to be reversed, with the over-all strategy in a unified Department of Defence plan dictating the contributions required of each service. Although tradition tends to preserve the rivalries between services, it is the mission which is pre-eminent and a service's importance depends on its potential contribution to missions. D. Novick (119) makes the following distinction between planning and programming:

Planning is the selection of courses of action through a systematic consideration of alternatives. Programming is the more specific determination of the manpower, material, and facilities necessary for accomplishing a programme. [p. 37]

A programme in this sense is thus an integrated set of activities designed for a military mission and within each programme are pro-gramme elements which are the forces, weapon systems and supporting activities. Thus, taking the mission 'Strategic Forces', programmes could be built up from elements such as the Polaris weapon system, Titan, and Minuteman. By way of contrast, budgeting under traditional appropriation categories would have involved consideration of Polaris alongside other Naval activities such as anti-submarine warfare and aircraft-carrier construction. A difficulty encountered in all programme budgeting systems is how to distribute general service costs among output categories.[13] As in conventional accounting practice, appor-tionment of such costs is a perennial problem and, at the best, one can only aim for stability and consistency in the procedures to ensure that comparisons are meaningful. To a certain extent the problem is less severe for PPBS than for conventional absorption costing systems, since cost comparisons for planning purposes frequently lend themselves to marginal (or incremental) analysis in which the additional or avoidable cost is less likely to be confounded by non-allocable elements. Assuming that programme costs can be ascertained on a comparable basis, decisions are made after projecting costs and assessing the effectiveness of the various feasible alternatives.

When a composite plan has been devised, covering all the mission-oriented programmes, the detailed programming can commence. This part of the process involves the drawing up of a five-year force structure and financial programme set out in terms of forces, man-power and dollar costs for each programme element. Thus planning and budgeting became harmonised, but previously they had operated independently. Military planners, prior to the 1960s, had considered defence needs over medium- to long-term time horizons while budgeting, undertaken by the civilian secretaries and the comptroller organisations, looked ahead mainly to the financial year ahead. The reform enabled the Basic National Security Policy, the Joint Strategic Objectives Plan (JSOP) and the plans for the services to be integrated within the Defence Secretary's five-year plan, using mechanisms which we shall describe shortly.

Long-term planning in an environment characterised by changing technology, uncertainty in cost estimation, and strategy needs which may themselves change, necessitates regular review and updating of the programmes. For example a new weapon system proceeds through three principal decision stages at each of which funds are committed: research and development, investment, and operations. It may become necessary to review costs during development, if there are short-comings in performance as compared with design objectives – short-comings which can only be remedied at a cost. Changing strategy needs may dictate that one weapon system be abandoned, while another development be accelerated and investment stepped up. In order to maintain an up-to-date five-year plan and budget, it was recognised in the early days of the new planning process that a programme change control system was absolutely essential. In this system, approval thresholds would be established to focus attention on major issues, thus applying the principle of management by exception. The updating procedure involved the use of standard forms for submitting proposed changes to programmes, in which projected cost estimates were an important feature. As part of the programme change control system a progress reporting procedure was adopted which required the establishing of 'milestones' with schedules which reflected the principal events and activities within the financial plan to cover about two hundred of the most important material items. Monthly performance, together with projections for the following quarter, would be compared with the milestones to indicate where corrective action or revision was necessary.

Having described the system in broad outline, let us now look at some of the principal features and mechanisms in greater detail. The central component is the Five-Year Defence Programme (FYDP) which is the name now given to what was the five-year force structure and financial programme.[14] The programme structure consists of mission-oriented programmes which cut across service boundaries. The major programmes[15] within the FYDP have been: strategic forces; general purpose forces; intelligence and communications; airlift and sealift; guard and reserve forces; research and development; central supply and maintenance; training, medical and other general personnel activities; administration and associated activities; and support of other nations. To emphasise the difference between planning for missions and planning according to services, we can see that within the first programme – strategic forces – there are programme elements such as B-52 bombers and B-1 supersonic bombers (aircraft forces), missile forces like Titan and Minuteman which are land-based and those like Polaris and Poseidon which are sea-based.

The planning cycle[16] starts when the Joint Chiefs of Staff (JCS) provide the Office of the Secretary of Defence (OSD) with their assessment of defence needs for up to eight years ahead, in relation to national security and military objectives. Their statement is in the form of the Joint Strategic Objectives Plan (JSOP). Around the same time, the Secretary receives advice from the National Security Council, and he subsequently issues strategic guidance on what appear to be the major military threats, together with fiscal constraints. The Joint Chiefs of Staff then issue a Joint Forces Memorandum (JFM) in which they estimate what is feasible within the budget available and provide data on programme costs over five years and associated manpower requirements. The services later submit more specific updating recommendations to the OSD for the forces, manpower and costs which are specified in Programme Objective Memoranda (POMs) (formerly the Programme Change Requests). The climax to this preparatory activity is a 'major force issues' meeting with the Defence Secretary, the Chiefs, and the service secretaries during which reconciliation between military needs and fiscal constraints is sought. The Secretary of Defence will subsequently issue Programme Decision Memoranda (PDMs) (formerly Programme Change Decisions) which are the official response to the POMs submitted by the services. The services are then required to draft their budgets in the light of proposed changes which have been agreed, following which final service issues are resolved and Programme Budget Decisions (PBDs) are issued by the OSD, and the FYDP is updated. The Office of Management and the Budget then prepares the defence budget for the President who resolves any outstanding issues. It should be noted that planning cycles overlap. Thus the cycle described by C.E. Stellini (152)[17] in 1971, starts in October and runs through to December of the following year, so that when one cycle begins, the previous year's is in its final phase with the services submitting their budget estimates to OSD. The result is a rolling plan in which the programmes inherited from the previous year have been updated, modified and re-negotiated.

In the UK, too, defence was the first ministry to adopt a programme budgeting approach, although the description 'functional costing system' was preferred to PPBS. The system, instituted in 1964, was similar in many ways to the early US version, notably in the major programme categories: nuclear strategic forces; European ground forces; general purpose combat forces (army, navy and air-force); air mobility; reserve and auxiliary formations; research and development; training; production; repair and associated research facilities in the UK; contingencies; other support functions; miscellaneous expenditure and receipts; and special materials. J.M. Bridgeman (27)[18] describes how the system facilitated the costing of alternative force structures during the defence reviews of the 1960s. A parallel development in the UK was the analysis and evaluation of alternative weapon systems and defence strategies by the Defence Operational Analysis Establishment, which brought together analytical staff who had previously worked for one service department or another. Budgetary control is still exercised through annual estimates prepared according to the traditional 'vote' headings on an input basis, rather than according to function or programme. However, the defence estimates are accompanied by an analysis according to programme and sub-programme which is given annually in the White Paper.

One of the explicit aims of PPBS, regardless of its sphere of application, is the facilitating of cost-effectiveness analysis. Its proponents claim that by classifying costs according to output, it becomes possible to weigh up decision alternatives against one another in terms of the contribution made to some objective per pound or dollar spent. Cost-effectiveness is thus an assessment of efficiency expressed in terms of output as a ratio of input. The measurement of input boils down to cost estimation, which as we have already suggested, is no easy matter in the complex world of defence planning. Quantifying output is more difficult still, with no satisfactory method available for translating outcomes into financial benefits. (If there were a method of so doing, the analysis would more properly be called 'cost-benefit' analysis). So we need criteria for determining effectiveness and, in turn, cost-effectiveness, but even assuming that satisfactory criteria are available, the problem still remains as to how input is related to output, that is, how cost is related to effectiveness. So, at best, PPBS provides a planning format conducive to evaluation of competing alternatives. It does not in itself provide the analytical capability which is essential if relationships are to be understood and quantified. The model building skills including the statistical and simulation techniques referred to in Chapter 1 are needed to obtain the maximum benefit from PPBS. The problems of evaluation in defence are compounded by the restrictions on experimentation which are dictated by the very nature of military activities, and the uncertainty which arises through the interdependence inherent in any 'game' of conflict. Apart from the problems on the cost side, then, there are difficulties in determining effectiveness in three areas: (1) finding suitable criteria; (2) measuring performance; and (3) anticipating the responses of opponents. Using the terminology of game theory, these are the problems of finding valid pay-off measures, calculating the pay-off values themselves, and enumerating and evaluating counter-strategies.

Figure 6.2: Comparing Cost with Effectiveness

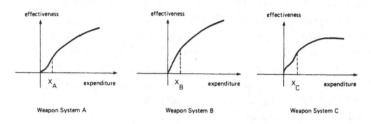

Let us imagine for a moment that these were not insurmountable obstacles and that the task of the analyst was just to relate cost to effectiveness. A plausible assumption is that expenditures on a given programme element will ultimately be subject to diminishing marginal returns, a phenomenon exhibited in Figure 6.2. In this diagram, three alternative weapon systems are compared in terms of their contributions to some mission-oriented programme and the expenditure necessary to bring about those contributions. After a certain level of expenditure, each programme element offers less and less benefit for additional monies spent. The analyst could find the maximum benefit for a given outlay by allocating funds between the three weapon systems so as to equate marginal effectiveness. This occurs in the diagram at X_A, X_B and X_C where the derivatives (slopes) of the three functions are all equal. If the over-all defence plan dictates that the expenditure on the programme in question should be expanded (or contracted), a new distribution of resources between the programme elements can be found in principle, again through marginal analysis. In the diagram, a substantial injection of cash would bring about a rather greater expansion for system B than for its competitors whose marginal returns fall off relatively faster. Of course marginal analysis would only be applicable if the three functions were independent and the curves were smooth and continuous.

Just how models are built and the relationships quantified involves analysis which receives scant attention in programme budgeting literature. Indeed, such a discussion in the present context would be inappropriate since it would inevitably encompass military matters outside the scope of this book. Obviously, weapon trials give an indication of capacity for destruction and accuracy in hitting targets. Military manoeuvres not only give experience to tacticians but also yield knowledge about equipment reliability, troop mobility, supplies reliability, etc. One would suppose that fairly accurate performance estimates could be made so far as conventional warfare is concerned. Indeed the US was, until recently, heavily committed in Indo-China and the use of American weapons systems elsewhere in the world enables estimates to be made of effectiveness. It is with nuclear weapons and inter-continental ballistic missiles that little is known about their performance in real warfare. Nevertheless in assessing the cost-effectiveness of alternative weapon systems and force deployments, attempts have been made to estimate performance according to criteria such as: enemy population and floor space destroyed and, on the debit side, the losses similarly measured for the US and her allies; number of targets destroyed of various types, for example military installations and large industrial complexes. The effectiveness of various tactical air force deployments might be compared using a format such as that given in Table 6.2 (see also Novick (120) p. 96).

Table 6.2: Format for Evaluation of Effectiveness

| | Tactical Air Forces (Attack Mission) | | | FY 1966 |
| | Alternative forces | | | |
	I	II	III	IV
Per day:				
Tons of ordnance delivered				
Aircraft hours on station				
Sorties				
Expected number of targets destroyed:				
Category I				
Category II				
Category III				
Category IV				
Others				

Source: C.J. Hitch (69).

On the cost side, apart from uncertainty in the estimation of expenditures, which is particularly difficult where development costs have to be ascertained, there is the problem of allowing for inflation and the time dimension. Inflation is normally eliminated by estimating at constant prices, but over time real salary costs may change relative to equipment or research and development costs, with the result that cost comparisons are no longer valid. The time dimension can be accommodated by discounting future expenditure streams at a pre-determined discount rate in which case cost-effectiveness could be expressed in units of, say, expected number of targets destroyed per dollar present cost. The present cost would include all relevant expenditures, including R & D, investment, and annual operating costs. Whatever cost-effectiveness criteria are used, the need to allow for uncertainty cannot be over-emphasised. Normal practice is to test options for sensitivity to a number of parameter changes, so that choices are not made on the basis of single-valued estimates of cost and/or effectiveness.

We intend to examine the implications of defence planning for other sectors, but before doing so we should point out that not all observers regard the US Department of Defence's system as an unqualified success. R.D. Lee and R.W. Johnson (82) describe how the plan starts with the JSOP prepared annually by the Joint Chiefs of Staff. In fact the JSOP originated in 1955, before the introduction of the PPB system, but the latter does not seem to have changed the character of the JSOP, which tends to be a long shopping list for the services drawn up without regard for the resources likely to be available. Just how far the JSOP influences decision making is unclear. Lee and Johnson cite references in which doubts are expressed as to whether it plays any major role at all (p. 128). The entire defence planning system came under fire during the 'Pentagon Papers' investigations into the US commitment to Vietnam in which serious questions were raised as to whether this commitment had been subject to thorough analysis. The cost and technical problems associated with the F.111 aircraft also provoked criticism of defence management, but it is interesting to note that the F.111 decision was made outside the PPBS process (p. 131), and in any case criticisms which are directed at errors of judgement do not necessarily imply faults in the planning system itself.

R.M. Cyert and J.G. March's (38) observations that budgets lend stability to coalition arrangements were obviously directed at conventional budgetary control systems, but one wonders whether

PPBS might achieve the same result unintentionally, thus retarding the process of change. In fact Stellini hints that this is the case when he states, 'What happens in the real world is that the precedents of previous years' allocations strongly influence subsequent years' allocations' (152, p. 234).

J.K. Galbraith in *Economics and the Public Purpose* (51) stresses the 'bureaucratic symbiosis' which exists between the manufacturers of weapons and the Department of Defence (p. 143). These manufacturers are alleged to have the same corporate growth objectives as any other large firms and their end products enhance the prestige and influence of the services. Furthermore, movements of personnel between weapons firms and the DoD are common, thus cementing the relationship. Galbraith takes an even stronger line in an earlier volume (49) in which weapons firms, in planning their own developments, are credited with a direct influence on defence policy. In conjunction with public agencies '. . . it [a weapons firm] helps to establish the official view of defence requirements and therewith of some part of the foreign policy' (p. 315).

Galbraith's main objection to bureaucratic symbiosis is that it contributes to unequal development of the economy. Weaker sectors such as agriculture, housing, education and health remain weak while defence and the large corporations in the private sector grow stronger. In the present context an interesting comment he made during the Nixon era, in the early seventies was, 'Despite peace and the avowed need to economise, and with no claims for their cost-effectiveness, defence expenditures are being increased' (51, p. 294). Another claim by the same author is that of all US government agencies, 'the largest and most powerful of all is the Department of Defence' (51, p. 297).

He cites evidence that, in the past, the budget requests of the Department of Defence have been largely immune to any interference from the Executive, and not subject to question by the President (51, p. 298). In contrast, Lee and Johnson (82) state that, despite the popular view that the Nixon Administration was more receptive to the military than were its predecessors, it did recognise the need for 'fiscal guidance' in defence planning, thereby imposing constraints on the DoD.

In an article published in 1966 entitled 'Six Business Lessons from the Pentagon', D.J. Smalter and R.J. Ruggles (147) argue that the concepts and principles of defence planning can usefully be applied to industrial corporate planning. The basis of their argument is that, despite the rather different nature of the problems encountered in the two environments, the structure of the problems and the techniques available for their solution are similar. Furthermore executives in both environments are responsible for the allocation of resources so as to maximise long-run effectiveness. The key characteristics of the DoD system listed in this article include:

(1)   strategic planning by missions, costed by programmes;
(2)   a large analytical and planning staff at the top organisational level;
(3)   a scheduled annual planning cycle which integrates strategy formulation with budgeting;
(4)   systems analysis and planning, embodying quantitative techniques;
(5)   'needs research' as a mechanism for perceiving problems and opportunities;
(6)   a planning process which proceeds in distinct steps which are themselves derived from military concepts;
(7)   network analysis used to co-ordinate project implementation;
(8)   a strategic planning 'decision centre'.

The six lessons for business represent an attempt to identify good planning practice and, although we shall not try to reproduce these lessons here, it is worth reiterating some of the more salient parts of the article by Smalter and Ruggles. The concept of 'missions' adopted by the DoD is certainly valid in industrial planning as we have already suggested in Chapter 4. The reorientation of budgeting towards missions by the DoD is reputed to have brought 'billion-dollar' changes in various parts of the defence budget, and although it is unlikely that such a parallel will be found in the business world, a change in perspective towards market missions, and away from the kind of introspective approach which characterises much of business decision analysis, would almost certainly result in a fundamental redirection of resources.

The idea of 'needs research' is akin to that of the intelligence activity we called 'problem recognition' in Chapter 1. We see this as a basic mechanism for any planning system, without which a systematic consideration of alternatives is impossible. We shall observe in the next section that the health planning system adopted in the re-organised National Health Service appears to possess the essential mechanisms of a planning system, but that the fundamental problem of assessing health needs is a major stumbling block in the functioning of the system.

Other aspects of the DoD system can undoubtedly be applied to virtually any planning system: the planning cycle, the decision making centre (with computer facilities, information retrieval systems and visual display equipment), the use of systems analysis and operational research techniques, and the sequencing of activities with the aid of network diagrams. Extravagant claims are made for network analysis, for example that the use of PERT (a form of network analysis) in the planning of the Polaris project in 1958 enabled two years to be lopped off its completion time. Further discussion of such techniques is inappropriate here, but we concur with the view that advances in management science should be recognised by business organisations and employed in the resolution of complex strategy issues wherever they can make a useful contribution.

6.5 Planning for Health

Corporate planning in most other sectors can proceed on the assumption that needs are finite in the sense that, if some specific objective is set for a given time horizon with which anticipated performance is compared, the more resources that are directed towards the attainment of that objective, the smaller will be any shortfall in performance. Ultimately, if sufficient resources are made available, needs will become sated. I. Illich (74) explains that the National Health Service in Britain, as conceived by Beveridge, was based on the assumption that treatment of a strictly limited quantity of illness would bring a reduction in subsequent sickness rates. The benefits were expected to be cumulative, with a healthier and healthier nation drawing less and less on health resources, and the annual cost of the health service falling in consequence. Nowadays it is still widely believed by the health-care professions that health levels will improve with the amount spent on medical services, but it is recognised that expectations of the population have outstripped the growth of resources available.[19]

A fundamental aim of the National Health Service was to give access to all in need as a human right, regardless of the individual's ability to pay. Certainly the bulk of the cost of the service is financed centrally with the patient paying but a small fraction directly, but Beveridge's expectation that expenditures would become self-eliminating has proved to be pure fantasy. M.H. Cooper (35) states, in the introduction to his book *Rationing Health Care* that 'need' as assessed by the medical professions is not finite, and he suggests that the stated resource requirements would absorb a proportion of the national product which would be inconsistent with the competing claims of other sectors. By the late 1960s, most advanced nations were, in fact, spending a greater proportion of the GNP on health services than the UK. B. Abel-Smith (2) provides evidence which shows that in 1969, Canada, the United States and Sweden were all spending about seven per cent of their GNP on health services as against less than five per cent for the UK (p. 122). Moreover, since these countries enjoy greater national incomes than the UK, the absolute sums allocated to health care are substantially higher. Even in the UK, health service expenditures have been growing in real terms although, at the time of writing (1977), prospects for further expansion are not good. Abel-Smith[20] gives six main reasons for the worldwide growth in health expenditure in recent years, which we summarise as follows:

(1)   increased involvement of the government, and wider coverage of government-sponsored health schemes, notably in the US;
(2)   increased expectations of the patient who seeks rapid cure of each and every ailment;
(3)   limited scope for productivity increases through mechanisation as compared with other sectors of the economy, with resultant high labour costs;
(4)   higher proportion of elderly in the population (which has itself been growing); the aged consume much more of health services than younger persons;
(5)   the expansion of medical knowledge, availability of new drugs, treatments and diagnostic procedures has extended the range of care which physicians can provide for the patient, but at an ever-increasing cost; moreover the success in combating infectious diseases has left less tractable forms of illness such as cancer at the forefront of the battle;
(6)   failure to differentiate, in some countries, between those services which are useful and those which are not, or are inappropriate (i.e. failure to control waste).

An interesting observation is that there is no obvious relationship between expenditures and level of health as indicated by mortality rates. For example, although the US spent more annually in the late 1960s than Sweden, France, Germany, the Netherlands, and the UK, it suffered the worst mortality rates for men aged 35-44 and 45-54 and women in the same age groups. Its perinatal mortality rates were the worst of the sample and its infant and maternal mortality rates also compared unfavourably. Of course, health services are not just about the postponement of death, so that we cannot measure effectiveness simply in terms of mortality rates, but a more important reason for the lack of correlation between input and output is that diet, living habits (especially smoking) and the environment in which we live, are now seen as the prime determinants of a nation's health status. From the foregoing discussion, it would seem that the economist has a central role to play in health planning, but at the same time it is obvious that the resource allocation problem in the health sector is a particularly complex one. A major difficulty is the confusion between supply and demand, and between demand and need. Demands originate from the wants of individuals. A demand exists when individuals present themselves for treatment and this may be translated into an identified health need by the doctor. The service may be able to provide for this need in which case the original demand is met, but there are identified needs which cannot be met and also needs which remain unidentified, either because the doctor fails to diagnose the need, or the patient does not visit the doctor. A King's Fund Working Party classified needs for health care in the following manner (77, p. 19): *met demand* which is identifiable in utilisation data; *identified but unmet need* where resources are not available, or only available after harmful delay, which is in part exhibited in waiting list statistics; and *unidentified need* which can only be assessed through *ad hoc* studies. However where supply is limited, utilisation statistics (i.e. number of cases treated per year) are indicative of supply rather than demand. Measures of demand are therefore, more often than not, measures of resource availability, so demand is confounded by supply parameters. It is apparent, then, that health needs are virtually unquantifiable, except in so far as waiting lists give some indication of identified but unmet need. Since needs are neither finite nor quantifiable, the foundation for health planning and the application of economic analysis looks distinctly shaky. This fundamental measurement difficulty pervades the entire planning process from the identification of problems and opportunities, through the evaluation of alternatives, to the monitoring of performance after implementation.

With these thoughts in mind let us consider what kind of health planning system might be feasible. The starting point must be the statement of an over-all goal for the health services such as that given by H.P. Hatry (64) in his discussion of programme planning. 'To provide for the physical and mental health of the citizenry, including reduction of the number, length, and severity of illnesses and disabilities' (p. 202). In striving for such a goal, the pattern of services provided must be reappraised in terms analogous to the re-examination of missions undertaken in other corporate planning environments, notably in defence planning.

The 'client group' concept is one means of classifying health services and this involves the identification of classes of patients whose needs are similar, for example, children could form one such group, the mentally ill another and so on. Changes in population structure and patterns of morbidity give some indication as to which client groups should receive priority over various time horizons. Thus, achievement of the basic health-planning goal might warrant a shift in resources from children's services to services for the elderly when the birth rate is falling and life expectancy is increasing. A client group orientation can also provide the basis for a PPB system in which costs would be grouped according to patients served rather than the facilities used, that is according to output rather than input. Within a client group it should be possible to translate the over-all health service goal into appropriate aims, but it is difficult to assess needs in absolute terms as we have already suggested. There is no completely satisfactory solution to this problem but needs may be established in relative terms by comparing indicators such as waiting lists for treatment, or prevalence of illness, in one region or area with those experienced nationally. Alternatively, policy makers may set norms or standards of good practive, based on medical advice, with which comparisons can be made. (It is inevitable, but often inappropriate, that provision and utilisation of resources will serve as the basis for comparison in many cases.) A need may therefore be recognised in the form of criteria such as morbidity or mortality rates which exceed the national average or some established norm. At this stage a more specific statement of objectives or targets for the long, medium and short term should be issued for the client group (or other mission-oriented group) and the units for which this target should be expressed will be the same as for the criterion used to indicate need. Thus, in planning maternity services, a region or area may be suffering from a higher perinatal mortality rate than is deemed acceptable.[21] The targets specified over the various time horizons would then normally be expressed in terms of intended reductions in that rate.

The time dimension in planning requires that analysis proceeds on the basis of forecasts and not just current indicators, also that the constraints on feasible options in the short and medium term are recognised. Thus strategic change may take ten or more years to accomplish. Strategic change would consist of major changes in the kind of product offered by the health service, for example a shift in emphasis to preventive rather than curative medicine, or providing for the patient in the community rather than in hospital. In the medium term (say three to ten years hence) it may be possible to make fairly substantial changes in the pattern of services, but the training of suitable medical manpower will limit possibilities, and in the short term (say within three years), most feasible alternatives will consist of minor redistributions within existing resources, improved methods of working, cutting out waste, etc. The alternatives should be assessed for cost-effectiveness which necessitates the calculation of capital and recurrent expenditures, and savings therein for all decision alternatives. The least demanding task for the analyst would seem to be finding the minimum cost way of meeting agreed objectives, in particular highlighting changes in resource allocation which will save money without reducing the standard of service offered. However, even this might prove difficult in the absence of a PPB system in which costs are grouped according to output categories. The efficacy of different treatments is often unknown before implementation, although part of the uncertainty could be removed by more widespread use of random-ised controlled trials (RCTs).[22] Indeed, A.L. Cochrane (33) cites numerous instances of treatments, regarded as highly respectable by the medical profession, which are shown to be most cost-ineffective when subject to the rigours of the RCT. One of the most startling results came from H.G. Mather's study (101) in Bristol in which hospital treatment for acute ischaemic heart disease was compared with treatment at home. The hospital treatment included a variable time in a coronary care unit: a facility well established in the USA but adopted in the UK to a lesser extent because of limited resources rather than doubts as to its efficacy. Mather found no medical gain in the hospital treatment compared with treatment at home and, although his results have been questioned on such issues as whether complete randomisation was achieved, the benefits of coronary care units must equally be questioned and compared with the high cost of installing and operating these units.

The key to successful planning may prove to be in the information system. The statistics routinely collected in the health service do provide some useful data on waiting lists, number of admissions for various kinds of treatments, etc., which enable inter-regional compari-sons to be made. Population statistics, including projections, are available from other sources and certainly the size and composition of the population are important parameters in health planning. In time, the use of computerised information systems may give access to data drawn from patient records, although privacy and confidentiality must be preserved. Until recently, data analyses in the health service have usually been classified by institution and activity rather than by individual, health care, group or health problem type. With the advent of the planning system, new information profiles for 'client groups' have been devised, but their usefulness in identifying problems has not yet been fully evaluated. While a collection of basic data presented in a standard format may satisfy some requirements, a more comprehensive, flexible system capable of providing information on demand, related to the particular problem under review is more important for planning purposes. In a WHO report on Statistical Indicators (168) a list of health services statistics considered relevant for planning purposes includes the following:

(1)   hospital discharge statistics — to enable comparisons to be made between different hospitals and communities as to their relative burdens of morbidity, the differences in the characteristics of the cases and populations;
(2)   ambulatory medical care statistics — providing data on care given outside hospital institutions; such information is necessary when planning primary medical care, e.g. general practice and health centres;
(3)   drug surveillance statistics — to detect trends in prescribing patterns of doctors and drug-taking habits of patients (although drugs supplied without prescription can only be estimated approximately);
(4)   health facilities statistics — to provide up-to-date information on the availability and use of institutions, beds, examination and treatment rooms, X-ray units, laboratories and other facilities;
(5)   health manpower and training statistics — including inventories of available manpower, and of educational and training resources; their current availability constrains short- and medium-term planning;
(6)   expenditure and financial statistics — given that cost-effectiveness criteria should be adopted in evaluating proposals, financial information is essential.

In the UK, information systems suited to planning are evolving, but there is still a predominance of information classified by institution rather than patient, by facility utilisation rather than patient need. In particular, costing tends to be according to input rather than to output or function. A major difficulty in re-casting budgets in programme form is that of apportioning the huge volume of general costs incurred in the health services. The DHSS, however, attempted to draw up a programme budget for health and personal social services in England.[23] The programmes are classified as follows: primary care, general and acute hospital and maternity services, services mainly for elderly and physically handicapped, services for the mentally handicapped, services for the mentally ill, services mainly for children, and other services (including social work, social services training, other LA services, and miscellaneous centrally financed services). The programme budget adopted is described as 'a crude method of costing policies based on past expenditure'. Its purpose is avowed to be 'to cost policies for service development across the board, so that priorities can be considered within realistic financial constraints' (43, p. 78).

As yet, then, the DHSS programme budget is not a particularly refined instrument, moreover the majority of health authorities, to whom local planning tasks are delegated, still rely on traditional budgeting techniques. The absence of an output-oriented costing system below DHSS level is a deficiency which is pervasive in its impact. It may retard the identification of needs, problems and opportunities for development, the evaluation of alternatives in cost-effectiveness terms, and the monitoring of performance, which in turn can hinder the identification of problems and so on.

Let us consider a particular planning problem to demonstrate the importance of information and measurement in health planning. W.A. Reinke (134) uses the following example concerned with respiratory diseases in an American state. The nature of the problem is specified in terms of mortality rates, days of restricted activity, days of hospitalisation, and out-patient visits. Specific objectives to be attained by a given point in time (2 years in this example) are stated in the form of target rates per 100,000 population,

(1)   decrease mortality to 50;
(2)   decrease days of hospitalisation to 25;
(3)   decrease out-patient visits to 340;
(4)   decrease days of restricted activity to 1,140.

The search for alternatives would typically begin by exploring causal factors for respiratory diseases, for example low immunisation levels, inadequate knowledge of health practices by the population, air pollution, the pollen count, and substandard or over-crowded housing. The feasibility of alternatives could only be determined by collaboration between various agencies, since the majority of the proposals would be outside the province of health service provision. The final list includes:

(1)   conduct monthly immunisation clinics;
(2)   conduct television and radio education programmes;
(3)   eliminate open burning of refuse;
(4)   extend weed control programmes (to cover 60 per cent of urban areas);
(5)   replace a proportion (3 per cent) of substandard homes.

Associated with this plan of action are a number of 'activity targets': immunise 80 per cent of high risk individuals against influenza, provide monthly public health nurse visits to 80 per cent of deprived homes, reduce air pollution (SO_2 levels) in metropolitan areas by 10 per cent, reduce average pollen count by 15 per cent. Details are not given in this illustration of how the final plan of action would be devised or a decision made as to the expenditure devoted to each aspect.[24] Despite this limitation, the example is useful because it shows the possibility of stating the nature of a problem and objectives in a quantifiable form which in principle would allow cost-effectiveness criteria to be applied if suitable models relating input to output were available. Follow-up of the implemented programme would also be facilitated through quantification with a gap between actual and intended rates indicating the need for further action.

Another useful aspect of this illustration is that it demonstrates the need to co-operate and collaborate with other bodies. In the British Health Service there is machinery for area health authorities to liaise with local authorities. Indeed, the boundaries of areas in the re-organised health service were drawn so as to achieve coterminosity with their local government counterparts. Let us now look more closely at the planning system in the NHS, paying particular attention to the activities contained in the planning cycle.

The reorganised Health Service came into being in 1974 and the general aims behind its restructuring were set out in the DHSS 'Grey Book' (42). These were:

(1)   the Health Service should be fully integrated so as to provide every aspect of health care provided by members of the health care professions;
(2)   this care should be provided locally as far as possible, and with due regard to the health needs of the community as a whole.

Within these two general aims, an important feature of the management arrangements was the intention to plan services in relation to needs of the people to be served, usually classified into client groups, for example the mentally handicapped, the elderly, children and so on. The planning was to be co-ordinated, so that all personal health services including health education, prevention, diagnosis, treatment and rehabilitation would be planned in conjunction with each other and with local government services. The planning system designed to satisfy these requirements marked a fundamental shift from previous thinking. Prior to reorganisation, planning had been mainly concerned with preparing the capital programme and this was highly developed since major hospital buildings absorb large capital sums and necessitate consideration of a long-time horizon. The new concept of 'service planning', as defined in another official publication[25] '. . . refers to the forward planning of the total range of health services – identifying the needs for services and then allocating resources (manpower and money as well as buildings) to meet needs' (165, p. 50). This more comprehensive, output-oriented approach was seen as essential for the Health Service to obtain the 'best value for the very substantial yet all too limited, resources available to it'.

In the system designed for health authorities in England, strategic and operational types of planning are distinguished, but the distinction lies primarily in the time horizon rather than the nature of change contemplated. Strategic planning is described by the DHSS as 'relatively long-term (up to 10-15 years)'. Operational planning is 'relatively short-term (1-3 years)' (44, p. 7). Obviously far-reaching developments are out of the question in the short term and the sort of changes which we would normally describe as 'strategic' will only be feasible over a longer period, so that in practical terms we need not be too concerned about the DHSS usage of the term. Below the DHSS, the administrative tiers are regions, areas and districts.[26] Each RHA (Regional Health Authority) and AHA (Area Health Authority) is required to produce a strategic plan and this is where the RHA makes its major contribution to planning. The AHA's planning assumptions are influenced by DHSS and regional guidance, but the area is also the focal point for collaboration with the local authority, and the area's boundaries were made coterminous with those of the latter to facilitate joint planning. Operational plans are produced by districts and areas, but it is thought that longer-term ideas will be developed at district level which the area will need to draw on in formulating strategy.

At the highest level, policies are reviewed periodically in the light of resource availability. The DHSS issues guidance to regions and areas to provide a framework for strategic planning. Guidance may include health care group priorities, for example, to urge the development of geriatric services, perhaps at the same time advocating lower priority to services for children. This kind of guidance may result from a central review of population projections in relation to resource provision and utilisation. National objectives and suggested strategies for their achievement may be given, and resource assumptions for current and capital expenditure in each region. Firm allocations can only be given for one year ahead, since the annual government review of public expenditure constrains what is available to the Health Service. However, it is envisaged that broad resource assumptions will be issued to regions, for the longer term.

At the time of writing (1977), health planning is evolving in an era of relative decline for the public sector. The economic and political background is that Britain's industrial performance has been harshly criticised for its failure to invest and maintain its share of world markets. Government policy of the 1960s and early 1970s increased the proportion of national resources used by the public sector and the extent of this can be seen in both expenditure and employment patterns. The government had decided by 1975 that the so-called 'industrial strategy' (i.e. the restoration of British industry both in terms of employment and share of national product) warranted substantial reductions in government expenditure. Many commentators were puzzled by the apparent repudiation of Keynesian principles implicit in the curtailing of government spending during a period of high unemployment, but international pressures forced the UK to adopt monetarist measures, and it was the need to control the growth in the money supply which ultimately brought home the need for stringency in the public sector. The Health Service came out of the ensuing cutbacks in expenditure growth rather better than some had dared hope, but, even so, expectations had to be lowered. At the same time a move towards equality in the geographical distribution of health care resources was set into motion. While some regions, previously less well endowed with resources would benefit from greater than average increases when prosperity returned, those which had always been relatively generously funded (for example regions in which teaching hospitals were concentrated) could expect no growth for many years to come.

The theme running through this book is that forward planning is

frequently directed towards growth, but although the NHS planning
system was conceived during an expansionary era, it now has to
function, in many instances, in a no-growth situation. Certainly the
shift in attitudes which this will entail cannot be overestimated, but
whether a change in the system is necessary is another matter. In fact
the requirements of an anticipatory decision making system are very
much the same whatever the objectives and constraints impinging upon
it. The major difference in a no-growth situation is that strategies will
be concerned with re-deployment within a given total, rather than
additions to the organisation's activities as is often, but not always,
the case with planning for expansion.

The mechanisms referred to in the accompanying charts
(Figures 6.3 and 6.4) should be capable of generating plans, whatever
the resource assumptions, if the system is a good one. In the first chart
(Figure 6.3) we see at district level that the DMT (District Management
Team) commences preparation/revision of district plans and issues
guidance to planning teams. These teams, formerly designated HCPTs
(Health Care Planning Teams) are fundamental mechanisms in the
planning process. They are multi-disciplinary teams and are composed
of general practitioners, consultants, hospital and community nurses,
health visitors, para-medical staff and representatives of local authority
services. The membership of each team will vary according to the
health care or client group concerned and may even vary for different
problems under consideration by a given planning team. The teams are
required to review existing services and to identify problems and
opportunities for development in the light of short- (up to 3 years),
medium- (3-10 years) and long-term (10-15 years) objectives which are
influenced by regional, area and district guidelines and the deliberations
of the team itself. The proposals submitted by planning teams to the
DMT are meant to be evaluated in cost-effectiveness terms and may
therefore include suggestions for reducing expenditure, but clearly
there is a greater incentive to participate when the team is discussing
ways of spending money rather than saving it. The consultation
process, which is an important component of the planning system, is
also more likely to run smoothly when facilities are being expanded
rather than contracted. Community Health Councils (CHCs) are
important agents in this process and their job is to represent the local
population when decisions are being made. Major changes in the
pattern of provision of health services, in particular rationalisation or
centralisation schemes, may meet with resistance from the local CHC
and, indeed, from representatives of health service employees if staff

Figure 6.3: NHS Planning System
A. Operational Planning Timetable

(Boxed items do not apply in the first year)

(Continuing activities are shown in square brackets)

Source: DHSS (44).

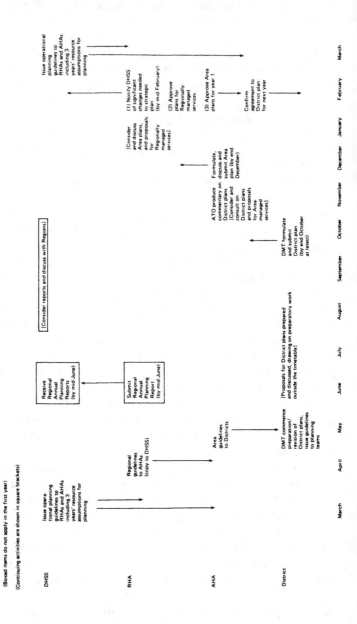

Figure 6.4: NHS Planning System
B. Typical Strategic Planning Timetable

Source: DHSS (44).

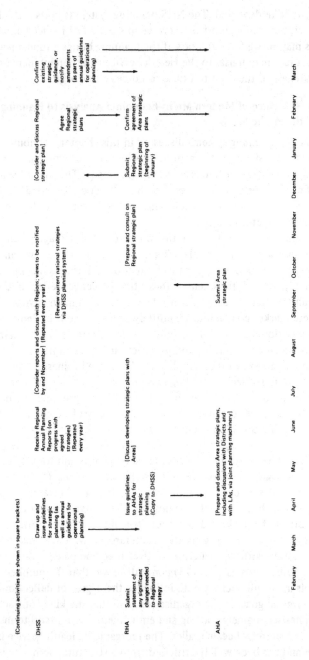

are to be re-deployed. The NHS planning system is in its early days
as yet, but although it has to evolve in a period of reduced expectations,
this may prove to be salutary if the planning brings a fundamental
corporate reappraisal to the Health Service and thereby increases
awareness of the need to utilise resources efficiently.

6.6 Relevance of Modern Micro-Economic Analysis to Planning in the Public Sector

In all the planning systems discussed in this chapter, economic analysis
can make a significant contribution when choices which involve
alternative resource allocations are being made. This contribution is
self-explanatory given concepts such as 'functional costing', 'cost-
effectiveness' and 'cost-benefit analysis' which pervade the literature
on public sector planning.

What concern us here are the implications of managerial and
behavioural theories for planning in this sector and the over-all
relevance of such theories outside their usual business organisation
context. Indeed, their central thesis that objectives reflect internal
organisational or managerial needs, is reinforced in an environment
where market constraints are entirely absent. Who is to deny that
organisational growth in the public sector is often sought as a means
of enhancing pay, promotion prospects and the security of
administrators and their employees? If private businesses exist with
organisational slack, including excessive staffs and perquisites, over-
allocation to subunits, and budgets justified by precedent, is it not
likely that other organisations will be similarly afflicted? In fact the
absence of a profit constraint means that slack may be pared or
eliminated less frequently than in an environment where external
pressures periodically bring a squeeze on profits and force a review of
the organisation's decisions and resource allocations. Of course,
governments do cut their spending from time to time and this brings
pressure to bear on public bodies, but their survival is assured unlike
the private firm which depends on its ability to make profit.

The questions of organisational hierarchies which we raised in
connection with the structure of diversified companies is also relevant
here. O.E. Williamson's (173) contention was that the number of
levels in the hierarchy would influence the degree of deflection from
the over-all goals of the organisation, and that the kinds of slack he
emphasised, namely staffing and emoluments would tend to increase
as the hierarchy became taller. The reorganised Health Service in
England has been widely criticised from a structural point of view

because there are now four main tiers: DHSS, Region, Area and
District and if one probes inside each of these a multitude of sub-
hierarchies is revealed. Undoubtedly the objective setting and
decision making process is complex with a heavy reliance on standard
procedures which govern the movement of plans, guidelines, requests,
reports and other communications within and between tiers. At the
time of writing, the functioning of the National Health Service is being
investigated by a Royal Commission, so we shall have to wait for
the results of this enquiry before passing judgement. However, it would
seem plausible to suppose that an intricate administrative structure
could retard strategic decision making in any kind of organisation
and provide the sort of surroundings within which organisational slack
can thrive.

We have made frequent references to this concept of organisational
slack, not to provide an explanation or justification for its presence,
but rather to indicate that, in so far as it exists, it can hinder the
achievement of corporate objectives. It is sometimes regarded
favourably since it acts as a cushion to protect the firm from adversity,
but we do not see this as an adequate reason for retaining slack when
there are opportunities for its removal. If an organisation plans towards
corporate objectives, then it can anticipate crisis, or at least take steps
to minimise its own vulnerability in adversity. The organisation should
therefore test existing internal allocations for consistency with corporate
objectives, at an early stage of the strategic decision making process.

As a conclusion to this chapter, and to the whole book, we re-
affirm our belief that the theories of modern micro-economics provide
a solid foundation for a deeper understanding of objectives and decisions
in organisations. Our emphasis has been on 'strategy' rather than
'operations' and we hope that our exploration of some of the major
issues in this context has helped to relate theory to practice.

Notes

1. For a further illustration in the public sector, namely that of local
    authorities, see R. Greenwood and J.D. Stewart (eds.) (59).
2. Known officially as the International Bank for Reconstruction and
    Development.
3. In contrast to the centralised planning of the USSR and others, the
    socialist but competitive planning of Yugoslavia and the more democratic
    competitive planning of say India. For a further coverage of these see
    A. Qayum (131).

4.   For a theoretical examination of indicative planning, see J.E. Meade (103).
5.   Also adopted by Belgium, Ireland and, in part, some African countries.
6.   Limited more to one and possibly two years ahead though the Plowden Report (128) in 1961 indicated a need for governments to develop longer-term programmes – say 5 years ahead on the public expenditure decisions.
7.   On the French model with a suggestion though not proven that there might be a connection between planning and greater growth.
8.   Similar to the French model with representatives from the government, TUC, industry and the academic world.
9.   For the period 1956-61 the growth rate was 2.7 per cent.
10. These objectives can change in terms of their primacy. For instance in the period 1976/7 the control of inflation has been seen as the main objective but one which can then itself help to achieve the other objectives.
11. And we can couple this with the current discussion on the Bullock Report (29) which has been one attempt at providing a structure for greater worker participation at board level.
12. D. Novick at this time was head of this department of RAND, a private consulting firm. See his article (119) 'Planning Ahead in the Department of Defence'.
13. The absence of a formal programme budgeting system in British Health Authorities reflects this difficulty. See Section 6.5.
14. In fact the projection of force-structure is now for 8 years ahead.
15. The actual classification has changed over the years, but the list given here is fairly representative.
16. The actual cycle has tended to vary over time, and the reader should verify the current position.
17. See Novick (121) (Appendix C).
18. In Novick (121) (Chapter 11).
19. I. Illich (74) (Chapter 2). Illich does not himself believe that health levels will improve with expenditure on medical services, nor is this contention supported by the statistics.
20. See Abel-Smith (2) (pp. 123-4).
21. The use of the word 'acceptable' implies that optimising has to be forsaken for satisficing in health planning. Whilst this is strictly true, we believe that it is still meaningful to seek a more efficient allocation of resources.
22. The randomised controlled trial is a method of testing the effectiveness of therapies which requires the random separation of similar patients into two groups – one which receives the therapy and one which does not.
23. See the 1976 Consultative Document on 'Priorities for Health and Personal Social Services in England' (43) (Annex 2, pp. 78-83).
24. The Department of Health, Education and Welfare in the USA did, however, in the 1960s examine a range of programmes aimed at various diseases and health problems and did provide estimates of cost-effectiveness. For a discussion of some of the applications by this agency see E.B. Drew (45).
25. Concerned with the arrangements for the Health Service in Wales.
26. Arrangements vary between the various parts of the UK. The structure described here refers to the set up in England, but in Wales there is no regional tier and Area Health Authorities report to the Secretary of State for Wales.

REFERENCES

1. Aaronvitch, S. and Sawyer, M.C. 'The Concentration of British Manufacturing', *Lloyds Bank Review*, October 1974, pp. 14-23
2. Abel-Smith, B. *Value for Money in Health Services – A Comparative Study*, London: Heinemann, 1976
3. Ackoff, R.L. *A Concept of Corporate Planning*, J. Wiley, 1970
4. Alchian, A.A. 'Advances in the Theory of Management of the Firm', *Journal of Industrial Economics*, November 1965, pp. 30-41
5. _____ 'Uncertainty, Evolution and Economic Theory', *Journal of Political Economy*, June 1950, pp. 211-21
6. Amey, L.R. 'Is Business Diversification Desirable', *District Bank Review*, June 1960
7. _____ 'Diversified Manufacturing Business', *Journal of the Royal Statistical Society*, Series A, 1964, pp. 251-90
8. Anderson, W.M.L. *Corporate Finance and Fixed Investment: An Econometric Study*, Cambridge, Mass.: Harvard University, Graduate School of Business Administration, 1965
9. Ansoff, H.I. 'A Model for Diversification', *Management Science*, 1958, pp. 392-414
10. _____ *Corporate Strategy*, New York: McGraw-Hill, 1965; Harmondsworth: Penguin, 1968
11. _____ 'Does Planning Pay? The Effect of Planning on Success of Acquisitions in America', *Long Range Planning*, March 1969 to December 1970
12. Ansoff, H.I. and Weston, J.F. 'Merger Objectives and Organisation Structure', *Review of Economics and Business*, August 1962, pp. 49-58
13. Bain, A.D., Day, C.L., Wearing, A.L. *Company Financing in the UK, A Flow of Funds Model*, London: Martin Robertson, 1975
14. Bain, J.S. 'Economies of Scale, Concentration and the Conditions of Entry in Twenty Manufacturing Industries', *American Economic Review*, vol. 64, 1954, pp. 15-39
15. Baldwin, W.L. 'The Motives of Managers, Environmental Restraints and the Theory of Managerial Enterprise',

Quarterly Journal of Economics, 1964, pp. 238-56

16. Barna, T. *Investment and Growth Policies in British Industrial Firms*, London: Cambridge University Press, 1962

17. Barnard, C.I. *Functions of the Executive*, Cambridge: Harvard University Press, 1938

18. Baumol, W.J. 'On the Theory of Oligopoly', *Economica*, vol. XXV, 1958, pp. 187-98

19. _____ *Business Behaviour, Value and Growth*, New York: Macmillan, 1959

20. _____ 'On a Theory of Expansion of the Firm', *American Economic Review*, December 1962, pp. 1078-87

21. Berle, A.A. and Means, G.C. *The Modern Corporation and Private Property*, revised edition, New York: Macmillan, 1968

22. Bond, R.S. 'A Note on Diversification and Risk', *Southern Economic Journal*, 41, October 1974

23. Boudreaux, K.J. 'Managerialism and Risk Return Performance', *Southern Economic Journal*, January 1973, pp. 366-72

24. Boulding, K.E. and Spivey, A.W. (eds.) *Linear Programming and the Theory of the Firm*, New York: Macmillan, 1960

25. Bowen, H.R. *Social Responsibilities of the Businessman*, New York, 1953

26. Bridge, J. and Dodds, J.C. *Managerial Decision Making*, London: Croom Helm, 1975

27. Bridgeman, J.M. 'Planning-Programming-Budgeting in the United Kingdom Central Goverment' (Chapter 2 in Novick, D. (ed.) [121])

28. Broke, M. and Turner, G. 'Why Managers Don't Dispose', *Management Today*, May 1971, pp. 86-9 and 144-8

29. Bullock Report *Report of the Committee of Inquiry on Industrial Democracy*, Cmnd. 6707, London: HMSO, 1977

30. Burns, T. and Stalker, G. *The Management of Innovation*, London: Tavistock, 1961

31. Clarkson, G.P.E. and Elliott, B.J. *Managing Money and Finance*, Gower Press, 1969

32. Cleland, S. 'A Short Essay on a Managerial Theory of the Firm', in Boulding, K.E. and Spivey, A.W. (eds.) (24)

33. Cochrane, A.L. *Effectiveness and Efficiency — Random Reflections on Health Services*, Oxford: Nuffield Provincial Hospitals Trust, 1972

34. Cohen, K.J. and Cyert, R.M. *Theory of the Firm: Resource Allocation in a Market Economy*, New York: Prentice-Hall, 1965

35. Cooper, M.H. *Rationing Health Care*, London: Croom Helm, 1975
36. Cosh, A. 'The Remuneration of Chief Executives in the UK', *Economic Journal*, March 1975, vol. 85, pp. 75-94
37. Cyert, R.M. and March, J.G. 'Organisational Structure and Pricing Behaviour in an Oligopolistic Market', *American Economic Review*, 45, 1955, pp. 129-39
38. _____ *A Behavioural Theory of the Firm*, New Jersey: Prentice-Hall, 1963
39. Davis, E.W. and Yeomans, K.A. *Company Finance and the Capital Market, A Study of the Effects of Firm Size*, Cambridge University Press, 1974
40. Dorfman, R. 'Operations Research', *American Economic Review*, 1960, pp. 575-623
41. Downie, J. *The Competitive Process*, London: Duckworth, 1958
42. DHSS *Management Arrangements for the Re-organised National Health Service*, London: HMSO, 1972
43. DHSS *Priorities for Health and Personal Social Services in England, A Consultative Document*, London: HMSO, 1976
44. DHSS *The NHS Planning System*, London: HMSO, 1976
45. Drew, E.B. 'HEW Grapples with PPBS', *The Public Interest*, Summer 1967, pp. 9-24
46. Eatwell, J. 'Growth, Profitability and Size, The Empirical Evidence' in Marris, R.L. and Wood, A. (98)
47. Elliott, D. 'Concentration in UK Manufacturing Industry', *Trade and Industry*, August 1974, HMSO, pp. 240-1
48. Florence, P.S. *Ownership, Control and Success of Large Companies, an Analysis of English Industrial Structure and Policy, 1936-51*, London: Sweet and Maxwell, 1961
49. Galbraith, J.K. *The New Industrial State*, London: Hamish Hamilton, 1967, and Harmondsworth: Penguin, 1969
50. _____ *Affluent Society* (2nd edition), Harmondsworth: Penguin, 1970
51. _____ *Economics and the Public Purpose*, London: André Deutsch, 1974
52. _____ *The Age of Uncertainty*, London: BBC Publications/ André Deutsch, 1977
53. George, K.D. 'The Changing Structure of Competitive Industry', *Economic Journal*, March 1972 (Supplement), pp. 353-68
54. _____ *Big Business Competition and the State*, Inaugural Lecture, Cardiff, 1974

55. Gordon, R.A. *Business Leadership in the Large Corporation*, Berkeley: University of California Press, 1961
56. Gorecki, P.K. 'An Inter-Industry Analysis of Diversification in the UK Manufacturing Sector', *Journal of Industrial Economics*, 1975
57. Gort, M. *Diversification and Integration in American Industry 1929-54*, National Bureau of Economics, Research General Series, Princeton University Press, 1962
58. Goyder, G. *The Responsible Company*, Oxford, 1961
59. Greenwood, R. and Stewart J.D. (eds.) *Corporate Planning in English Local Government, An Analysis with Readings 1967-72*, London: Charles Knight & Co. Ltd, 1974
60. Hall, M. 'Sales Revenue Maximisation, An Empirical Examination', *Journal of Industrial Economics*, April 1967, pp. 143-56
61. Hannah, L. *The Rise of the Corporate Economy*, London: Methuen, 1976
62. Hannah, L. and Kay, J.A. *Concentration in Modern Industry, Theory, Management and the UK Experience*, London: Macmillan, 1977
63. Hansard, 6 April 1970
64. Hatry, H.P. 'Criteria for Evaluation in Planning State and Local Programmes', ch. 10 in Lyden, F.J. and Miller, E.G. (eds.) (88)
65. Hawkins, C.J. 'On the Sales Revenue Maximisation Hypothesis', *Journal of Industrial Economics*, April 1970
66. Heald, M. 'Management's Responsibility to Society, The Growth of an Idea', *Business History Review*, vol. 31, 1957, pp. 375-84
67. Hicks, J.R. *Value and Capital* (2nd edition), London: Oxford University Press, 1965
68. Hindley, B. 'Separation of Ownership and Control in the Modern Corporation', *Journal of Law and Economics*, April 1970, pp. 185-221
69. Hitch, C.J. *Systems Development and Management (Part 2) Hearings before a Subcommittee of the Committee on Government Operations* (House of Representatives 87th Cong. 2nd session), Washington DC: US Government Printing Office, 1962 (tables reproduced in Novick, D. (ed.) (120), p. 96)
70. HMSO *The Task Ahead, Economic Assessment to 1972*, Department of Economic Affairs, HMSO, 1969

71. HMSO White Paper: *The Regeneration of British Industry*, Cmnd. 5110, HMSO, 1974
72. Holl, P. 'Effect of Control Type on the Performance of the Firm in the UK', *Journal of Industrial Economics*, June 1975, pp. 257-71
73. Howe, M. 'Competition and the Multiplication of Products', *Yorkshire Bulletin of Economic and Social Research*, vol. 12, no. 2, November 1960, pp. 57-72.
74. Illich, I. *Medical Nemesis, The Expropriation of Health*, London: Marion Boyars, 1975
75. Kamerschen, D.R. 'Influence of Ownership and Control on Profit Rates', *American Economic Review*, June 1968, pp. 432-47
76. King, M.A. 'Dividend Behaviour and the Theory of the Firm', *Economica*, 1974, pp. 25-34
77. King's Fund Working Party on the application of economic principles to health service management, *Accounting for Health*, London: King Edward's Hospital Fund for London, 1973
78. Kuehn, D.A. 'Stock Market Valuation and Acquisitions: An Empirical Test of One Component of Management Utility', *Journal of Industrial Economics*, April 1969, pp. 132-44
79. _____ *Takeovers and the Theory of the Firm*, London: Macmillan, 1975
80. Lackman, C.L. and Craycraft, J.L. 'Sales Maximisation and Oligopoly, A Case Study', *Journal of Industrial Economics*, December 1974, pp. 81-95
81. Larner, R. *Management Control and the Large Corporation*, New York, 1970
82. Lee, R.D. and Johnson, R.W. *Public Budgeting Systems*, Baltimore: University Park Press, 1973
83. Leibenstein, H. 'Allocative Efficiency versus X-Efficiency', *American Economic Review*, June 1966, pp. 392-415
84. Levitt, T. 'Exploit the Product Life-Cycle', *Harvard Business Review*, vol. 43, no. 6, 1965, pp. 81-94
85. Lewellen, W.G. 'Management and Ownership in the Large Firm', *Journal of Finance*, May 1969, pp. 299-322
86. _____ 'A Pure Financial Rationale for the Conglomerate Merger', *Journal of Finance*, May 1971, pp. 521-37
87. Lintner, J. 'Distribution of Incomes of Corporations among Dividends, Retained Earnings and Taxes', *American Economic Review*, vol. 46, May 1956 (supplement), pp. 97-113

88.   Lyden, F.J. and Miller, E.G. (eds.) *Planning – Programming –*
      Budgeting: A Systems Approach to Management (2nd edition),
      Chicago: Markham Publishing Company, 1972
89.   Lynch, H.H. *Financial Performance of Conglomerates*, Division
      of Research, Graduate School of Business Administration,
      Harvard University, 1971
90.   Manne, H.G. 'Mergers and the Market for Corporate Control',
      Journal of Political Economy, April 1965, pp. 110-20
91.   Mansfield, E. *The Economics of Technological Change*, New
      York: Norton, 1968
92.   Marris, R.L. 'A Model of the Managerial Enterprise', *Quarterly*
      Journal of Economics, 1963, pp. 185-209
93.   –––––––   *The Economic Theory of Managerial Capitalism*, London:
      Macmillan, 1964 and 1967 (with corrections)
94.   –––––––   'An Introduction to Theories of Corporate Growth' in
      Marris, R.L. and Wood, A. (98)
95.   –––––––   'The Modern Corporation and Economic Theory' in
      (98)
96.   –––––––   'Some New Results on Growth and Profitability' in (98)
97.   –––––––   'Why Economics needs a Theory of the firm', *Economic*
      Journal, March 1972 Supplement, pp. 321-41
98.   Marris, R.L. and Wood, A. (eds.) *The Corporate Economy,*
      Growth, Competition and Innovative Power, London:
      Macmillan, 1971
99.   Marshall, A. *Principles of Economics* (8th edition), London:
      Macmillan, 1920
100. Masson, R.T. 'Executive Motivation and Earnings and Consequent
      Equity Performance', *Journal of Political Economy*, December
      1971, pp. 1278-92
101. Mather, H.G. *et al.* 'Acute Myocardial Infarcation: Home and
      Hospital Treatment', *British Medical Journal*, 3.334 (1971)
102. McGuire, J.W., Chiu, J.S.Y., and Elbing, A.O. 'Executive Incomes,
      Sales and Profits', *American Economic Review*, September
      1962, pp. 753-61
103. Meade, J.E. *The Theory of Indicative Planning*, Manchester
      University Press, 1970
104. Meeks, G. and Whittington, G. 'Giant Companies in the United
      Kingdom, 1948-69', *Economic Journal*, December 1975,
      pp. 824-43
105. –––––––   'The Financing of Quoted Companies in the UK'
      Background Paper to Report No. 2, 'Income from Companies

and its Distribution', Royal Commission on the Distribution of Income and Wealth, HMSO, 1976

106. Merrett, A.J. and Sykes, A. *Capital Budgeting and Company Finance* (2nd edition), London: Longmans, 1973

107. Midgley, K. 'How Much Control Do Shareholders Exercise?', *Lloyds Bank Review*, October 1974, pp. 24-37

108. Miller, M.H. and Modigliani, F. 'Dividend Policy, Growth and the Valuation of Shares', *Journal of Business*, October 1961, pp. 411-33

109. Mitchell, J. *Groundwork to Economic Planning*, London: Secker and Warburg, 1966

110. Modigliani, F. and Cohen, K.J. 'The Role of Anticipations and Plans in Economic Behaviour and their Use in Economic Analysis', *Studies in Business Expectations and Planning*, no. 4, Urbana, University of Illinois, Bureau of Economic and Business Research, 1961

111. Modigliani, F. and Miller, M.H. 'The Cost of Capital Corporation Finance and the Theory of Investment', *American Economic Review*, 1958, pp. 261-97

112. _____ 'Corporate Income Taxes and the Cost of Capital, A Correction', *American Economic Review*, 1963, pp. 433-43

113. Monsen, R.J. and Downs, A. 'A Theory of Large Managerial Firms' Firms', *Journal of Political Economy*, June 1965, pp. 221-36

114. Moon, R.W. *Business Mergers and Take-Over Bids. A Study of the Post-War Pattern of Amalgamations and Reconstructions of Companies* (4th edition), London: Gee and Co, 1971

115. Morgan, E. 'Social Responsibility and Private Enterprise in the United Kingdom', *National Westminster Bank Review*, May 1977, pp. 25-67

116. Newbould, G.D. *Management and Merger Activity*, Liverpool: Guthstead, 1970

117. Newbould, G.D., Stray, S.J. and Wilson, K.W. 'The Benefits of Company Size: The Case of Shareholders', *Scottish Journal of Political Economy*, vol. 24, no. 1, February 1977, pp. 77-82

118. Nichols, T. *Ownership, Control and Ideology*, London: Allen and Unwin, 1969

119. Novick, D. 'Planning Ahead in the Department of Defence', *California Management Review*, Summer 1963, pp. 35-42

120. _____ (ed.) *Programme Budgeting – Programme Analysis and the Federal Budget*, Cambridge: Harvard University Press, 1967

121. Novick, D. (ed.) *Current Analysis in Programme Budgeting (PPBS) – Analysis and Case Studies Covering Government and Business*, New York: Crane, Russak and Company Inc., 1973
122. Palmer, J. 'Extent of the Separation of Ownership from Control in Large UK Corporations', *Quarterly Review of Economics and Business*, Autumn 1972
123. Panic, M. and Close, R.E. 'Profitability of British Manufacturing Industry', *Lloyds Bank Review*, July 1973, pp. 17-30
124. Papandreou, A. 'Some Basic Problems in the Theory of the Firm', in Haley, B.F. (ed.), *Survey of Contemporary Economics*, vol. 2, Homewood, Illinois: Richard D. Irwin, 1952, pp. 183-219
125. Parker, J.E.S; 'Profitability and Growth of British Industrial Firms', *Manchester School*, May 1964, pp. 113-29
126. Patton, P. 'Top Executives' Pay: New Facts and Figures', *Harvard Business Review*, 44, September 1966, pp. 94-9
127. Penrose, E.T. *The Theory of the Growth of the Firm*, Oxford: Blackwell, 1959
128. Plowden Committee Report *Control of Public Expenditure*, Cmnd. 1432, London: HMSO, 1961
129. Prais, S.J. 'Size, Growth and Concentration', ch. 8 in Tew, B. and Henderson, R.F. (156)
130. _____ *The Evolution of Giant Firms in Britain*, London: Cambridge University Press, 1976
131. Qayum, A. *Techniques of National Economic Planning*, Bloomington: Indiana University Press, 1975
132. Radcliffe Report *Committee on the working of monetary system*, Cmnd. 827, HMSO 1959
133. Radice, H.K. 'Control Type. Profitability and Growth in Large Firms. An Empirical Study', *Economic Journal*, September 1971, pp. 547-62
134. Reinke, W.A. *Health Planning – Qualitative Aspects and Quantitative Techniques*, Baltimore: Department of International Health, The John Hopkins University School of Hygiene and Public Health, Waverly Press Inc, 1972
135. Roberts, D.R. *Executive Compensation*, Glencoe: Free Press, 1959
136. Robinson, E.A.G. *The Structure of Competitive Industry*, Cambridge University Press, 1958
137. Samuels, J. 'Size and Growth of Firms', *Review of Economic Studies*, 1965, pp. 105-12

138. Samuels, J. and Smyth, D. 'Profits, Variability of Profits and Firm Size', *Economica*, May 1968, pp. 127-39

139. Sawyer, M.C. 'Concentration in British Manufacturing Industry', *Oxford Economic Papers* (New Series), November 1972, pp. 438-47

140. Schumacher, E.F. *Small is Beautiful, A Study of Economics as if People Mattered*, London: Blond and Briggs, 1971

141. Selznick, P. *TVA and the Grass Roots*, Berkeley: University of California Press, 1949

142. Shepherd, W.G. 'On Sales Maximising and Oligopoly Behaviour', *Economica*, November 1962, pp. 420-24

143. Simon, H.A. *Administrative Behaviour* (2nd edition), New York: Macmillan, 1957

144. Singh, A. *Take-Overs: Their Relevance to the Stock Market and the Theory of the Firm*, London: Cambridge University Press, 1971

145. ―――― 'Take-Overs, Economic Natural Selection and the Theory of the Firm', *Economic Journal*, vol. 85, September 1975, pp. 497-515

146. Singh, A. and Whittington, G. *Growth, Profitability and Valuation*, London: Cambridge University Press, 1968

147. Smalter, D.J. and Ruggles, J. 'Six Business Lessons from the Pentagon', *Harvard Business Review*, vol. 44, no. 2, March-April 1966, pp. 64-75

148. Smith, K.V. and Schreiner, J.C. 'A Portfolio Analysis of Conglomerate Diversification', *Journal of Finance*, June 1969, pp. 413-27

149. Solow, R.M. 'Some Implications of Alternative Criteria for the Firm', in Marris, R.L. and Wood, A. (98)

150. Sorensen, R. *Some Economic Implications of the Separation of Ownership and Control in the Large Firm*, unpublished PhD thesis, Virginia Polytechnic Institute State University, 1974

151. Staudt, T.A. 'Programme for Product Diversification', *Harvard Business Review*, vol. 32, no. 6, November/December 1954, pp. 121-31

152. Stellini, C.E. 'The New PPBS: A Framework for Decision', Appendix C in Novick, D. (ed.) (121)

153. Stock Exchange, *Stock Exchange Fact Book*, London

154. Stone, R.G. and Roe, A.R. *The Financial Interdependence of the Economy 1957-1966*, London: Chapman Hall, 1971

155. Sweezy, P.M. 'Demand under Conditions of Oligopoly', *Journal*

of Political Economy, 1939, pp. 568-73

156. Tew, B. and Henderson, R.F. (eds.) *Studies in Company Financing*, Cambridge University Press, 1959

157. Thane, S.S. and House, R.J. 'Where Long Range Planning Pays Off', *Business Horizons,* August 1970

158. Turner, G. *Business in Britain* (revised edition), Harmondsworth: Penguin, 1971

159. Utton, M.A. 'Mergers, Diversification and Profit Stability', *Business Ratios*, 3 (1), 1969

160. _____ 'Large Firm Diversification in British Manufacturing Industry', *Economic Journal*, March 1977, pp. 96-113

161. Vice, A. *The Strategy of Takeover – a casebook of international practice*, London: McGraw-Hill, 1971

162. Walker, J.L. 'Structure of Company Financing', *Economic Trends*, no. 263, September 1975, HMSO, pp. 96-116

163. _____ 'Estimating Companies' Rates of Return on Capital Employed', *Economic Trends*, November 1974, pp. 30-39

164. Waverman, L. 'Sales Revenue Maximisation: A Note', *Journal of Industrial Economics*, 1968, pp. 73-7

165. Welsh Office, *Management Arrangements for the Reorganised Health Service in Wales*, Cardiff: HMSO, 1972

166. Weiner, J.L. 'The Berle-Dodd dialogue in the Concept of the Corporation', *Columbia Law Review*, vol. 64, 1964, pp. 1458-67

167. Whittington, G. 'The Profitability of Retained Earnings', *The Review of Economics and Statistics*, May 1972, pp. 152-60

168. WHO, *Statistical Indicators for the Planning and Evaluation of Public Health Programmes,* Fourteenth Report of the WHO Expert Committee on Health Statistics, Geneva: World Health Organisation, 1971

169. Williamson, J.H. 'Profit, Growth and Sales Maximisation', *Economica*, February 1966, pp. 1-16

170. Williamson, O.E. 'Managerial Discretion and Business Behaviour', *American Economic Review*, 1963, pp. 1032-57

171. _____ *The Economics of Discretionary Behaviour: Managerial Objectives in a Theory of the Firm*, New Jersey: Prentice-Hall, 1964

172. _____ *Corporate Control and Business Behaviour: an Inquiry into the Effect of Organisational Form on Enterprise Behaviour*, Eaglewood, New Jersey: Prentice-Hall, 1970

173. _____ 'Managerial Discretion, Organisation Form and the

Multi-Division Hypothesis', in Marris, R.L. and Wood, A. (98)

174. Wood, A. 'Diversification, Merger and Research Expenditure:
A Review of Empirical Studies', in Marris, R.L. and Wood, A.
(98)

175. _____ *A Theory of Profits*, Cambridge University Press, 1975

176. Wynn, J. *Trends in Life Assurance and Related Savings Schemes*,
SSRC, HR 1826, September 1973

INDEX

206

Printed in the United States
by Baker & Taylor Publisher Services